Trade Policy Developments
in the Middle East
and North Africa

Bernard Hoekman
Hanaa Kheir-El-Din
Editors

THE WORLD BANK
WASHINGTON, D.C.

ISBN 0-8213-4614-8

Library of Congress Cataloging-in-Publication Data

Trade policy developments in the Middle East and North Africa / edited by Bernard
    Hoekman, Hanaa Kheir-El-Din.
        p. cm.
      ISBN 0-8213-4614-8
        1. Middle East—Commercial policy. 2. Africa, North—Commercial policy.
    3. Free trade—Middle East. 4. Free trade—Africa, North. 5. Middle East—
    Economic integration. 6. Africa, North—Economic integration.   I. Hoekman,
    Bernard M., 1959– .   II. Kheir-El-Din, Hanaa, 19— .

HF1583.3 .T7 2000
382'.3'0956—dc21

                                                                         99-058630

Contents

TABLES

FIGURES

Contributors

George T. Abed
Senior Advisor, Fiscal Affairs Dept., The International Monetary Fund,
Washington, D.C.

A. Halis Akder
Professor of Economics, Middle East Technical University, Turkey

Benita Cox
Senior Lecturer, The Management School, Imperial College for Science,
Technology and Medicine, London

Annette I. De Kleine
Economist, The World Bank, Washington, D.C.

Ahmed Galal
Executive Director, The Egyptian Center for Economic Studies (ECES),
Cairo, Egypt

Sherine Ghoneim
Economist, Economic Research Forum for the Arab Countries, Turkey and Iran,
Cairo, Egypt

Bernard Hoekman
Principal Trade Economist, The World Bank, Washington, D.C. and Fellow,
Center for Economic Policy Research (CEPR)

Hanaa Kheir-El-Din
Professor of Economics, Cairo University, Egypt

Mustapha K. Nabli
Chief Economist and Sector Director, Middle East and North Africa Region,
The World Bank, Washington, D.C.

Kishore Rao
President and CEO, The Services Group, Inc., Arlington, Virginia, USA

Amal Refaat
Economist, The Egyptian Center for Economic Studies (ECES), Cairo, Egypt

Sübidey Togan
Professor of International Economics, Bilkent University, Turkey

Jamel Zarrouk
Senior Economist, Arab Monetary Fund, United Arab Emirates

Foreword

This is the second book published by the World Bank on behalf of the Mediterranean Development Forum (MDF) partnership of 10 Middle East and North Africa region (MENA) think tanks and the World Bank Institute. The volume is a joint publication with the Economic Research Forum for the Arab Countries, Iran and Turkey (ERF). Most of the contributors are researchers from the region, many of whom are active ERF Fellows. We hope that the studies presented here will contribute to the ongoing debate on the trade opportunities and challenges facing the countries in the Middle East and North Africa.

The MDF publication series is based on conferences that the MDF partnership holds every 18 months. This particular volume on trade policy developments in the Middle East and North Africa includes papers discussed at the second Mediterranean Development Forum, which took place in Marrakech, Morocco, in September 1998.

We would like to express our thanks to those who contributed to the sessions on trade and global integration challenges facing the region at both MDF1 and MDF2. Hana' Al Sagban of the ERF played a major role in organizing the workshops and ensuring that they went smoothly. In addition to the ERF, other think tank representatives who contributed to the trade sessions were Faycal Lakhoua (Institut Arabe des Chefs d'Entreprise, Tunisia), Nabil Sukkar (Syrian Consulting Bureau), and Imed Limam (Arab Planning Institute, Kuwait).

Heba Handoussa, Director
Economic Research Forum for the
Arab Countries, Iran, and Turkey

Vinod Thomas, Director
World Bank Institute

About MDF

The MDF partnership, launched in 1997, is composed of 10 Middle East and North Africa region (MENA) think tanks and the World Bank Institute. The partnership is dedicated to providing policy support among development actors, research and capacity building of think tanks, and creating networks in the MENA region. The partnership's work culminates in a forum held every 18 months. The MDF represents a vital opportunity for some of the region's most influential thinkers and practitioners to affect regional policy.

The forum is a crucial component of the MDF partnership because it provides a rare opportunity for MENA experts, high-level government officials, and civil society representatives to meet and engage in a dialogue to set the region's development agenda. The MDF already has a unique impact on the region. Its first conference, MDF1—held in May 1997—focused on the interplay of civil society, business, and government in boosting the region's competitiveness. The discussions at MDF2 in September 1998 revolved around the theme of enhancing public participation in the development process. More than 100 speakers debated innovative and cutting-edge development issues with an audience of over 500 of the region's most influential thinkers and practitioners, including high-level government officials, think tank representatives, private sector leaders, academics, and civil society.

As a direct result of the MDF partnership, a number of projects have emerged, including programs on decentralization and governance in the West Bank and Gaza; programs on quality education, emphasizing gender; the Network of Women Evaluators; the Network of Lawyers Reforming NGO Laws; the "Meet the Civil Society Initiative"; the MENA Data Initiative; and the MDF publication series.

The next Forum, MDF3, will take place in Cairo, Egypt, on March 5–8, 2000. Based on the theme "Voices for Change, Partners for Prosperity," MDF3 will emphasize an inclusive approach toward development and the importance of partnerships in the new millennium. For more information on the conference, please contact the partner in your region listed on the back cover of this publication.

Introduction

Bernard Hoekman and Hanaa Kheir-El-Din

The extent to which countries in different parts of the world have increased their integration into the world economy varies substantially. Some countries, such as China or the former centrally planned economies of Europe, have greatly increased their participation in the international economy in the last decade. Others, including many countries in the Middle East and North Africa (MENA), have been less dynamic. Although almost all MENA countries have pursued economic reforms, including trade liberalization, the pace of integration into the world economy achieved by the region has been slow. As pointed out by Mustapha Nabli and Annette De Kleine in chapter 1 of this volume, the trade integration ratio for MENA economies (that is, trade in goods and nonfactor services trade as a share of GDP) was stagnant over the 1990–97 period, whereas it increased in all other regions of the world.

The factors that constrain the ability of Arab businesses to confront import competition and compete in world markets are numerous. Some are exogenous— for example, political and foreign policy related—and give rise to significant disincentives for investment in the region. Others reflect the large role of the state in the economy, which crowds out the private sector, generates excessive transactions costs, and raises the costs of intermediate inputs (both goods and services) that are a determinant of the competitiveness of enterprises. The focus of the contributions in this book is on trade and trade policy–related factors. Contributors—almost all economists from the region—review recent trends in trade performance, assess current trade and investment regimes, and discuss some of the emerging microeconomic policy challenges that confront governments and firms seeking to expand trade.

Topics addressed include the need for and scope of using regional integration and economic free zones as a tool of development, mobilization of nontrade tax bases to offset revenue losses as tariffs are lowered, establishment of more efficient mechanisms to enforce product standards to ensure health and safety of citizens, and implementation of modern information technologies to expedite customs clearance.

A number of chapters reveal that, although tariffs have fallen and quotas have largely been abolished, transactions costs associated with international trade frequently are high in MENA countries. Inefficiencies in customs clearance procedures, in port and ancillary services, and in transportation and telecommunications services impose excess costs on economic actors. Administrative red tape and redundant procedures imposed at the border are a major problem in some economies in the region. Relatively high import duties and inadequate duty drawback mechanisms—in part because para-tariffs in many countries are significant—add an additional burden by raising the costs of imported inputs and technology.

There are three major policy options for governments seeking to liberalize trade—unilateral (autonomous) reform, opening of markets in the context of (reciprocal) bilateral or regional trade agreements, and multilateral liberalization in the World Trade Organization (WTO) forum. Many countries all over the world are complementing autonomous economic reform programs with reciprocal trade agreements and WTO commitments. Arab countries are no exception, although unilateral and regional approaches have tended to dominate. Starting in the mid-1990s, many MENA countries began trade liberalization programs in the context of broader economic reform efforts. A number of Mediterranean Arab countries complemented such unilateral reforms with reciprocal free trade agreements (FTAs) with the European Union (EU) covering all manufactures. These imply that by the end of the next decade EU goods will enter the relevant MENA markets duty free.

A primary motivation for the FTAs with the EU was the collapse of communism in Central and Eastern European countries (CEECs) and the conclusion of FTAs between these countries and the EU. The advent of EU-CEEC free trade raised concerns that the Mediterranean Arab countries might be "marginalized" in EU markets, as the competitive advantage that they used to enjoy in those markets (through geographic proximity and preferential access) would be eroded. So far, Tunisia, Morocco, and Jordan have concluded so-called Euro-Mediterranean (Euro-Med) Partnership Agreements, while Israel and Turkey have somewhat different arrangements that also imply virtual free trade with the EU (the notable exception being agriculture). Lebanon and Egypt are actively negotiating with the EU to conclude similar agreements, and the intention of the EU is that agreements will be concluded with all countries around the Mediterranean (and beyond—for example, with the Gulf Cooperation Council).

The impact of such FTAs with the EU has been the subject of a substantial amount of work.[1] To some extent, the Euro-Med FTAs led to a revival in interest in intra-MENA integration, as exemplified in the 1998 Greater Arab Free Trade Area agreement. In chapter 2 of this volume, Ahmed Galal assesses the prospects and preconditions for greater economic integration within the MENA region (including Israel as well as Arab countries). To a significant extent, the prospects and payoffs of intraregional integration are determined by the interaction of noneconomic (especially political) and economic factors. Galal argues that preconditions for regional integration are implementation of the FTAs with the EU, more far-reaching domestic economic reforms, and a clear perception on the part of all countries' leaderships that there are political gains from integrating. In his view, these conditions have yet to be satisfied.

One reflection of the differences in preparedness of economies in the region is the variation that is observed in the content and depth of the agreements with the EU. These differences are assessed in chapter 3 by Sübidey Togan, who compares in some detail three of the trade agreements involving the EU. Although there are important gaps in all of the EU agreements, both in terms of sectoral coverage and the extent to which the agreements ensure effective market access, some Mediterranean countries have concluded more comprehensive deals than others.

A recent report by the World Bank (2000) notes among other things that:

- Realization of economic gains from regional integration depends on securing an effective increase in competition in the regional market. Increasing openness to trade with the outside world is a key ingredient in maximizing the gains from regional trade agreements.

- Although there are clear advantages associated with selecting high-income countries (such as those in the EU) as partners in terms of the potential for income convergence over time, attaining the desired increase in growth depends importantly on the coverage of the agreement. In particular, realization of competition and scale effects may require abolition of antidumping, cooperation on customs practices and product standards, and liberalization of investment regimes and service sectors ("deeper integration").

A problem affecting both the autonomous trade reforms and the trade agreements that have been concluded among countries in the region is that their coverage is relatively narrow. As a result, the potential gains from reforms are reduced. A major hole in the EU agreements—and in unilateral reform efforts as well[2]—is agriculture. In chapter 4, A. Halis Akder assesses the extent to which southern Mediterranean countries produce and export similar agricultural commodities, or compete in the same EU countries. He concludes that a number of MENA countries have a great interest in improving their access to EU markets. The issues here are relatively well-known—what is of interest in this chapter is the use of statistical techniques to assess the similarity of countries' export agricultural bundles and identify which countries are, and which are not, competitors. Improving agricultural market access conditions in EU markets should be a priority for many Mediterranean countries.

More generally, the focus in many MENA countries is arguably too much on the "traditional" trade agenda—elimination of quotas, reduction in tariffs—and not enough on the complementary regulatory and institutional reforms that are needed to ensure that antitrade biases are removed and a strong supply response emerges. Many of the chapters in this volume discuss the outstanding reform agenda. However, even on the traditional front there is still a significant amount of work to be done. Chapters 5, 6, and 7 by Amal Refaat, Riad al Khouri, and Jamel Zarrouk, respectively, document both the progress that has been made to liberalize trade in a number of MENA countries and the challenges that remain. Average tariffs remain relatively high, and nontariff barriers, including para-tariffs, can be a significant burden. In general, the conclusion of these chapters is that trade regimes could be made more transparent, in the process lowering transactions costs.

The trade policy agenda extends well beyond traditional tariff and para-tariff issues. Priority areas that are discussed in a number of chapters are domestic regulatory regimes and administrative procedures related to trade. Administrative procedures and requirements associated with importing into MENA countries are often burdensome, increasing the cost of imports substantially and thereby lowering the competitiveness of MENA firms on world markets. Many government bodies are involved in the import process, either collecting taxes or import duties, or authorizing the release of imports. The many administrative controls can delay customs clearance by anything from a few days to several weeks. Customs officials in many MENA countries appear to be generally suspicious of invoice values, relying on price lists and declared values of "bona fide" importers of particular goods to determine the value of goods. To some extent, burdensome customs procedures and relatively high tariffs are motivated by government revenue objectives. In chapter 8, George Abed provides a comprehensive survey of the dependence of MENA governments on trade taxes; assesses the fiscal impact of trade liberalization, especially the Euro-Med agreements with the EU; and discusses the options for mobilizing alternative tax bases.

Two specific issue areas that are attracting a lot of attention—both inside and outside the region—are discussed in some detail in this book. In chapter 9, Hanaa Kheir-El-Din discusses the enforcement of mandatory product standards in Egypt, which is regarded as a serious nontariff barrier by many exporters to Egypt. In chapter 10, Benita Cox and Sherine Ghoneim focus on the scope for using modern informatics techniques—in particular electronic data interchange—to reduce transactions costs related to customs procedures. In both cases, progress is not easy to achieve—in contrast to tariff reforms, which can be implemented at the stroke of a minister's pen—reduction in transactions costs and facilitation of trade require institutional changes and strengthening. Greater reliance on information technologies, international norms and good practices, and market forces can help trade, but progress requires that all stakeholders be consulted and involved in the process of reform.

Regional integration initiatives of the type discussed in chapters 2 and 3 can play an important role in advancing regulatory reform by acting as focal points and commitment mechanisms, but they are simply tools, not panaceas. Many of the actions that are required will have to be pursued by governments and stakeholders autonomously. In the transition toward a more open economy, one instrument that could be used is the economic free zone or free trade zone. Such zones have been used to good effect by a number of countries—both developing and developed—but have not been very prominent in the MENA region. In chapter 11, Kishore Rao discusses the global experience with free zones and reviews the status quo in the MENA region. He concludes that MENA countries could benefit greatly from more widespread use and more effective implementation of such zones.

In conclusion, the contributions to this volume illustrate that a lot has been achieved in the last decade, but that a lot also remains to be done on the trade policy–related front. This is an issue area that is receiving substantial attention from both policymakers and the research community in the region. The contributions to this volume illustrate that the policy challenges extend beyond traditional trade policies, and include domestic regulatory regimes, administrative procedures, and the performance of public institutions. Complementary reforms that center on reduction of transactions costs and improving the performance of infrastructure service providers—for example, transport, port services, telecoms, and finance—are as important, if not more important, than trade policy reforms narrowly defined.

Notes:

1. See Galal and Hoekman (1997), Safadi (1998), Joffé (1999), and Hoekman and Zarrouk (2000).

2. See, for example, De Rosa (2000) and Chaherli and El Said (1999).

References

Chaherli, Nabil, and Moataz El Said. 1999. "Impact of the WTO Agreement on MENA Agriculture," Economic Research Forum, Cairo. Mimeo.

De Rosa, Dean. 2000. "Agricultural Trade and Rural Development in the Middle East and North Africa." In B. Hoekman and J. Zarrouk, eds., *Catching Up with the Competition: Trade Opportunities and Challenges for Arab Countries*. Ann Arbor: University of Michigan Press.

Galal, Ahmed, and Bernard Hoekman, eds. 1997. *Regional Partners in Global Markets: Limits and Possibilities of the Euro-Med Agreements*. London: Centre for Economic Policy Research.

Hoekman, Bernard, and Jamel Zarrouk, eds. 2000. *Catching Up with the Competition: Trade Opportunities and Challenges for Arab Countries*. Ann Arbor: University of Michigan Press.

Joffé, George, ed. 1999. *Perspectives on Development: The Euro-Mediterranean Partnership*. London: Frank Cass Publishers.

Safadi, Raed, ed. 1998. *Opening Doors to the World: A New Trade Agenda for the Middle East*. Cairo: American University of Cairo Press for the Economic Research Forum.

World Bank. 2000. *Trade Blocs and Beyond: Political Dreams and Practical Decisions*. Policy Research Report. Washington D.C.

CHAPTER 1

Managing Global Integration in the Middle East and North Africa[1]

Mustapha K. Nabli
Annette I. De Kleine
The World Bank

In the aftermath of the Asian crisis, questions regarding the role and implications of increased integration into the world economy for developing countries are again at center stage. A renewed debate and assessment of the issues involved is taking place. While little has changed in the terms of the debate and policy implications for trade and trade policy, it has been heated about financial integration. The role of capital inflows and the pertinence of prescriptions for capital account liberalization are being reassessed in view of their potential contribution to financial crisis.

While very diverse in many respects, the Middle East and North Africa (MENA) countries nevertheless also share some common characteristics, including a number of important shared challenges for policymakers. On the domestic front, low labor productivity and high unemployment are critical issues to be dealt with to secure improved future growth prospects. These generally reflect the need throughout MENA to redefine the role of the state, linked to the pursuit of increased private sector participation and financial sector reform. The public sector still plays a dominant role, especially compared with other developing regions. For example, MENA governments spend 9.8 percent of GDP on wages, in contrast to less than 5.0 percent in the OECD countries, Asia, and Latin America (World Bank, 1999). This is intricately linked to the region's high unemployment rate, which makes government downsizing especially difficult. MENA governments on the whole have also been under pressure to introduce fiscal reforms and cut public spending programs—including even the Gulf petroleum exporters, which have faced generally weak oil markets since the mid-1980s and made huge outlays tied to the Gulf War.

The policies with regard to integration into the world economy are central to the MENA countries' response to deal with these challenges. The debate about globalization is, therefore, of particular interest for the MENA region, especially because it has lagged behind other regions, in part reflecting skepticism about the benefits of integration in both academic and policymakers' circles.

Goods trade has expanded as a percentage of national output in real terms (purchasing power parity, or PPP) for all regions except MENA between 1986 and 1996 (Table 1.1). However, during this period, MENA's integration declined on the whole: while its level of trade integration ratios were highest or among the highest in 1986, it lost this position by 1996. The same observation applies to capital inflow ratios. In sum, the worldwide trend of increased cross-border trade in goods and capital has bypassed the MENA countries as a group. Examination of individual MENA countries, where data are available, reveals that only a few of the North African countries diverged from the regionwide trends: Tunisia shows an across-the-board improvement in the four integration measures presented in Table 1.1, below. And, while Egypt and Morocco both exhibit deterioration in the private capital flow indicators, they were the only other MENA region countries to show improvement in the two merchandise trade integration indicators (Table 1.1).

Given these regional and international developments in trade and finance, this chapter aims to (a) present an update and overview of the extent and main characteristics and trends of integration of MENA countries into the world economy; (b) review the terms of the debate about globalization and development and, more specifically, the issues of risks and benefits of financial integration; and (c) present a brief discussion of the implications and lessons for managing MENA's integration into the world economy in the future in light of the experience of other countries.[2] Given the terms of the debate, highlighted most recently by the East Asian crisis and its spread, the chapter discusses the issues of trade integration, globalization of production, and financial integration.

MENA and Trade Integration in Global Markets

Trends in Trade Integration in MENA

A variety of measures of trade integration can be used, and they all lead to the same conclusion: The MENA region as a whole has lagged behind other regions, despite a far stronger level of integration achieved by a limited number of the individual countries.

VOLUME OF EXPORTS AND IMPORTS

Using a broader measure of trade integration—including nonfactor services trade as a share of GDP, in contrast to using only merchandise trade in Table 1.1—Figure 1.1 shows an increase in openness for all regions since the late 1980s or early 1990s,

TABLE 1.1. OVERVIEW OF INTEGRATION WITH THE GLOBAL ECONOMY: MENA, CENTRAL EASTERN EUROPEAN, SOUTHERN MEDITERRANEAN, AND EAST ASIAN COUNTRIES

	Merchandise trade, % of GDP PPP		Merchandise trade, % of goods GDP PPP		Gross private capital flows, % of GDP PPP		Gross FDI, % of GDP PPP	
	1986	*1996*	*1986*	*1996*	*1986*	*1996*	*1986*	*1996*
MENA								
Algeria	17.3	15.0	41.1	66.7	0.8	—	0.0	—
Egypt	13.6	14.8	60.9	70.6	4.6	2.5	1.5	0.4
Iran	9.7	9.6	17.1	—	2.0	1.5	0.0	0.0
Jordan	36.8	36.6	123.8	172.4	3.3	4.7	0.4	0.4
Kuwait	54.3	45.8	158.2	132.4	41.1	16.8	1.0	1.7
Libya	—	—	91.9	—	—	—	—	—
Morocco	12.6	14.0	66.8	69.3	2.8	1.7	0.0	0.4
Oman	52.9	45.4	136.7	—	10.2	2.5	1.4	0.2
Saudi Arabia	36.2	41.2	110.2	—	14.2	5.5	0.9	1.0
Syria	20.0	19.6	64.5	—	6.1	5.0	0.0	0.2
Tunisia	20.6	30.2	84.6	—	3.8	5.8	0.3	0.6
UAE	83.6	135.7	160.8	—	—	—	—	—
Central Europe								
Czech Republic	—	46.3	—	187.2	—	10.9	—	1.3
Estonia	—	77.4	—	280.4	—	13.7	—	3.2
Hungary	34.5	41.4	126.9	137.1	5.4	14.0	0.0	2.8
Poland	15.9	26.5	50.6	107.2	3.8	9.3	0.0	2.0
Slovenia	—	74.0	—	184.5	—	9.5	—	0.8
Southern Mediterranean								
Greece	21.2	27.9	58.6	50.4	4.3	10.9	0.6	0.8
Portugal	23.2	43.1	106.1	—	4.5	19.0	0.4	1.0
Spain	18.4	36.8	64.8	—	4.6	10.3	1.1	1.9
East Asia								
Indonesia	10.7	13.6	55.0	69.7	2.0	2.1	0.1	0.8
Korea, Rep. of	33.6	46.7	115.0	118.0	3.5	11.1	0.8	1.1
Malaysia	33.6	70.2	163.5	269.0	2.8	4.6	0.7	2.0
Philippines	8.0	21.3	57.4	98.8	2.3	4.8	0.1	0.8
Thailand	14.7	31.3	85.8	138.2	1.6	5.0	0.2	0.8
By income group								
Low	7.1	7.9	33.8	56.9	2.0	2.1	0.2	1.0
Middle	12.5	21.8	53.3	81.1	4.0	5.8	0.3	0.9
High	26.5	38.9	70.4	178.8	11.4	19.3	1.6	2.7
Low- and middle-income group by region								
East Asia and Pacific	9.1	13.0	48.1	127.3	1.7	1.9	0.2	1.0
Europe and Central Asia	—	25.5	57.2	79.7	—	9.2	—	0.8
Latin America and Caribbean	7.9	17.3	40.6	61.7	4.6	6.6	0.3	1.1
MENA	19.4	18.9	52.1	78.4	5.0	3.2	0.4	0.4
South Asia	4.9	5.8	22.1	39.2	1.2	0.9	0.0	0.2
Sub-Saharan Africa	15.8	18.9	70.3	102.5	4.8	5.7	0.3	0.4

— Not available.
Note: Trade comprises the sum of exports and imports.
Source: World Bank, *World Development Indicators, 1998c.*

except for MENA. In other words, both goods and services trade integration in MENA has deteriorated. After a period of continuous declines in the early 1980s, the MENA region did witness an increase in integration in the mid-1980s, much of which it lost after the Gulf War.

The performance by country within the MENA region varies (see Table 1.A.1 in the Annex). Largely reflecting the impact of civil strife and/or regional conflict, trade volume ratios for Algeria, Syria, Kuwait, Iran, and Iraq show stark downward trends. Bahrain and Egypt's ratios have also deteriorated markedly. Morocco, Tunisia, Saudi Arabia, the UAE, and Jordan have, in contrast, expanded real goods and services trade as a share of national output. Morocco, Tunisia, and Jordan have reaped these gains in large part as a result of market reforms introduced in the 1980s and early 1990s. In the case of Saudi Arabia, expansion of trade integration stems in part from significantly increased petroleum export volumes following the sanctions imposed on Iraq in 1990. The UAE's growth in integration are due to its greatly expanded port and free trade zone activity.

FIGURE 1.1. TOTAL TRADE INTEGRATION: VOLUME OF GOODS AND NONFACTOR SERVICE TRADE RATIO TO GDP

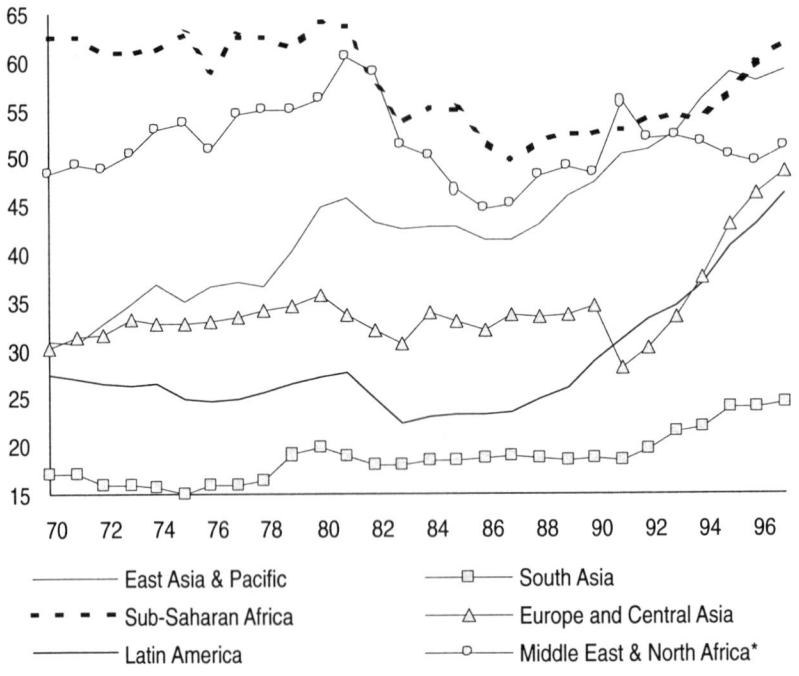

* Excludes Libya, Lebanon, and Qatar.
Source: World Bank.

Aside from the 1970s, the MENA region's rate of integration has lagged behind that of most other low- and middle-income country regions (Table 1.2). The largest gap in MENA's relative performance is evident in the 1990s, when most other developing regions witnessed a surge in trade integration. The only countries markedly boosting the regional rate of trade integration over 1990–95 are Morocco, Jordan, Saudi Arabia, the UAE, and Yemen. A similar pattern is evident when the speed of export integration as a share of national output is considered (Table 1.3). Algeria, Morocco, and Yemen also show robust export integration growth in the early 1990s. However, in 1996 and/or 1997 the trend reversed and became negative in Morocco, Tunisia, Egypt, Jordan, and Yemen.

EXPORTS

In real terms, MENA's goods and services exports as a percentage of total world exports have declined since the oil boom period in the 1970s, from 10.5 percent in 1980 to 2.1 percent in 1997 (Table 1.4). The level of MENA exports volumes as a share of total international exports used to place it behind that for Europe and Cen-

TABLE 1.2. SPEED OF TOTAL TRADE INTEGRATION[a]

(Percentage change over previous period, negative values underlined)

	1975	*1980*	*1985*	*1990*	*1995*	*1996*	*1997*
Volumes							
Low- and middle-income regions							
East Asia and Pacific	12.7	28.7	_4.4_	10.5	24.0	_1.3_	2.1
South Asia	_11.7_	32.1	_7.4_	1.0	28.2	0.4	1.8
Sub-Saharan Africa	0.5	2.2	_14.4_	_4.7_	8.1	5.1	4.3
Europe and Central Asia	8.9	8.6	_7.8_	5.4	24.2	7.4	5.1
Latin America	_9.4_	9.4	_14.2_	23.5	41.3	6.1	7.2
MENA[b]	10.7	4.8	_16.9_	3.5	3.6	_1.2_	3.1
Algeria	13.6	_17.7_	0.3	_18.5_	_5.3_	_2.2_	6.9
Morocco	8.9	_12.8_	_6.3_	25.6	25.8	_9.7_	6.9
Tunisia	14.3	21.3	_16.4_	27.7	0.0	_7.6_	0.6
Egypt	30.4	_16.5_	_21.5_	_19.3_	_4.3_	2.2	_0.4_
Jordan	78.2	33.6	23.4	39.6	3.7	8.7	_0.9_
Syria	48.2	_15.8_	_7.9_	_17.5_	_35.0_	4.9	_0.4_
Bahrain	55.7	_10.8_	7.6	10.5	_15.5_	_3.6_	_7.1_
Saudi Arabia	11.3	_3.1_	2.4	_4.8_	38.1	0.0	0.0
Kuwait	3.4	28.9	_1.3_	_38.7_	_11.7_	_5.9_	5.2
UAE	7.2	_5.5_	_16.2_	34.4	9.6	3.1	10.2
Oman	16.8	9.4	_22.2_	4.2	_13.1_	1.0	4.1
Iran	13.8	_56.1_	_4.8_	26.1	_35.9_	_2.3_	_0.2_
Iraq	1.9	_5.9_	_10.8_	4.2	_78.3_	8.8	169.4
Yemen	56.7	37.7	_52.7_	23.9	32.5	_2.3_	_1.7_

a. (Exports + Imports of GNFS)/GDP.
b. Excluding Lebanon, Libya, and Qatar.
Source: World Bank.

TABLE 1.3. SPEED OF EXPORT INTEGRATION, AS A SHARE OF GDP
(Percentages, negative values underlined)

	1975	1980	1985	1990	1995	1996	1997
Real							
Low- and middle-income regions							
East Asia & Pacific	16.0	16.9	−12.5	26.3	19.9	−1.1	6.8
South Asia	6.5	9.0	−9.0	17.3	44.6	−0.3	3.7
Sub-Saharan Africa	−11.0	3.6	−6.9	2.4	5.9	5.4	4.4
Europe and Central Asia	1.1	11.5	9.3	−3.7	24.5	5.6	5.2
Latin America	−26.9	2.0	15.7	20.7	28.8	6.7	4.2
MENA total	−8.5	−8.9	−35.8	20.9	5.0	−1.4	2.6
Algeria	−20.6	−24.6	−1.8	17.2	2.4	5.6	9.8
Morocco	−14.0	−5.7	7.1	23.4	25.5	−4.7	5.0
Tunisia	11.4	19.8	−16.1	37.3	4.8	−6.0	−1.0
Egypt	0.7	−3.2	−22.2	21.1	2.5	3.2	−4.2
Jordan	163.5	28.5	33.2	45.4	5.9	6.6	−0.7
Syria	−19.1	−36.2	1.5	6.3	−24.0	−0.5	−3.3
Bahrain	13.6	−8.9	13.3	7.1	−13.5	−6.7	−8.5
Saudi Arabia	5.8	−19.1	−34.7	1.0	43.1	0.0	0.0
Kuwait	−6.8	−11.9	−19.6	−23.1	−21.3	−5.5	2.0
UAE	−17.0	−3.8	−19.3	56.6	1.6	−0.8	8.8
Oman	−16.1	19.8	−24.9	10.9	−9.3	−1.0	3.9
Iran	−18.3	−77.6	21.8	66.9	−20.6	−5.0	0.1
Iraq	−20.6	−14.6	−31.7	18.0	−80.3	7.9	168.1
Yemen	161.9	30.1	−36.6	368.5	63.6	−4.9	−4.0

Source: World Bank.

tral Asia in the 1970s, but by the mid-1980s, it came to be outranked by Latin America and East Asia and the Pacific as well. MENA's goods and services imports as a share of total world imports have also fallen, dropping to 1.9 percent in 1997, less than a third of the 6.9 percent share in 1980. Import volumes as a share of total world imports from East Asia and the Pacific have grown to outstrip those of MENA, and those of Latin America, Europe and Central Asia have remained above the MENA region's level, in both real and nominal terms.

Despite the Maghreb countries' dependence on EU export markets, the region's exports to the EU as a share of total world merchandise exports to the EU have dropped markedly since the early 1980s, from 10.6 percent in 1980 to 2.3 percent in 1995 (Table 1.4). Over the same period, MENA has come to represent a smaller export market for the EU, although the decline has not been as sharp.

The decline in importance of MENA's exports compared with other regions is strikingly evident when comparing real GNFS exports as a share of GDP (Figure 1.2). The MENA countries had the highest export volumes as a share of GDP throughout the 1970s, despite a consistent decline in the ratio during the period. In the 1980s, due to an acceleration of the drop in the ratio, MENA's share fell below that of Sub-Saharan Africa. Despite a resumption of export growth in the mid-1980s,

TABLE 1.4. SHARE IN WORLD EXPORTS AND IMPORTS, 1970–97
(Percentages, nominal unless otherwise noted)

	1970	1975	1980	1985	1990	1995	1996	1997
MENA's share of intraregional								
goods trade	5.6	4.2	4.0	6.0	9.2	8.1	7.3	7.2
Share in total world exports, GNFS								
Current prices								
East Asia and Pacific	2.1	2.4	3.1	3.8	3.8	6.4	6.6	7.0
South Asia	1.0	0.8	0.7	0.9	0.8	1.0	1.0	1.1
Sub-Saharan Africa	3.2	2.7	3.5	2.3	1.8	1.3	1.4	1.4
MENA[a]	2.8	7.0	8.5	4.3	3.3	2.3	2.2	2.2
Europe and Central Asia	13.1	14.9	6.4	6.4	4.3	3.6	3.8	3.8
Latin America	4.5	4.0	4.6	5.2	4.0	4.3	4.6	5.0
Constant prices								
East Asia and Pacific	2.3	3.2	3.8	4.1	4.0	5.9	6.3	6.6
South Asia	1.1	1.0	0.9	0.9	0.8	0.9	1.0	1.0
Sub-Saharan Africa	3.6	3.6	4.3	2.4	1.9	1.2	1.3	1.3
MENA[a]	3.1	9.2	10.5	4.7	3.4	2.1	2.1	2.1
Europe and Central Asia	14.7	19.4	8.0	6.9	4.5	3.3	3.6	3.6
Latin America	5.0	5.2	5.7	5.7	4.1	4.0	4.4	4.7
Share in total world imports, GNFS								
Current prices								
East Asia and Pacific	2.2	2.5	2.8	4.3	3.7	6.7	6.7	6.5
South Asia	1.4	1.0	1.2	1.4	1.1	1.3	1.3	1.4
Sub-Saharan Africa	3.5	3.2	3.1	2.1	1.7	1.5	1.4	1.4
MENA[a]	2.2	5.0	5.6	5.0	3.2	2.1	2.0	2.0
Europe and Central Asia	13.8	17.6	6.6	6.1	4.7	4.3	4.7	4.8
Latin America	4.7	4.7	5.0	3.7	3.4	4.4	4.7	5.3
Constant prices								
East Asia and Pacific	2.4	3.2	3.5	4.7	3.8	6.1	6.4	6.2
South Asia	1.5	1.3	1.5	1.6	1.2	1.2	1.3	1.4
Sub-Saharan Africa	3.7	4.2	3.8	2.3	1.8	1.3	1.4	1.4
MENA[a]	2.4	6.6	6.9	5.5	3.3	1.9	1.9	1.9
Europe and Central Asia	14.9	23.1	8.1	6.8	4.9	4.0	4.5	4.6
Latin America	5.1	6.2	6.1	4.1	3.5	4.1	4.5	5.0
Memo items								
MENA's share in total world								
goods *X* to the EU	4.5	7.9	10.6	6.3	3.5	2.3	2.5	2.7
MENA's share in total world								
goods *M* from the EU	2.7	6.6	6.7	6.2	3.5	3.2	3.3	3.8

a. Excludes Kuwait, the UAE, Lebanon, Libya, and Qatar.
Source: IMF, *Direction of Trade*; World Bank.

MENA was overtaken in 1990 by East Asia and the Pacific. While the ratio increased during the late 1980s, the rate of increase leveled off and remained flat throughout the 1990s, in contrast to other regions, with the exception of South Asia. (Table 1.A.2 in the Annex presents a breakdown by country.)

FIGURE 1.2. RATIO OF GNFS EXPORT VOLUMES TO GDP
(Percentage shares, real)

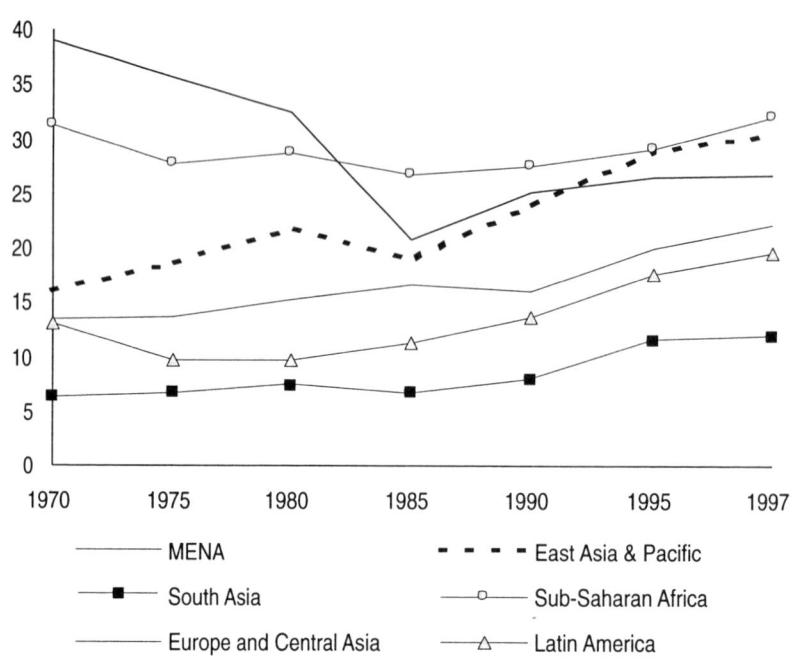

MENA   — — — East Asia & Pacific

South Asia   —□— Sub-Saharan Africa

Europe and Central Asia —△— Latin America

Source: World Bank.

Per capita exports for the region (in real terms) also reveal a pattern of declining integration, indicating a progressive tightening of the external constraint on growth. This translates into a falling standard of living. Decreasing real exports per capita also imply falling import-purchasing power. Declines are sharpest from the early 1970s through the mid-1980s, when real per capita exports declined from $5,238 in 1970 to less than half, at $2,192, in 1985 (Table 1.5). In the decade since 1985, exports per capita have, however, remained fairly stable. Among the countries for which data are available, Jordan is the only one that has expanded strongly and consistently over the last 25-years, increasing more than 10-fold, albeit from an extremely low base of $74 per capita to $1,027 in 1997. Morocco, Tunisia, and Egypt also witnessed a fairly steady increase over the period from 1970 to 1997. However, they reaped more modest gains: Morocco's exports doubled to $300 per capita, and Tunisia and Egypt's tripled to $646 and $150 per capita, respectively. Sharp declines in exports per capita were experienced by Kuwait, the UAE, and Iraq, pulling down the region's aggregate performance.

FUELS AND NONFUELS EXPORTS

Clearly, the large geographical grouping of MENA countries masks great variability among the individual countries due to factors such as size (both geographical
and population), role of fuels, and trade policies. It is therefore useful to use the
following sub-groupings: *Gulf Cooperation Council (GCC)* (and Libya)—that is,
oil exporters with low population density, Saudi Arabia, the UAE, Kuwait, Bahrain,
Oman, and Qatar; *oil exporters with large populations*—Algeria, Iraq, and Iran; and
diversified exporters—Egypt, Jordan, Lebanon, Morocco, Tunisia, Syria, and Yemen.
With respect to trade profiles, the percentage share of fuel exports as share in total
goods and services exports provides one indication of regional diversity (Table 1.6).

Not surprisingly, for the GCC, Syria, and Algeria, the bulk of foreign export
earnings is composed of fuel exports (Table 1.6). Only a limited number of MENA
economies have a significant ratio of nonfuels exports to GDP: Morocco, Tunisia,
Egypt, Jordan, Bahrain, and, more recently, Oman.[3] Morocco has not increased its
ratio of nonfuels to exports significantly since the mid-1980s, while Egypt made
some gains up to the early 1990s, which it lost over the last few years. Oman has
experienced a surge in nonfuels exports since the early 1990s, as has Bahrain. Tunisia achieved a very rapid increase in nonfuels since the structural adjustment program in the mid-1980s, but the rate of increase has stagnated since 1994.

TABLE 1.5. PER CAPITA EXPORTS AND POPULATION

	1970	1975	1980	1985	1990	1995	1996	1997[a]
Per capita exports								
(Real 1987 US$)								
MENA, average[b]	5,238	3,988	3,795	2,192	2,344	2,339	2,299	2,256
Algeria	470	411	376	409	423	391	421	452
Morocco	142	136	151	175	238	286	298	301
Tunisia	196	299	430	390	551	635	629	646
Egypt	66	75	105	102	134	144	153	150
Jordan	74	196	487	641	794	945	1,034	1,027
Syria	164	209	156	155	150	138	140	136
Bahrain	4,570	5,349	8,307	7,269	7,447	7,108	6,605	6,070
Saudi Arabia	4,691	7,254	6,691	2,401	2,491	3,247	3,217	3,197
Kuwait	27,711	17,388	11,674	5,776	4,622	5,142	4,921	4,996
UAE	24,825	15,640	16,039	8,372	10,637	9,546	9,757	9,325
Oman	2,176	2,055	2,367	1,768	2,251	2,564	2,433	2,659
Iran	532	538	82	109	153	121	136	143
Iraq	2,477	2,294	2,475	919	499	49	53	151
Yemen	—	—	—	12	77	89	85	81

— Not available.

a. Underlined values are based on estimates for population figures for 1997.

b. Excludes Yemen.

Sources: IMF, *International Financial Statistics*; World Bank.

TABLE 1.6. FUEL AND NONFUEL EXPORTS
(Percentage shares of GDP, nominal)

	1985	1990	1991	1992	1993	1994	1995	1996
Fuel exports/GDP								
Algeria	17.1	17.2	24.7	21.7	19.3	19.7	19.6	—
Morocco	0.7	0.6	0.4	0.4	0.4	0.3	0.3	0.2
Tunisia	8.2	4.9	4.1	3.9	3.0	2.8	2.6	3.0
Egypt	3.6	1.8	5.4	3.2	3.3	2.6	2.2	2.5
Jordan	0.0	0.0	0.0	0.0	0.0	0.0	0.0	—
Syria	7.4	15.5	—	16.2	—	—	—	—
Bahrain	66.7	73.3	64.7	59.8	52.4	42.3	—	—
Saudi Arabia	29.9	38.3	37.0	37.8	32.6	—	—	—
Kuwait	—	34.7	7.9	31.3	41.8	45.4	46.0	—
UAE	—	—	—	—	—	—	—	—
Oman	—	48.0	41.8	40.3	37.4	36.6	38.4	—
Iran	—	—	—	—	—	—	—	—
Iraq	—	—	—	—	—	—	—	—
Yemen	—	—	0.0	—	—	—	20.8	—
Nonfuel GNFS exports								
Algeria	6.5	6.1	4.2	3.1	2.5	4.0	7.8	—
Morocco	24.8	25.9	23.7	24.7	26.2	25.1	26.6	24.9
Tunisia	23.9	38.6	36.3	35.6	37.5	42.1	42.1	39.3
Egypt	16.3	18.3	22.4	25.8	24.4	20.3	22.1	18.1
Jordan	38.7	61.9	59.5	52.1	51.6	49.8	52.4	—
Syria	4.9	12.3	—	2.9	—	—	—	—
Bahrain	35.0	48.6	50.0	51.8	52.2	62.8	—	—
Saudi Arabia	6.1	7.9	7.6	7.3	7.8	—	—	—
Kuwait	—	10.2	9.0	9.1	6.0	5.7	8.8	—
UAE	—	—	—	—	—	—	—	—
Oman	—	4.7	6.5	9.3	11.0	12.8	14.2	—
Iran	—	—	—	—	—	—	—	—
Iraq	—	—	—	—	—	—	—	—
Yemen	—	—	14.2	—	—	—	4.1	—
Total GNFS exports								
East Asia and Pacific	17.0	23.7	25.2	25.7	25.0	28.9	28.7	27.1
South Asia	7.1	9.0	10.8	11.6	12.5	12.4	13.6	13.8
Sub-Saharan Africa	26.2	27.7	26.3	26.7	26.4	28.0	28.2	28.8
MENA[a]	20.7	30.2	30.0	29.6	29.2	30.7	29.5	29.3
Europe and Central Asia	17.8	14.4	13.0	28.9	20.0	17.8	17.2	16.1
Latin America	16.6	15.0	14.8	14.5	13.9	13.8	15.5	16.3

— Not available.
a. Excludes Kuwait, the UAE, Libya, and Qatar.
Source: World Bank.

SERVICES: THE CASE OF TOURISM

Tourism revenues represent a large component of foreign exchange receipts for a number of MENA countries, especially the North African countries of Egypt, Morocco, and Tunisia, as well as Jordan and Syria. As a share of total exports, there has been a striking expansion of tourism exports share in total exports in Egypt, from 12.9 percent in 1980 to 21.0 percent in 1996, and in Syria, from 6.3 percent in 1980 to 24.1 percent in 1996 (Table 1.7). Compared with other low- and middle-income regions, MENA tourism revenues as a percentage of total GNFS are comparable or high at 8.2 percent in 1996. However, as a percentage of total world tourism, the region only captures a marginal share of 2.6 percent in 1996, down significantly from 4.2 percent in 1980. In contrast, as a group, low- and middle-income countries were able to increase their share of total world tourism receipts from 22.2 percent to 26.8 percent, at the expense of high-income countries.

This reflects the strong growth of tourism in East Asia and the Pacific and Europe and Central Asia, which offsets declines in world market shares in Latin America and the Caribbean, MENA, South Asia, and Sub-Saharan Africa.

INTRAREGIONAL TRADE

Another important feature of the MENA region's global trade integration is the fact that export and import product profiles are similar—that is, intraregional demand for MENA goods and services is generally weak. The predominance of primary goods in the product mix also constrains the intraregional market potential. As a result, there is little opportunity for intraindustry trade growth, which is more generally associated with trade in manufactured goods.

Intraregional trade as a share of the region's total trade first declined and then expanded during the 1970s and 1980s. The pattern was repeated in the late 1980s, peaking in the early 1990s, and then deteriorating again through 1997 (Figure 1.3). MENA's low level of intraregional integration (even within subregions such as the Maghreb and the Gulf) makes the countries more dependent on extraregional trading partners and correspondingly constrains their export market diversity. For example, the Maghreb's export dependence on EU markets is immense: In 1997, exports to the EU as a percentage of total merchandise exports were close to 60 percent for Algeria, 70 percent for Morocco, and as much as 80 percent for Tunisia. In contrast, exports to one another are marginal and came to less than 5 percent.

Trade Policy and Liberalization in MENA

PAST AND PRESENT

Over the period from the mid-1960s through the mid-to-late 1980s, MENA countries as a group implemented some of the most restrictive trade regimes in the developing world. Import substitution industrialization was pursued throughout the region. While varying in degree and form from country to country, these policies include(d) an extensive and complex system of import controls, tariff rates, and exchange controls. Additionally, MENA governments also put in place comprehensive systems to support domestic import-substituting industries, including investment, credit, prices, and trade support programs.

TABLE 1.7. INTERNATIONAL TOURISM RECEIPTS

	$ (millions)		Export, %		World receipts, %	
	1980	1996	1980	1996	1980	1996
MENA						
Algeria	115	16	0.8	0.1	0.1	0.0
Egypt	808	3,200	12.9	21.0	0.8	0.8
Iran	54	165	0.4	0.8	0.1	0.0
Iraq	170	13	—	—	0.2	0.0
Jordan	431	744	36.5	20.3	0.4	0.2
Kuwait	377	109	1.7	0.7	0.4	0.0
Libya	10	6	0.0	—	0.0	0.0
Morocco	397	1,381	12.3	14.9	0.4	0.3
Oman	—	99	—	1.3	—	0.0
Qatar	—	—	—	—	—	—
Saudi Arabia	1,344	1,308	1.3	2.2	1.3	0.3
Syria	156	1,478	6.3	24.1	0.2	0.4
Tunisia	601	1,436	18.4	17.6	0.6	0.3
UAE	—	—	—	—	—	—
Yemen	24	42	—	1.7	0.0	0.0
World	101,016	421,783	4.6	6.4	100.0	100.0
Low-income	3,055	16,722	3.5	5.4	3.0	4.0
Middle-income	19,388	96,400	4.7	8.8	19.2	22.9
Low- and middle-income	22,443	113,122	4.5	8.0	22.2	26.8
East Asia and Pacific	2,480	32,450	5.1	7.3	2.5	7.7
Europe and Central Asia	1,358	32,820	4.0	10.2	1.3	7.8
Latin America and Caribbean	11,262	27,993	9.2	8.1	11.1	6.6
MENA	4,260	10,903	2.3	8.2	4.2	2.6
South Asia	1,485	3,774	8.5	5.8	1.5	0.9
Sub-Saharan Africa	1,598	5,182	1.9	5.4	1.6	1.2
High-income	78,573	308,661	4.6	5.9	77.8	73.2

— Not available.

Source: World Bank, *World Development Indicators*, 1998.

Beginning in the mid-1980s, a few countries (Jordan, Algeria, Morocco, Tunisia, and Egypt) began to pursue extensive economic reform programs. Trade reform measures, including a general dismantling of quantitative import controls, cuts in tariff levels, streamlining of tariff systems, and current account convertibility, were introduced. Policies to promote nonoil and nonmineral exports were also implemented. In most of these countries where reforms were introduced, the impetus for change came in response to major balance-of-payments difficulties. Overall, greater progress was made in liberalizing quantitative restrictions than in reducing tariffs, due largely to the continued reliance on international trade taxes as a source of budgetary revenue.

FIGURE 1.3. MENA'S INTRAREGIONAL TRADE: SHARE OF EXPORTS
(Percentages)

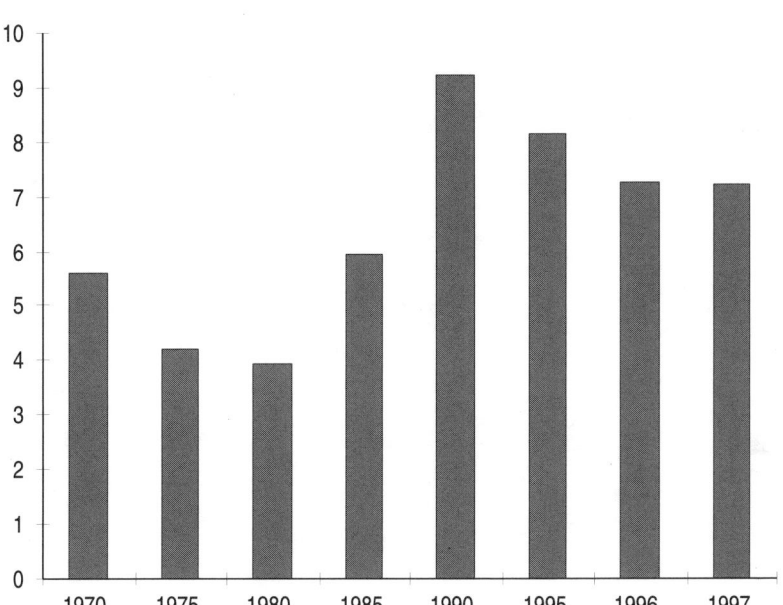

Source: IMF, *Direction of Trade.*

Despite these advances in trade liberalization in some countries, MENA economies remain relatively closed on the whole, with high average tariffs compared with
the other developing countries (Table 1.8). If average tariff and paratariff levels are
compared with other countries', only a few MENA countries—Bahrain, Oman, and
Saudi Arabia (all GCC members)—have levels below 15 percent, for example, while
most are close to or above 30 percent. Quantitative restriction (QR) ratios are also
very high compared with those in other regions. Again, only in the three GCC states
are QR ratios comparably low, less than 5 percent. Despite the fact that some GCC
countries have more open trade regimes than other countries in MENA, they have
heavy protection of import-substituting activities. Moreover, trade institutions, such
as customs, financial services, and export promotion, function far less well in MENA
than in more integrated economies (for example, East Asia), creating further deter-
rents to trade expansion.

Where data are available, weighted average tariffs rates in all MENA countries
are more than double the international average, and are either higher or just below

TABLE 1.8. COMPARISON OF TRADE POLICY INDICATORS FOR SELECTED COUNTRIES

Country	Average tariff[a] (%)	Average tariff + paratariff[a] (%)	QR coverage ratios[a] (%)
MENA			
Algeria	22.9	24.9	9.5
Bahrain	7.1	7.1	1.5
Egypt	33.5	33.5	45.2
Iran	20.7	100.9	99.3
Jordan	13.8	28.0	12.9
Kuwait	—	—	—
Libya	18.3	34.7	10.3
Morocco[c]	23.5	36.1	27.6
Oman	2.9	2.9	3.6
Qatar	—	—	—
Saudi Arabia	12.1	12.1	3.9
Syria	14.8	27.5	36.6
Tunisia	27.5	30.6	32.7
UAE	n.a.	n.a.	n.a.
Other selected countries			
Colombia	11.8	11.8	1.7
Costa Rica	21.1	61.7	0.8
Korea, Rep. of	11.1	12.3	2.6
Singapore	0.4	0.4	0.3
Sri Lanka	26.1	29.2	3.8

— Not available.
a. Data are unweighted averages for most recent year available in the early 1990s.
b. Unweighted averages for number of items covered by quantitative restrictions (QR) for most recent year in the 1990s.
c. For the late 1980s.
Source: World Bank.

the average for developing countries (Table 1.9). Effective import duties tend to be lower in the GCC countries, ranging from less than 0.1 percent in the UAE to 5.8 percent in Bahrain, with the exception of Saudi Arabia, where they are estimated at 10 percent. Aside from rates of 8 percent in Yemen and Jordan, among the MENA countries, diversified exporters' effective import duty rates range from 11.3 percent in Lebanon to 20 percent in Syria. Trade taxes in the region represent from 2.8–8.1 percent of GDP in more diversified MENA exporters, and from 0.4–4.2 percent of GDP for MENA oil exporters.

PROSPECTS: FREE TRADE AGREEMENTS WITH THE EU AND WORLD TRADE ORGANIZATION MEMBERSHIP

Jordan, Tunisia, and Morocco recently signed Euro-Mediterranean Free Trade Agreements (FTAs). Egypt, Lebanon, and Algeria are in the process of negotia-

TABLE 1.9. TRADE TAXES IN MENA COUNTRIES

Country/region	Weighted average tariff (as of March 1996) (%)	Effective import duties[a] (%)	Trade taxes as % of GDP (1994)
GCC			
Bahrain	—	5.8	2.8
Kuwait	—	3.8	0.9
Oman	—	2.7	1.0
Qatar	—	—	0.8
Saudi Arabia	—	10.0	0.4
Other oil exporters			
Algeria	21.6[b]	15.1	3.2
Iran	—	4.0	1.0
Libya	—	8.9	4.2
Diversified exporters			
Egypt	28.0	17.3	4.2
Jordan	19.8	8.2	8.1
Lebanon	24.2	11.3	5.2
Morocco	20.3	16.2	4.4
Syria	17.2	20.1	3.0
Tunisia	31.7	17.4	7.6
Yemen		8.0	2.8
Developing countries			
All developing countries	21.4	—	—
East Asia and Pacific	21.3	—	—
Latin America	14.1	—	—
South Asia	47.1	—	—
Central Europe	9.1	—	—
Sub-Saharan Africa	14.8	—	—
Memo			
World	8.2	—	—

— Not available.
Note: East Asia: Indonesia, Korea, Macao, Malaysia, Philippines, Thailand. Latin America: Argentina, Brazil, Chile, Colombia, Jamaica, Mexico, Peru, El Salvador, Uruguay, Venezuela. South Asia: India, Sri Lanka. Central Europe: Czech and Slovak Republics, Hungary, Poland, Romania. Sub-Saharan Africa: Senegal, Zimbabwe.
a. Import taxes as a percentage of value of total imports.
b. 1992.
Source: Alonso-Gamo, Fennell, and Sakr 1997, Tables 6, 8.

tions. These bilateral FTAs with the EU will serve as one of the main forces driving trade liberalization in the MENA region in the coming 15 to 20 years, as well as influence economic performance. Additionally, they have stimulated regional integration, evidenced by the recent Arab Free Trade Area Agreement negotiated within the Arab League. While the EU FTAs entail significant opening, the pace of liberalization is slow. EU FTAs with the MENA countries do not envisage eventual accession to the EU.

The most significant feature of the EU FTA agreements is the implied unilateral liberalization and opening to imports of manufactured products. The Euro-Med agreements include the following shared objectives: (a) progressive elimination of all tariffs on industrial goods, over 12 years; (b) gradual and limited trade liberalization for agricultural products; (c) measures to liberalize services and rights of establishment; and (d) adoption of a wide range of trade-related EU regulationsthat is, harmonization of rules and regulations to facilitate trade, especially in the areas of competition policy and intellectual property rights. Additionally, the agreements open further liberalization prospects with planned negotiations on agriculture and services.[4] This is important in that, while these EU-FTAs are expected to improve growth prospects as they are implemented, competition to export to the EU is increasing, especially by the Central and Eastern European EU applicant countries (or CEECs), but also by now more price-competitive East Asian exporters.

Another factor advancing trade liberalization in a number of MENA countries is GATT/WTO membership. As of the end of 1997, Bahrain, Egypt, Kuwait, Morocco, Qatar, Tunisia, and the UAE were members of the WTO. Algeria, Jordan, Oman, and Saudi Arabia have all applied to join, and currently have observer status. Jordan's accession negotiations were completed at the end of 1999.

Benefits, Costs, Risks, and Challenges

While the path to greater trade integration may be paved with a number of hurdles in the MENA countries, benefits are potentially as large as the scope for liberalization, in part because of the high initial level of protection. Prospects are promising, given the EU agreements and forthcoming WTO negotiations. In the wake of the recent financial crisis in East Asia, the challenge may have become greater, but—given the associated drop in import demand from East Asia and consequent decline in world trade—introduction of reforms has become more of an imperative.

BENEFITS

Evidence indicates that implementation of more rapid trade liberalization paves the way for better economic performance. This has been the experience of the MENA reformers, Jordan, Morocco, and Tunisia, which were able to not only increase their integration with the rest of the world, but also to achieve higher rates of GDP growth compared with other MENA countries. The extent and speed of liberalization that other countries in the region will implement, however, may vary because of country-specific circumstances. Strength and resistance by protected industries, other policy objectives (for example, raising fiscal revenue through trade taxes), and administrative and institutional inefficiencies are some factors that could hinder the pace of reforms. Conflicts between policy reform and stabilization goals, including social adjustment costs, could slow the process of liberalization. Low or negative economic growth could also reduce popular support for reforms.

Estimates of static benefits from greater trade openness due to improved resource allocation generally show only modest gains in welfare. Empirical evidence has, however, shown significant GDP growth gains, which indicate the presence of significant dynamic effects.[5] In a recent study of these dynamic gains, Wacziarg

(1998) calculates that a one standard deviation increase in an index of trade policy openness is associated with a 0.9 percentage point higher per capita GDP growth. This effect of trade policy openness on growth can be separated into a number of different channels, one of which is the impact on investment (Figure 1.4). Indeed, about half of the positive effect of trade policy openness on growth is due to its effect on the investment rate. Other channels include improvements in macroeconomic policies induced by greater openness and increased technology transfer. Specifically, gross domestic investment (GDI) accounts for 0.42 percentage point of the overall effect, followed by a 0.23 percentage point–induced improvement in macroeconomic policy quality, with FDI accounting for a 0.12 percentage point increase in per capita GDP growth.

Other benefits associated with trade liberalization include the reduction of risks and vulnerabilities of export revenues, which the region experiences as a result of the high concentration of exports in hydrocarbons and other primary goods. Strikingly, over the extended period from 1970 through 1993, the purchasing power of MENA's exports[6] has been twice as volatile as that for other developing regions, and nearly four times that of industrial countries (Figure 1.5). Of course, the volatility in export earnings among the region's countries varies widely. Instability for

FIGURE 1.4. EFFECT ON PER CAPITA GDP GROWTH OF ONE STANDARD DEVIATION INCREASE IN TRADE POLICY OPENNESS INDEX
(Percentage points)

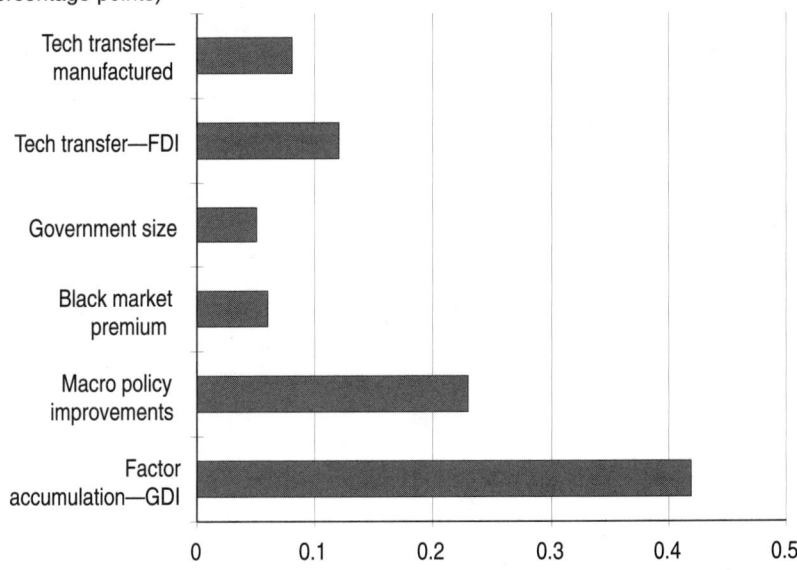

Source: World Bank 1997a.

the oil exporters exceeds that of the non-oil-exporting group by a factor of three, and, in general, the closer a country's links are to the fuel exporters, the higher the variability in revenues tends to be. In contrast, more diversified economies (for example, Morocco) tend to display a more stable pattern in export earnings (Figure 1.6).

It should also be noted that, in general, trade liberalization can yield important net social gains. It can play a significant role in poverty reduction by raising returns to unskilled labor (where it is the relatively abundant factor of production) and, as already noted, by contributing to faster overall growth.

ADJUSTMENT COSTS

Although over the medium and long term, trade liberalization is beneficial, it involves short- and medium-term adjustment costs. The benefits are a large multiple of the costs. These costs are associated with losses incurred by resources idled as a consequence of the introduction of trade reforms. Sectors protected by tariffs, quotas, and other governmental interventions are the most vulnerable, as firms will likely face lower production and downsizing, including employee layoffs. The unemployed workers may not be readily absorbed in other expanding sectors of the economy, in turn also reducing aggregate demand. Correspondingly, other workers and entrepreneurs (especially those employed in the tradables sectors) will benefit. Until other sectors benefit enough from the introduced trade reforms and associated efficiency gains, such that their expansion outweighs the decline in the formerly protected sectors, output will fall.

Various studies have shown that the implementation of the Uruguay Round agreements would imply net losses to the MENA region in the medium term. They result from higher food prices and the dismantling of the multifiber agreement (and the resulting loss of preferences). The implementation of the EU FTA agreements will also result in adjustment costs, in terms of temporary unemployment, due to intersectoral shifts of resources.[7] There may also be a temporary negative effect on investment because of increased uncertainty, particularly in view of the length and timing of the lifting of trade restrictions.

CHALLENGES

Greater trade integration is key to overcoming the MENA countries' many challenges to achieving better growth performance and improved standards of living and poverty reduction, and to achieving a significantly faster rate of employment growth. It should also help improve performance in terms of productivity growth, faster capital accumulation, and greater diversification of output and exports, in all of which MENA has lagged behind other regions. But the challenges of greater trade integration alone are significant.

Given its characteristics and endowments, the MENA region occupies an intermediate place on the ladder of comparative advantage and is being squeezed from above and below. On the one hand, the more advanced developing countries

FIGURE 1.5. VOLATILITY OF PURCHASING POWER OF EXPORTS, 1970–93:
RATIO OF REGION STANDARD ERROR TO ALL LMICs

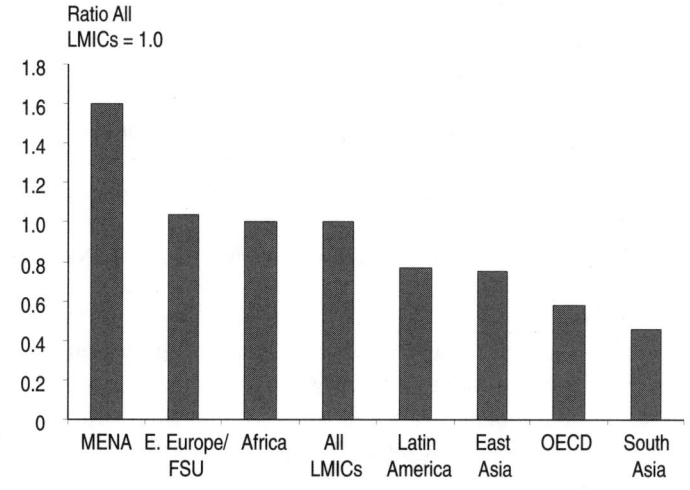

FIGURE 1.6. VOLATILITY OF PURCHASING POWER OF EXPORTS, 1970–93:
STANDARD ERROR IN PERCENTAGE POINTS

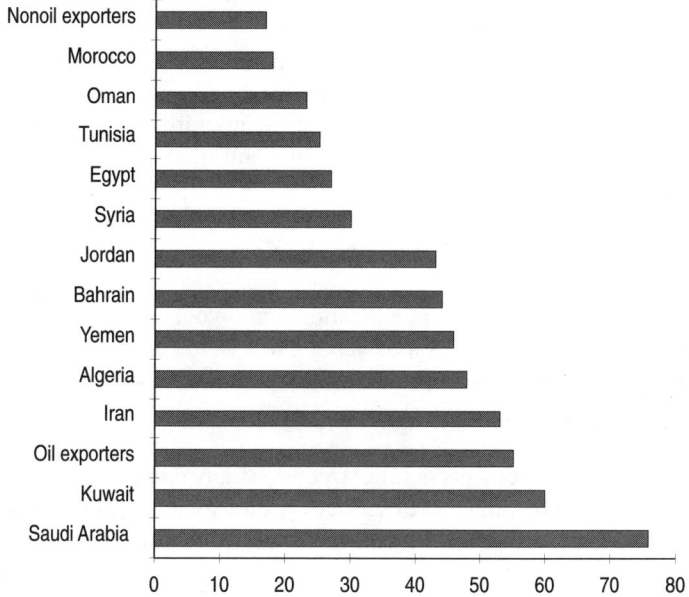

Note: The measure of volatility used is the standard error (in percent) of a time trend
regression of the purchasing power of exports covering the period 1970–93.
Source: Development Economic Prospects Group.

(such as in East Asia) have gone upscale in their production structure toward more skilled and capital-intensive activities. On the other hand, large and unskilled, labor-abundant countries (China, India, Bangladesh) are integrating fast into the world economy, putting strong pressure on countries (such as Egypt, Tunisia, and Morocco), which have specialized in low-skills intensive manufactures. The Central European countries, which are closer to MENA in terms of endowments and geographically closer to its main trading partner (the EU), are on track for accession to the EU and to gain a competitive edge. The MENA countries have to quickly position themselves in this context, so as not to be squeezed out of international markets, particularly the EU.

The management of increased and faster trade integration in the MENA region calls for

- Recognizing and dealing with the adjustment costs of the transition to a more liberalized trading system: retraining programs, measures to facilitate restructuring of companies (labor severance, financial restructuring), government support of technology acquisition, and improved quality control processes.

- Addressing the trade diversion effects that may result from the EU FTA agreements. This requires trade liberalization with the rest of the world, and particularly within the region, in step with that of the EU.

- For countries already advanced on the path of reform, deepening of reforms that help reduce the adjustment costs and maximize the long-term benefits: public administration, legal infrastructure, labor markets, state-owned enterprises, domestic competition, and financial markets.

- For countries still at the beginning of their reform programs, implementation of aggressive liberalization and opening.

- Improved and more efficient educational and vocational training systems to enhance labor market responsiveness, that is, to create a labor force with more appropriate skills, improved ability to innovate, and increased capacity to adjust to change.

- Significant improvements in infrastructure (transport and communications networks) and liberalization of services related to international trade (transport, insurance, cross-border services), to reduce transaction costs.

- Institutional development and policies for acquisition, adaptation, and dissemination of technology.

MENA and the Globalization of Production

Globalization of production has expanded rapidly over the last two to three decades, driven by a number of factors: the liberalization of trade and investment policies, privatization, the rapid fall in transport and communications costs, and the growing importance of knowledge and other intangible assets in world production. An increasing share of world output is generated by cross-border production by multinational affiliates. It is estimated that, in 1990, about 22.0 percent of world GDP was produced by multinationals at home and abroad. The share of value added by multinationals *abroad* was 6.4 percent of world GDP in 1990 (up from 4.5 percent in 1970), which increased to 7.5 percent in 1995. This share is much higher when only manufacturing industry is considered: it increased from 11.5 percent in 1977 to 17.5 percent in 1992. This trend of expanding global production networks has contributed to increased integration of the developing economies and expands opportunities for developing countries to participate in international specialization.

The share of production of affiliates of multinationals in developing country GDP increased from 4.4 percent in 1982 to 6.3 percent in 1995, close to the international average.[8] FDI flows accounted for about 5–6 percent of aggregate investment in developing countries in the 1990s, significantly above the 1–2 percent share of the previous 15 years (World Bank 1997a) (Table 1.10).

TABLE 1.10. NET FDI FLOWS TO THREE GROUPS OF COUNTRIES
(Percentage of GDP)

Country	1993	1994	1995	1996	1997(e)	Mean	Standard deviation
MENA							
Egypt	1.05	2.35	0.84	0.94	1.21	1.28	0.61
Jordan	0.36	0.43	0.61	0.81	1.12	0.67	0.31
Morocco	1.75	1.74	0.84	0.77	3.51	1.72	1.10
Tunisia	3.85	2.73	1.50	1.30	1.35	2.14	1.12
Central Europe							
Czech Rep.	1.80	2.10	5.70	2.50	2.30	2.90	1.60
Estonia	4.00	5.50	4.50	2.50	6.10	4.50	1.40
Hungary	6.10	2.60	10.00	4.40	6.60	5.90	2.80
Poland	0.70	0.60	1.00	2.00	2.10	1.30	0.70
Slovenia	0.90	0.90	0.90	1.00	1.60	1.10	0.30
East Asia							
Indonesia	1.00	0.90	1.90	3.00	1.50	1.70	0.90
Korea, Rep. of	−0.20	−0.50	−0.40	−0.40	−0.60	−0.40	0.10
Malaysia	8.00	6.10	4.90	5.40	5.90	6.10	1.20
Philippines	1.60	2.00	1.50	1.70	1.40	1.60	0.20
Thailand	1.30	0.60	0.70	0.80	1.50	1.00	0.40

Note: 1997(e): estimate.
Sources: World Bank staff, from IMF, *Balance of Payments*; World Bank, *Global Development Finance*.

FDI Benefits and Risks

The benefits from FDI and participation in global production networks are large. They are partly related to the complementarity between trade and FDI. The overseas production of multinationals is increasingly oriented toward exports rather than domestic markets in the host countries.[9] Intrafirm trade as a percentage share of total trade has been increasing. Open trade economies tend to attract more FDI, and the benefits from FDI tend also to be larger with a more open trade regime.[10] Unlike other forms of financial flows, the risks associated with FDI are low, since they are less volatile and not subject to quick reversals. Developing countries, therefore, stand to gain from FDI, and policies should be geared to promote this type of financial integration.

BENEFITS

Access to FDI flows allows countries to benefit more quickly and effectively from improved investment opportunities, such as new natural resource discoveries or major structural policy reforms. The evidence suggests that FDI tends to "crowd in" more domestic investment: a dollar of FDI in developing countries is associated with a $0.50–$1.30 of additional domestic investment, that is, faster capital accumulation and aggregate growth. Additional indirect benefits accrue from spillover effects, such as labor market spillovers (through improved skills), market access and demonstration effects, and supplier spillovers, among others. While it is difficult to establish causality, increased FDI flows are generally associated with faster aggregate long-run growth (and total factor productivity growth), with each percentage increase in the FDI to GDP ratio associated with a 0.3–0.4 percentage point faster per capita GDP growth.[11] However, the increase in GNP would be smaller when repatriation of profits is taken into account.

RISKS AND VOLATILITY

FDI inflows to developing countries are relatively stable and have been rising on the whole, during periods of both crisis and noncrisis in the developing world. This contrasts with non-FDI private net inflows, which show far greater volatility with sudden reversals (Figure 1.7). This general characteristic of persistence is even more strongly and clearly evident in specific country episodes (Figures 1.8, 1.9, and 1.10). For Argentina, Mexico, and Hungary, FDI flows have proven to be much less volatile than non-FDI flows (portfolio or other flows). Among non-FDI flows, the behavior of portfolio equity flows most closely resembles that of FDI, but is more volatile. Debt portfolio flows have been far more volatile compared to FDI and magnify the amplitude of boom-bust cycles.

The low volatility and associated lower risks of reversal of FDI capital inflows is also seen in Figure 1.11 (see Table 1.A.3 in the Annex), which presents data on a number of MENA countries, as well as selected Central European and East Asian countries for the 1993–97 period. The standard deviation for FDI flows (as percent of GDP) and (the absolute value of the) coefficient of variation over this period is much lower (by a large multiple) for FDI flows.

FIGURES 1.7 – 1.10. NET PRIVATE CAPITAL FLOWS TO DEVELOPING COUNTRIES

Figure 1.7. All Developing Countries
(1975–96, Percentage share of GDP)

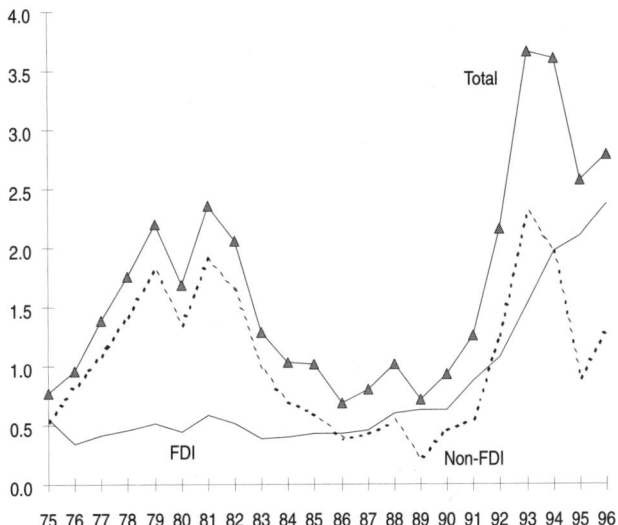

Note: Weighted average.
Source: WDI.

Figure 1.8. Argentina
(US$ millions)

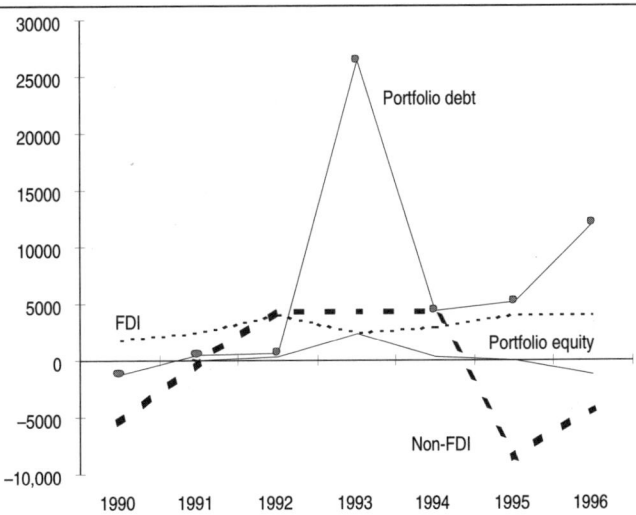

Source: IMF, World Bank.

Figure 1.9. Mexico
(US$ millions)

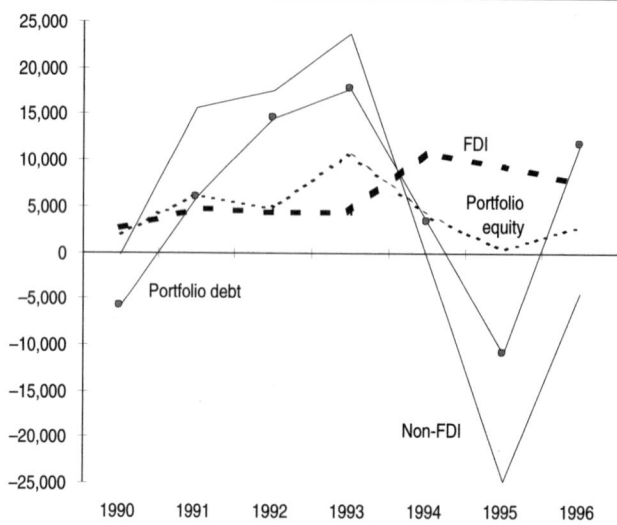

Source: IMF, World Bank.

Figure 1.10. Hungary
(US$ millions)

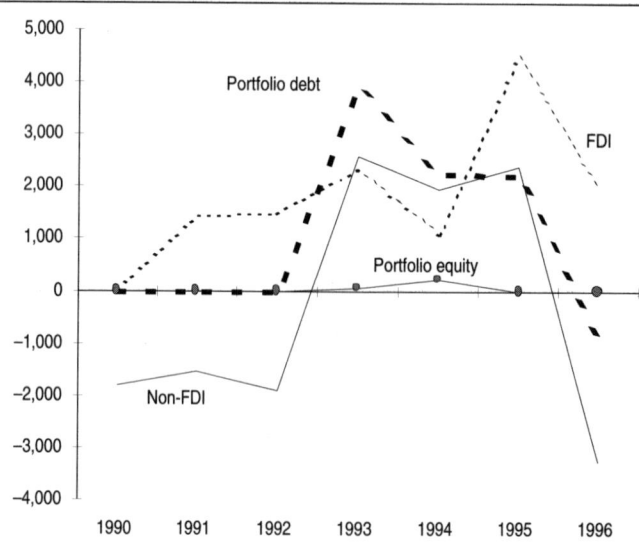

Source: IMF, World Bank.

FIGURE 1.11. COEFFICIENT OF VARIATION FOR FDI AND NON-FDI PRIVATE INFLOWS
(Percentage of GDP, 1993–97)

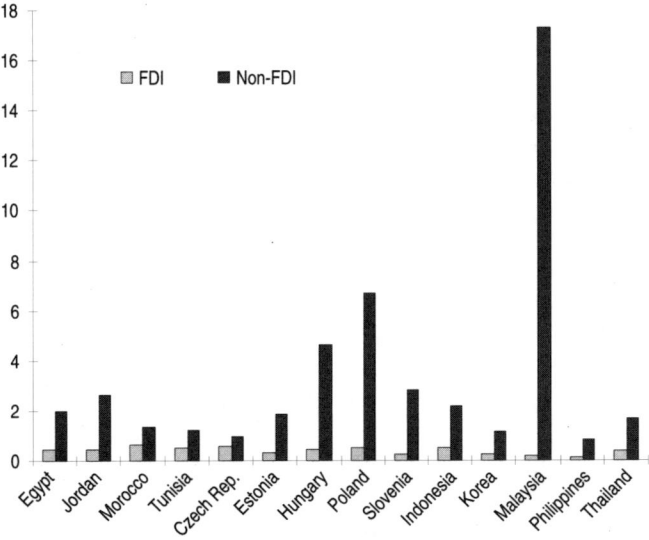

Source: Development Economic Prospects Group, World Bank.

FIGURE 1.12. NET FDI FLOWS TO MENA AND OTHER REGIONS
(Percentage share of GDP)

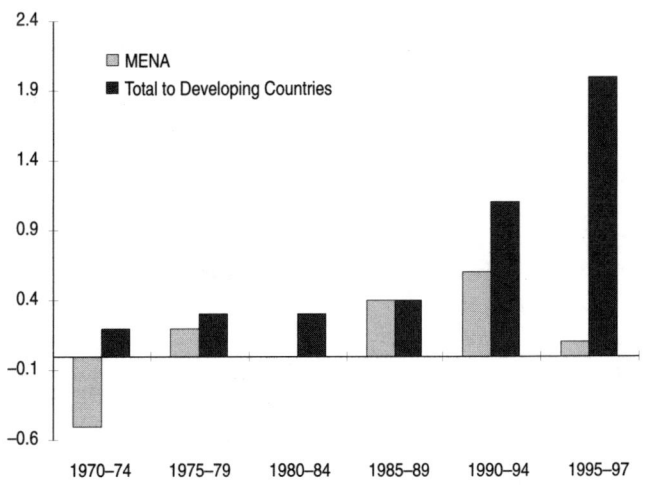

Source: Development Economic Prospects Group, World Bank.

FDI in MENA

Net FDI inflows in the MENA region have been *consistently* lower than the average for developing countries (as a percentage of GDP) (Figure 1.12; see Table 1.A.4 in the Annex). There was a temporary surge during the second half of the 1980s and first half of the 1990s, but the region lagged behind considerably during 1995–97. The total net inflow was 0.1 percent of GDP, compared with an average of 2.0 percent for all developing countries, and was the *lowest* among all regions. The region has not been a full participant by any measure in the globalization of production trends, and has been missing important opportunities to bolster growth.

In terms of attracting FDI, the best-performing countries of the region (Egypt, Jordan, Morocco, and Tunisia) show a mixed experience with respect to the level, variability, and trend of FDI inflows. Their experience is comparable to that of some well-performing countries in East Asia and Central Europe, but much less successful than the most "attractive" countries in these regions. FDI has been especially strong in low-skill-intensive activities.

Attracting FDI

In order to both attract more FDI and reap the potentially very large gains from it, countries of the MENA region need to follow the same policies that have been found to be successful in other countries and regions. These are

- openness to trade, which as discussed above has been found conducive to attracting FDI, and also is associated with greater gains from FDI

- improved infrastructure in terms of availability and quality

- more active privatization

- public administration and legal structures, which enhance the rule of law and improve the predictability and enforceability of contracts

- improved transparency of corporate activities and corporate governance, and greater development of capital markets.

Entry of Foreign Financial Institutions in Domestic Markets

A specific type of FDI involves *foreign financial institutions that are allowed to enter domestic markets.*[12] For this type of FDI, the level of capital inflow is much less important than the introduction of greater competition in domestic banking markets and the associated reduction in domestic bank costs.[13] At the same time, entry by internationally active foreign banks—which are also more diversified in terms of their activities—can help strengthen the domestic financial system.

Table 1.11 shows that MENA countries vary significantly in terms of extent of foreign bank participation. Gulf oil-producing countries are generally closed to for-

eign banks, while the more open and diversified economies have a significant foreign bank presence.

The average level of openness, as measured by the share of foreign banks in the
total number of banks and in bank assets, is comparable to the average for industrial
countries. It is lower, however, than for other developing regions, particularly transition
economies. The indicators of performance for MENA banks compare favorably with
other developing regions with respect to overhead costs and net margins (which are
relatively low), but tend to have lower profits and lower provisioning (in total assets).[14]

Non-FDI Flows and Financial Integration in MENA

Non-FDI Flows in MENA

On average, the MENA region has also tended to attract less net non-FDI capital
than all developing countries as a group (Figure 1.13; see Table 1.A.5 in the Annex).
In the early 1990s (1990–94), net non-FDI inflows were, on average, negligible.
Although they increased sharply in 1995–97 to reach 0.9 percent of GDP, this was
still below the 2.0 percent average for developing countries.

Non-FDI capital flows involve a variety of financial instruments, and their composition differs considerably among countries. Portfolio inflows to MENA have

TABLE 1.11. SHARE OF FOREIGN BANKS IN DOMESTIC BANKING SYSTEMS
(Average period 1988—95)

Country/region	Share in number of banks (%)	Share in bank assets (%)	Total number of banks [a] (1995)
Egypt	10	1	9
Jordan	43	95	7
Lebanon	49	57	5
Morocco	33	21	8
Oman	0	0	6
Qatar	0	0	3
Saudi Arabia	34	43	4
Tunisia	39	35	7
Yemen	0	0	3
MENA	26	19	...
Africa	31	27	...
Asia	28	30	...
Latin America	25	28	...
Transitional economies	54	52	...
Industrial economies	25	15	...

... = Not available.
Note: A foreign bank is defined as having at least 50 percent foreign ownership.
a. Banks included in the BankScope database of IBCA.
Source: Claessens, Demirgurc-Kunt, and Huizinga 1997.

FIGURE 1.13. NET NON-FDI PRIVATE FLOWS TO MENA AND OTHER REGIONS
(Percentage share of GDP)

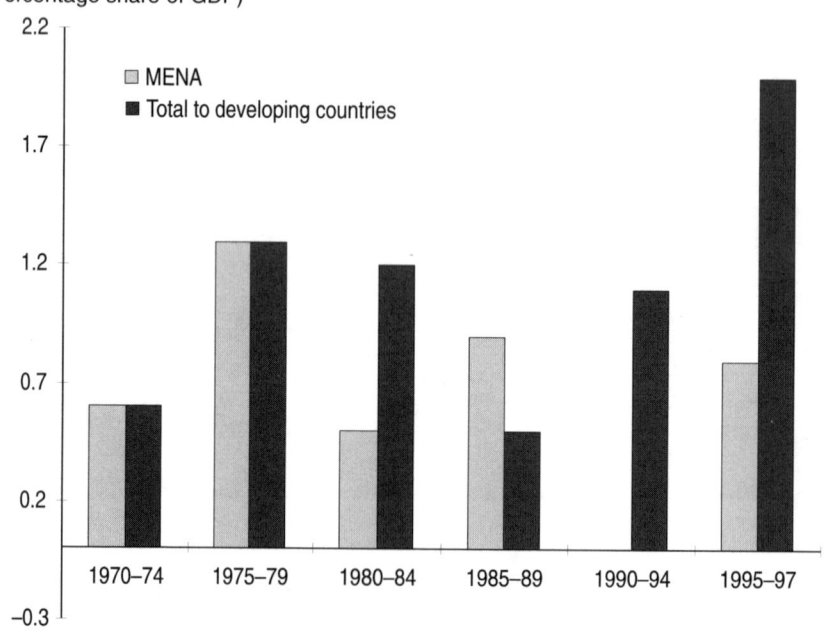

Source: Development Economic Prospects Group, World Bank, based on *Global Develop-ment Finance.*

been close to zero until the 1995–97 period, when they reached around $1 billion per year. Commercial bank loans and bonds have been the main instruments used.

The diversity of experience across the region in terms of non-FDI (particularly private-to-private) inflows is great (Table 1.12). Egypt and Jordan had negative net private-to-private non-FDI inflows during 1993–97. Tunisia and Morocco experienced significant inflows on average, but at declining levels, and then negative flows in 1997. Portfolio flows were very low for the region as a whole.

A comparison with a number of East Asian and Central European countries reveals the limited extent of non-FDI private-to-private inflows in the MENA countries (Table 1.13). Many countries in the other regions experienced large surges in such flows, which have been associated with subsequent financial problems in some cases (including Thailand, Korea, and the Czech Republic).

While the MENA region has not attracted large amounts of capital flows, it has been a large exporter of capital looking for higher returns, lower risks, and greater diversification of portfolios. In the future, the reversal of such outflows could help increase net inflows into the region.

TABLE 1.12. NET NON-FDI CAPITAL FLOWS TO SELECTED MENA COUNTRIES, 1993–97
(Percentage of GDP)

Indicator	Country	1993	1994	1995	1996	1997(e)	Mean	Standard deviation
Total non-FDI	Egypt	−1.40	−0.10	0.26	−0.05	0.86	−0.09	0.83
flows	Jordan	3.77	9.79	5.90	3.94	5.67	5.82	2.43
	Morocco	1.25	1.85	1.18	1.41	−2.01	0.74	1.56
	Tunisia	5.66	4.11	3.09	3.54	2.32	3.74	1.25
Portfolio	Egypt	0.01	0.01	0.03	0.81	1.93	0.56	0.84
investment	Jordan	0.00	0.00	0.00	0.00	0.00	0.00	0.00
	Morocco	0.09	0.78	0.06	0.39	0.00	0.26	0.33
	Tunisia	0.12	0.10	0.14	0.74	0.00	0.22	0.29
Other investment	Egypt	1.82	−0.60	−0.22	−0.75	−0.46	−0.04	1.06
	Jordan	−1.66	10.72	11.02	8.87	0.11	5.81	6.10
	Morocco	1.18	1.19	−0.75	−0.52	−2.01	−0.18	1.37
	Tunisia	4.70	4.50	3.60	2.10	2.27	3.43	1.22
Other investment	Egypt	0.68	−1.72	0.37	0.98	0.59	0.18	1.09
(of which by	Jordan	−4.69	5.73	6.63	2.40	0.00	2.01	4.59
banks)	Morocco	0.00	−0.06	−0.36	−0.14	0.00	−0.11	0.15
	Tunisia	0.43	1.50	1.08	−1.02	0.68	0.53	0.96
Net errors	Egypt	−3.24	0.49	0.45	−0.11	−0.61	−0.60	1.54
& omissions	Jordan	5.43	−0.93	−5.11	−4.93	5.56	0.00	5.29
	Morocco	−0.02	−0.13	1.87	1.54	0.00	0.65	0.97
	Tunisia	0.84	−0.49	−0.65	0.71	0.05	0.09	0.67
Total	Egypt	−1.83	1.47	1.38	1.03	2.21	0.85	1.56
private	Jordan	3.73	7.46	−2.65	−2.75	1.25	1.41	4.35
flows	Morocco	3.10	5.54	3.43	2.78	2.43	3.46	1.22
	Tunisia	7.61	5.11	4.10	4.55	2.93	4.86	1.74
Private to	Egypt	−2.48	1.16	0.97	0.66	1.89	0.44	1.69
private	Jordan	1.77	4.46	−5.61	−4.88	−0.77	−1.01	4.30
	Morocco	2.70	5.11	3.27	2.22	2.06	3.07	1.23
	Tunisia	7.00	4.34	1.33	2.59	1.17	3.28	2.43
Non-FDI	Egypt	−3.53	−1.19	0.13	−0.27	0.69	−0.84	1.66
private to	Jordan	1.41	4.03	−6.22	−5.69	−1.89	−1.67	4.44
private	Morocco	0.95	3.37	2.42	1.45	−1.44	1.35	1.82
	Tunisia	3.15	1.61	−0.17	1.29	−0.19	1.14	1.39

Note: 1997(e): estimate.
The calculations to obtain the data are as follows:
Total private-to-private capital flows = total private capital flows - public and publicly guaranteed private creditors.
Total private capital flows = total flows - official flows - net use of IMF credit.
Total flows = FDI + portfolio investment + other investment + net errors and omissions.
Total non-FDI private-to-private capital flows = total private-to-private capital flows − FDI.
Sources: World Bank staff, from IMF, *Balance of Payments*; World Bank, *Global Development Finance*.

TABLE 1.13. NON-FDI NET PRIVATE-TO-PRIVATE CAPITAL FLOWS TO THREE
GROUPS OF COUNTRIES, 1993–97
(Percentage of GDP)

Country	1993	1994	1995	1996	1997(e)	Mean	Standard deviation
MENA							
Egypt	−3.53	−1.19	0.13	−0.27	0.69	−0.84	1.66
Jordan	1.41	4.03	−6.22	−5.69	−1.89	−1.67	4.44
Morocco	0.95	3.37	2.42	1.45	−1.44	1.35	1.82
Tunisia	3.15	1.61	−0.17	1.29	−0.19	1.14	1.39
Central Europe							
Czech Rep.	3.9	8.3	9.8	−1.0	1.9	4.6	4.5
Estonia	−1.7	−1.7	0.1	8.2	11.6	3.3	6.2
Hungary	6.7	4.7	5.3	−7.3	−2.8	1.3	6.1
Poland	−0.2	−1.5	1.2	0.4	0.9	0.2	1.1
Slovenia	−1.6	−0.3	0.1	1.4	4.6	0.8	2.4
East Asia							
Indonesia	−1.5	0.0	1.8	3.43	0.5	0.8	1.9
Korea, Rep. of	1.3	2.5	3.7	5.4	−1.6	2.3	2.6
Malaysia	14.3	−4.5	−1.0	2.1	−8.4	0.5	8.7
Philippines	2.3	4.5	3.4	8.5	0.1	3.8	3.1
Thailand	6.4	7.6	11.2	7.6	−9.1	4.7	7.9

Sources: World Bank staff, from IMF, *Balance of Payments*; World Bank, *Global Development Finance*.

Benefits, Risks, and Vulnerability[15]

Theory suggests that there are several potential benefits for developing countries
that pursue capital account liberalization.[16] These include increased access to (and
lower costs of) capital, faster productivity growth, risk diversification, consumption
smoothing, and improved domestic financial intermediation.[17]

Non-FDI flows are associated with increased domestic investment, but at a lower
rate than FDI flows. There is little evidence of a significant positive association
between non-FDI inflows, particularly shorter-term and more volatile flows, and
productivity growth. The benefits associated with this type of flow are much less
certain than for FDI. There is no evidence that countries with fewer capital controls
have grown faster.

As many developing economies have relatively concentrated exports and economic
activity, opening capital accounts allows risk sharing and asset diversification. Here
again, there is limited empirical evidence about the significance of these effects.

In the face of high income volatility in developing countries, another potential
source of welfare improvement from greater capital flows is increased opportunities for consumption smoothing.[18] If isolated financially, a country that experiences
an external shock must accommodate it through changes in consumption and investment. In contrast, if it is well integrated into world financial markets, it can lend

and borrow and thus maintain consumption and investment closer to desirable levels. Potential gains may be larger for developing countries with more income volatility.[19] However, the general observation that capital flows tend to be pro-cyclical in developing countries is an indication that actual consumption smoothing may not be significant. More detailed evidence suggests, also, that while capital inflows may have sometimes provided for some consumption smoothing and reduction of volatility of consumption relative to that of income, on average they are associated with increased volatility.

Increased capital flows can help the development of capital markets and allow more banking system intermediation, both of which have been shown to affect growth positively.[20] Additionally, increased international competition enhances the quality of the financial system. Allowing domestic banks to diversify their portfolios helps reduce their vulnerability to external (terms of trade) and internal output shocks.

The Risks Associated with Capital Account Openness

Capital account liberalization and capital flows are also associated with increased risks, which are a function of both the risk absorption capacity (or robustness) of the domestic economy and the volatility and changed perceptions it may be subject to. Different classes of internationally traded financial assets vary in their volatility and implications for increased vulnerability to crisis.

There are four channels that link financial integration to increased risks of financial crises:

1. Exogenous factors, such as international interest rates, are an important determinant of capital flows. Independently of their actions and policies, developing countries may witness surges and reversals of capital flows (and crises). Under such conditions, openness to capital flows may be said to increase the risks of currency crises. When there is an upturn in interest rates, international investors are unwilling to continue, and are more likely to decrease, their financing to developing countries. At the same time, the capacity of developing country banks, firms, and governments to service their debt is reduced.

2. The presence of potentially serious international capital market failures can aggravate domestic financial weaknesses and produce contagion effects on others. Models of self-fulfilling expectations of currency crisis imply that the intrinsic instability of the international financial system is a major contributor to currency crises, and, therefore, complete openness of the capital account implies greater risks for developing countries.

3. Capital flows may make macroeconomic management much more difficult and lead to excessive borrowing and macroeconomic instability.

4. Capital flows may amplify preexisting weaknesses of the domestic financial system. Domestic financial liberalization may interact with external capital account liberalization and increase the risks of crisis because of the "overborrowing syndrome." With inadequate supervision and the presence of moral hazard, possibly due to government guaranties, unrestricted access to external finance may result in excessive borrowing and risk taking.

There is little *direct* empirical evidence about the role of either capital account liberalization or capital inflows in financial crises. There is only some *indirect evidence*, such as the association between surges in capital inflows and subsequent occurrence of crises.[21]

Vulnerability
The risks associated with large and rapid increases in capital flows include possible increased vulnerability to sudden shifts in market sentiment and reversals in these flows. Loss of confidence, which may be triggered by any major domestic change or shock, and external shocks in international capital markets or the terms of trade may bring about a sudden reversal of flows and an attack on the currency. A currency crisis could result. If the domestic financial system is fragile, a currency crisis could also be accompanied by a banking crisis, which is the most damaging and costly "twin-type" of crisis.

The MENA region has attracted limited volumes of non-FDI flows and has been less exposed to vulnerabilities of the type experienced in East Asia, for example. Figures 1.14 to 1.17 show a number of the indicators of vulnerability that have been extensively used to assess the risks of crisis in East Asia. The ratio of foreign liabilities to foreign assets, as a proxy for foreign currency exposure, remained low for the MENA countries (Figure 1.15), except for Tunisia, as compared to the very large values observed in Thailand, Malaysia, the Philippines, the Republic of Korea, and Indonesia, as well as the Czech Republic, before the onset of crisis. Also, the ratio of short-term debt to total debt (Figure 1.14), and that of short-term debt to reserves (Figure 1.16), remained low (except for Lebanon, with a very high ratio of short-term to total debt). On the other hand, M2/reserves ratios are high in many MENA countries (Figure 1.17).

Implications for MENA
The previous brief discussion and lessons from the East Asia crisis suggest that there are benefits, the size of which is uncertain, from financial integration involving the more volatile type of capital flows; but attendant risks are significant, especially when the domestic financial system is weak. Hence, the particular conditions of developing countries need to be taken into account. The implications are not that developing countries should close their capital account and systematically impose controls on capital flows. Rather, the process and pace of capital account liberalization has to take account of the potential risks. Policies toward capital account openness should

FIGURE 1.14. RATIO OF SHORT-TERM DEBT TO TOTAL DEBT
(1996, e.o.p.)

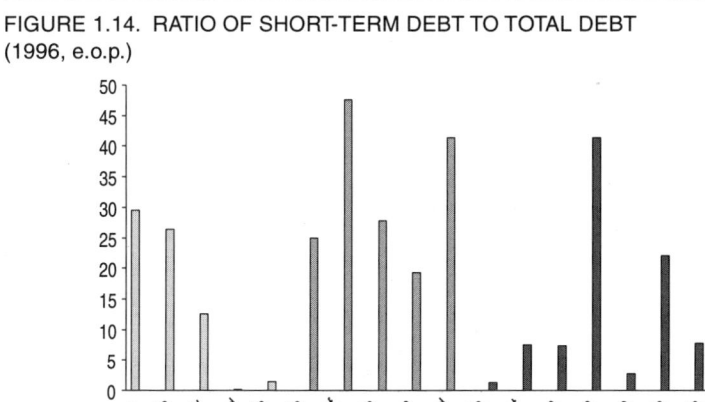

Source: GDF 1998.

FIGURE 1.15. FOREIGN EXCHANGE EXPOSURE: RATIO OF FOREIGN LIABILITIES TO
FOREIGN ASSETS OF BANKS
(Percentages)

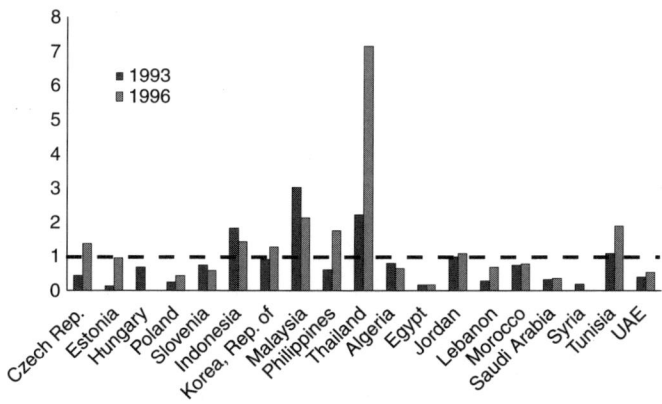

Source: IFS.

aim at determining the origin of the distortions that are the source of vulnerability of a given country to a financial crisis and try to address them directly.[22]

As the empirical evidence shows, the main problem in MENA is its relative unattractiveness to capital flows. Overall, there is no problem of managing capital inflows as experienced by other regions. This suggests that the benefits of financial

FIGURE 1.16. RATIO OF SHORT-TERM DEBT TO RESERVES
(Percentages, 1996, e.o.p.)

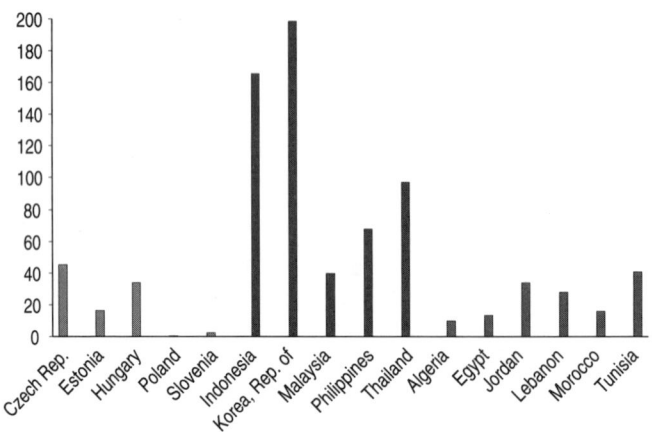

Source: GDF 1998, IFS.

FIGURE 1.17. M2/RESERVES, 1996

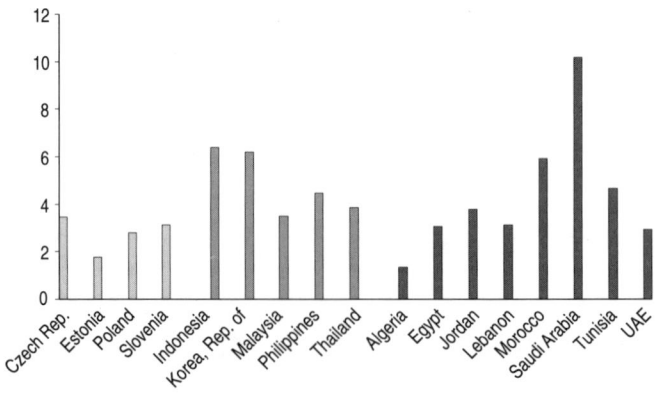

Source: IFS.

integration may be even higher for MENA countries than for other regions, given the larger volatility the region faces. But the risks are also significant because of the weaknesses of their financial systems and the presence of other traditional vulner-abilities. Despite significant improvements over the last decade, many MENA countries still have high debt ratios, relatively large budget deficits (possibly larger than the official numbers show because of contingent liabilities), and a prevalence of implicit and explicit guarantees.

MENA countries need to develop policies that allow increased financial integration, but in such a way as to avoid financial crises in the event they face incipient surges in capital inflows (possibly as a reversal of previous outflows). MENA countries need to aim at maximizing the benefits while minimizing the risks of crisis. To this end, recommended steps include:

- The crucial issues of domestic financial sector reform need to be addressed. Weaknesses in these systems are prevalent, given low capital adequacy ratios, large nonperforming loans, large role and weight of government, and low capacity for risk management. This implies improving capitalization, dealing with the nonperforming loan overhang, privatizing banks, and enhancing the human capital capacity in banks.

- Resolute domestic financial liberalization programs need to be implemented, but carefully managed with improved and adequate supervision and regulatory framework. This should include introducing and forcefully enforcing prudential regulations on foreign currency exposure by banks, in addition to those on other high-risk activities.

- Regulation must be complemented with improved incentives for owners and managers of banks for prudent risk taking.

- Corporate governance, transparency, and the capacity for enforcement of contracts need to be improved. This helps to support the domestic financial system and improve the efficiency of resource allocation.

- Promotion of capital markets development would help reduce the high debt-to-equity ratios and reduce the vulnerability of the corporate sector.

- The process of opening the capital account has to take into consideration the state of development of the domestic financial system. In addition to FDI, trade-related credit should be facilitated and controls phased out. Long-term borrowing, particularly bonds, with improved information and transparency of borrowing corporations and banks should be encouraged. However, the process has to be more careful with short-term debt for both banks and firms.

- Macropolicy should continue to aim, as is the case generally in MENA, to preserve stability. The appearance of large distortions (such as large foreign-domestic interest differentials and perceptions that underestimate currency risk), which may encourage excessive borrowing, needs to be avoided. For that purpose, flexibility of exchange rate policy is desirable, especially in a region where inflation has been mostly moderate, and the benefits from the exchange rate as an anchor for expectations are low.

Notes

1. This chapter was presented at the workshop, Benefiting from Globalization, at the Mediterranean Development Forum, September 3–5, 1998, Marrakesh, Morocco. We are grateful for research assistance from Carol Gabyzon and Eung Ju Kim. Special thanks to E. Mick Riordan and Himmat Kalsi. The findings, interpretations, and conclusions are the authors' own and should not be attributed to the World Bank, its Executive Board of Directors, or any of its member countries.

2. The chapter draws heavily on work of the World Bank Development Economic Prospects Group on these issues, particularly Riordan et al. (1998), World Bank (1998a), and World Bank (1998b).

3. Countries for which data are available.

4. The agreements also cover human rights and social, cultural, and environmental issues.

5. Sachs and Warner 1995; Edwards 1998.

6. Defined as exports of goods and all factor and nonfactor services, adjusted for inflation by the U.S. private consumption deflator.

7. See Nabli (1997) and Galal and Hoekman (1997).

8. World Bank 1997a, chapter 2.

9. The share of exports in sales of U.S. majority-owned foreign affiliates has increased from 20 percent in 1966 to 40 percent in 1993 (World Bank 1997a).

10. World Bank 1997a, chapter 2.

11. World Bank 1997a, chapter 2.

12. This may be part of external financial liberalization, but is not formally part of capital account liberalization.

13. Claessens, Demirgurc-Kunt, and Huizinga 1997.

14. Claessens, Demirgurc-Kunt, and Huizinga 1997.

15. These issues are discussed in detail in World Bank 1998b.

16. World Bank (1997b) discusses these benefits at length.

17. Another benefit that is sometimes cited is that financial openness submits governments to the hard scrutiny of international markets and would restrain any tendencies for mismanagement.

18. Low-income developing countries may also benefit from long-term consumption smoothing. They may borrow and increase their consumption now in view of increased future income.

19. The precise welfare improvement associated with increased consumption smoothing depends on a number of factors, such as the time preference and the shape of the utility function, as well as assumptions about market structure, country size, and technology.

20. Levine and Zervos 1998.

21. World Bank 1998b.

22. Obstfeld 1998.

References

Alonso-Gamo, Patricia, Susan Fennell, and Khaled Sakr. 1997. "Adjusting to New Realities: MENA, the Uruguay Round, and the EU-Mediterranean Initiative." IMF Working Paper. Washington, D.C.

Claessens, Stijn, Asli Demirgurc-Kunt, and Harry Huizinga.1997. "How Does Foreign Entry Affect the Domestic Banking Market?" World Bank, Washington, D.C., processed.

Edwards, Sebastien. 1998. "Openness, Productivity and Growth: What Do We Really Know?" *Economic Journal* 108 (March):383–98.

Galal, Ahmed, and Bernard Hoekman, eds. 1997. *Regional Partners in Global Markets: Limits and Possibilities of the Euro-Med Agreements.* London: CEPR and ECES.

Levine, Ross, and Sara Zervos. 1998. "Stock Markets, Banks, and Economic Growth." *American Economic Review* 88 (June):pp. 537–558.

Nabli, Mustapha K. 1997. "Trade Liberalization in the Maghreb Countries in the Context of the Free Trade Area Agreements with Europe in a Comparative Perspective." *Journal of Economic Cooperation among Islamic Countries* 18(4):1–22.

Obstfeld, Maurice. 1998. "The Global Market: Benefactor or Menace?" Boston: NBER. Working Paper 6559.

Riordan, E. Mick, Uri Dadush, Jalal Jalali, Shane Streifel, Milan Brahmbatt, and Kazue Takagashi. 1998. "The World Economy and Its Implications for the Middle East and North Africa, 1995–2010." In Nemat Shafik, ed., *Prospects for Middle Eastern and North African Economies: From Boom to Bust and Back.* Economic Research Forum for the Arab Countries, Iran and Turkey. London: Macmillan.

Sachs, Jeffrey, and Andrew Warner. 1995. "Economic Reform and the Process of Economic Integration." *Brookings Papers on Economic Activity.* Vol. 1. Washington: Brookings Institution.

Wacziarg, Romain. 1998. "Meauring the Dynamic Gains from Trade." Harvard University, Department of Economcis. Cambridge, Mass., mimeo.

World Bank. 1997a. *Global Economic Prospects 1997.* New York: Oxford University Press.

———. 1997b. *Private Capital Flows to Developing Countries: The Road to Financial Integration.* New York: Oxford University Press.

———. 1998a. "Financial Integration Vulnerabilities to Crisis and EU Accession in Five Central European Countries." Development Prospects Group. Washington, D.C.: World Bank, mimeo.

———. 1998b. *Global Economic Prospects 1998.* forthcoming.

———. 1998c. *World Development Indicators.* Washington, D.C.: World Bank.

———. 1999. *World Development Report.* Washington, D.C.: World Bank.

Annex

TABLE 1.A.1. GOODS AND SERVICES TRADE INTEGRATION RATIOS[a]
(Percentages)

Country/region	1970	1975	1980	1985	1990	1995	1996	1997
Volume ratios								
East Asia nad Pacific	30.9	34.8	44.8	42.8	47.3	58.7	57.9	59.1
South Asia	17.0	15.1	19.9	18.4	18.6	23.9	23.9	24.4
Sub-Saharan Africa	62.5	62.8	64.2	55.0	52.4	56.7	59.5	62.1
Europe and Central Asia	30.1	32.7	35.6	32.8	34.6	42.9	46.1	48.5
Latin America	27.4	24.8	27.1	23.3	28.7	40.6	43.1	46.2
MENA[b]	48.4	53.5	56.1	46.6	48.3	50.0	49.4	51.0
Algeria	39.0	44.3	36.4	36.6	29.8	28.2	27.6	29.5
Morocco	52.1	56.7	49.4	46.3	58.2	73.2	66.1	70.6
Tunisia	60.8	69.4	84.3	70.4	89.9	90.0	83.1	83.6
Egypt	52.5	68.5	57.2	44.9	36.2	34.7	35.4	35.3
Jordan	40.5	72.2	96.4	119.0	166.1	172.2	187.3	185.6
Syria	41.4	61.3	51.6	47.6	39.3	25.5	26.8	26.7
Bahrain	121.0	188.4	168.0	180.8	199.7	168.9	162.7	151.2
Saudi Arabia	80.3	89.3	86.6	88.6	84.4	116.6	116.6	116.6
Kuwait	81.7	84.4	108.8	107.4	65.8	58.1	54.7	57.5
UAE	87.7	94.0	88.9	74.5	100.1	109.7	113.0	124.5
Oman	74.5	87.0	95.2	74.0	77.1	67.0	67.7	70.4
Iran	18.7	21.2	9.3	8.9	11.2	7.2	7.0	7.0
Iraq	63.1	64.2	60.4	53.9	56.2	12.2	13.2	35.6
Yemen	23.9	37.4	51.5	24.4	30.2	40.0	39.1	38.4
Nominal ratios								
MENA[b]	52.6	84.3	80.9	49.2	64.7	64.0	63.0	62.2
Algeria	51.0	76.5	64.7	43.9	48.4	58.6	56.2	57.1
Morocco	39.2	55.8	45.3	59.7	59.0	61.3	55.0	59.5
Tunisia	46.7	64.0	85.8	70.2	94.2	93.4	86.0	86.3
Egypt	32.9	61.5	73.4	52.0	52.8	53.0	45.6	47.7
Jordan	41.9	95.1	124.1	113.1	154.6	126.2	125.1	120.4
Syria	38.6	55.4	53.7	37.2	55.1	40.9	41.1	33.7
Bahrain	253.4	195.0	239.3	191.6	221.7	206.6	216.7	186.6
Saudi Arabia	89.0	99.2	101.0	80.0	82.4	69.6	70.1	70.2
Kuwait	83.9	106.5	112.6	96.4	103.0	103.8	96.0	93.1
UAE	113.1	103.2	112.4	89.7	107.3	125.6	125.3	128.9
Oman	93.4	118.2	100.3	87.0	83.3	92.7	96.6	97.5
Iran	41.9	76.0	29.7	16.0	45.5	36.4	34.7	27.0
Iraq	52.4	86.7	102.0	53.8	38.1	4.1	4.8	13.3
Yemen	15.1	21.6	37.5	28.3	35.1	72.9	90.7	104.6

a. (Exports + Imports of GNFS)/GDP.
b. Excluding Lebanon, Libya, and Qatar.
Source: World Bank.

TABLE 1.A.2. GOODS AND NONFACTOR SERVICES EXPORTS AS A SHARE OF GDP
(Percentages)

	1970	1975	1980	1985	1990	1995	1996	1997
Low- and middle-income regions								
East Asia and Pacific	16.0	18.6	21.8	19.0	24.0	28.8	28.5	30.4
South Asia	6.4	6.8	7.4	6.8	7.9	11.5	11.4	11.8
Sub-Saharan Africa	31.2	27.8	28.8	26.8	27.5	29.1	30.6	32.0
Europe and Central Asia	13.5	13.6	15.2	16.6	16.0	19.9	21.0	22.1
Latin America	13.1	9.6	9.8	11.3	13.7	17.6	18.8	19.6
MENA total	39.0	35.7	32.5	20.9	25.2	26.5	26.1	26.8
Algeria	23.4	18.6	14.0	13.8	16.1	16.5	17.4	19.2
Morocco	24.7	21.2	20.0	21.4	26.5	33.2	31.7	33.3
Tunisia	27.4	30.5	36.5	30.6	42.1	44.1	41.4	41.0
Egypt	16.3	16.4	15.9	12.4	15.0	15.4	15.9	15.2
Jordan	9.2	24.2	31.1	41.5	60.3	63.8	68.1	67.6
Syria	25.9	20.9	13.3	13.5	14.4	10.9	10.9	10.5
Bahrain	81.4	92.5	84.3	95.5	102.2	88.4	82.5	75.5
Saudi Arabia	76.4	80.9	65.4	42.7	43.1	61.7	61.7	61.7
Kuwait	76.8	71.6	63.1	50.7	39.0	30.7	29.0	29.6
UAE	65.1	54.0	52.0	42.0	65.7	66.8	66.2	72.0
Oman	58.4	49.0	58.7	44.1	48.9	44.4	44.0	45.7
Iran	15.1	12.3	2.8	3.4	5.6	4.5	4.2	4.2
Iraq	56.3	44.7	38.2	26.1	30.8	6.1	6.5	17.5
Yemen	1.3	3.5	4.5	2.9	13.5	22.1	21.0	20.2

Source: World Bank.

TABLE 1.A.3. VOLATILITY OF FDI AND NON-FDI PRIVATE-TO-PRIVATE CAPITAL
INFLOWS, 1993–97
(% of GDP)

Country	Mean	FDI standard deviation	Coefficient of variation[a]	Mean	Non-FDI standard deviation	Coefficient of variation[a]
MENA						
Egypt	1.28	0.61	0.48	−0.84	1.66	1.98
Jordan	0.67	0.31	0.46	−1.67	4.44	2.66
Morocco	1.72	1.1	0.64	1.35	1.82	1.35
Tunisia	2.14	1.12	0.52	1.14	1.39	1.22
Central Europe						
Czech Rep.	2.9	1.6	0.55	4.6	4.5	0.98
Estonia	4.5	1.4	0.31	3.3	6.2	1.87
Hungary	5.9	2.8	0.47	1.3	6.1	4.6
Poland	1.3	0.7	0.54	0.2	1.1	6.68
Slovenia	1.1	0.3	0.27	0.8	2.4	2.81
East Asia						
Indonesia	1.7	0.9	0.53	0.8	1.9	2.21
Korea, Rep. of	−0.4	0.1	0.25	2.3	2.6	1.17
Malaysia	6.1	1.2	0.20	0.5	8.7	17.3
Philippines	1.6	0.2	0.13	3.8	3.1	0.83
Thailand	1	0.4	0.40	4.7	7.9	1.68

a. Absolute value.
Source: Development Economic Prospects Group, World Bank.

TABLE 1.A.4. NET FDI FLOWS TO MENA AND OTHER REGIONS

	MENA	Sub-Saharan Africa	East Asia and Pacific	Latin America and Caribbean	South Asia	Europe and Central Asia	Total to developing countries
			US$ billion				
1970–74	-0.8	0.7	0.4	1.5	0.0	0.1	2.0
1975–79	0.5	0.8	1.0	3.5	0.1	0.1	6.0
1980–84	0.0	0.9	2.3	5.4	0.2	0.1	8.9
1985–89	1.7	1.3	5.0	6.0	0.4	0.4	14.7
1990–94	2.8	1.8	25.5	15.2	0.9	4.6	50.8
1995–97	0.8	3.4	54.0	36.2	3.5	15.6	113.6
			Percentage share of total				
1970–74	−365.5	151.5	81.5	209.4	10.9	12.2	100.0
1975–79	6.2	14.4	17.9	58.5	1.8	1.2	100.0
1980–84	−8.2	8.8	27.1	68.6	2.1	1.7	100.0
1985–89	12.1	9.0	33.1	41.1	2.6	2.0	100.0
1990–94	6.5	3.7	48.1	31.3	1.7	8.8	100.0
1995–97	0.7	3.0	47.7	31.7	3.0	13.9	100.0
			Percentage share of GDP				
1970–74	-0.5	0.8	0.2	0.7	0.0	0.0	0.2
1975–79	0.2	0.5	0.3	0.7	0.1	0.0	0.3
1980–84	0.0	0.3	0.5	0.7	0.1	0.0	0.3
1985–89	0.4	0.5	0.9	0.7	0.1	0.0	0.4
1990–94	0.6	0.7	3.0	1.2	0.2	0.4	1.1
1995–97	0.1	1.1	3.9	2.2	0.6	1.3	2.0

Source: Development Economics Prospect Group, World Bank, based on *Global Development Finance*.

TABLE 1.A.5. NET NON-FDI PRIVATE FLOWS TO MENA AND OTHER REGIONS

	MENA	Sub-Saharan Africa	East Asia and Pacific	Latin America and Caribbean	South Asia	Europe and Central Asia	Total to developing countries
			US$ billion				
1970–74	0.5	0.5	0.9	4.9	0.0	0.5	7.4
1975–79	3.4	2.2	2.7	15.4	0.0	3.2	26.9
1980–84	2.2	2.8	6.1	19.1	1.5	5.4	37.1
1985–89	4.0	0.2	4.9	0.0	3.4	4.7	17.1
1990–94	−0.1	−0.6	16.7	21.8	3.8	7.7	49.3
1995–97	4.9	4.1	37.0	47.8	4.7	18.6	117.1
			Percentage share of total				
1970–74	7.3	7.1	11.7	67.1	0.0	6.8	100.0
1975–79	12.6	8.2	10.0	57.1	0.1	12.0	100.0
1980–84	6.0	7.6	16.3	51.5	3.9	14.5	100.0
1985–89	23.1	0.9	28.6	−0.1	20.0	27.5	100.0
1990–94	−0.1	−1.2	33.8	44.3	7.7	15.5	100.0
1995–97	4.2	3.5	31.6	40.8	4.0	15.9	100.0
			Percentage share of GDP				
1970–74	0.6	0.6	0.4	1.9	0.0	0.1	0.6
1975–79	1.3	1.1	0.9	3.2	0.0	0.5	1.3
1980–84	0.5	1.0	1.4	2.5	0.6	0.6	1.2
1985–89	0.9	0.1	0.9	0.0	1.1	0.4	0.5
1990–94	0.0	−0.2	2.0	1.6	0.9	0.7	1.1
1995–97	0.8	1.3	2.6	2.8	0.8	1.5	2.0

Source: Development Economics Prospects Group, World Bank, based on *Global Development Finance.*

Chapter 2

Incentives for Economic Integration in the Middle East[1]

Ahmed Galal
Egyptian Center for Economic Studies

Notwithstanding the slow progress of the Middle East peace talks, what has been accomplished to date was unimaginable a few years earlier. In 1993—14 years after the peace agreement between Egypt and Israel was signed—the first stage of a peace agreement between the Palestinians and Israel was reached, and in 1994 another was concluded with Jordan. Much is still to evolve on the Palestinian front, with Syria and with Lebanon. The rest of the Arab countries will eventually follow suit.

While the road to peace is long and far from easy, the remarkable achievements so far suggest that peace is inevitable. The alternatives are costly to all parties. The key question now and in the future is: What kind of economic cooperation, if any, will peace permit? This question raises a set of subsidiary questions. For example, will the preferential trade liberalization prompted by the agreements with the EU serve to stimulate further trade liberalization in the Middle East and North African countries? Will these agreements serve to promote trade and other forms of cooperation within the region and with the Israeli-Palestinian-Jordanian triad? What are the prospects for extending the incipient steps toward integration within the triad to Egypt and other countries?

This chapter makes and evaluates a very simple proposition: Regional integration becomes a reality when the parties involved have sufficient economic and political incentives. When such incentives are lacking, regional integration does not occur, no matter how many times politicians declare their intentions to the contrary. The limited integration in the region, despite repeated attempts at an Arab common market, is a prime example of this. Arab nationalism was not enough—nor will the peace euphoria necessarily be sufficient—to bring about economic cooperation in the region. Any serious consideration of the prospects of regional integration must therefore be grounded in the economic and political incentives to integrate.

The next section documents the degree of intraregional trade and factor movements in the last few years. This is followed by an assessment of the current economic and political incentives to integrate in the region, focusing on Egypt and the triad, and explores the prospects of regional integration in the medium run.

Intraregional Trade and Factor Movements

Peace was viewed by many as a turning point toward political reconciliation and economic opportunities. However, significant regional integration has yet to be seen. The data on regional trade in goods and services, capital movements, and labor mobility show limited progress. Similarly, the data for Egypt suggest limited progress on integrating with the triad of Israel, the Palestinian National Authority (PNA), and Jordan.

Trade in Goods

Intraregional trade in merchandise averaged only 9 percent of total exports over the period 1989–97 (Table 2.1). This average compares with over 60 percent for the EU, and over 35 percent for Asia. In addition, intraregional trade is in fact shrinking, down from 11 percent in 1989 to 7 percent in 1997.

Egypt's exports to the region (relative to its total exports) are also modest (Table 2.2). While the EU countries absorb close to 50 percent of Egypt's exports, Jordan and the PNA import less than 2 percent from Egypt. Although Israel imports a notable fraction of Egypt's exports, its share declined from a peak of 10 percent in 1991 to less than 1 percent in 1997. Arab countries, other than Jordan and the PNA, account for a little over 10 percent. This pattern has not changed significantly over the period 1989–97.

Although data are not presented on traded commodities, mineral fuels account for the bulk of intraregional trade and no category of commodities is very important (El Erian and Fischer 1996). The Arab-Israeli conflict virtually meant no trade between Israel and its neighbors. Egypt is an important exception, although there has been a dramatic decline in Israel's share in Egypt's exports in the last few years.

Capital Mobility

Although the region includes relatively capital-abundant countries (oil exporters) and relatively capital-scarce countries (such as Egypt), intraregional capital transactions have also been limited. The exception was the large official flows from the oil exporters to other Arab countries, especially in the wake of the 1973–74 and 1979–80 oil price increases (Van den Boogaerde 1991). The information available for the inflows of FDI into the region (North Africa and West Asia) indicates that the FDI share of the total inflows is less than 1 percent. Egypt and Israel receive more FDI than Jordan, and the trend is favorable for both countries. (See Table 2.3.)

TABLE 2.1. INTRAREGIONAL EXPORTS IN PERCENT OF TOTAL EXPORTS

	1989	1991	1993	1995	1997	Average 1989-97
Industrialized countries	76	76	73	72	71	74
EU[a]	60	61	59	64	64	61
Developing countries	36	38	39	42	43	39
Africa	7	8	9	10	10	9
Asia	33	37	38	40	41	38
Europe	28	20	22	30	29	25
Middle East[b]	11	8	7	7	7	8

a. As of 1995, the EU includes 15 countries.
b. The Middle East includes Bahrain, Egypt, Iran, Iraq, Israel, Jordan, Kuwait, Lebanon, Libya, Oman, Qatar, Saudi Arabia, Syria, the United Arab Emirates (UAE), and the Republic of Yemen.
Source: IMF, *Direction of Trade Statistics*, 1996.

TABLE 2.2. EGYPT'S TRADE PATTERN: EXPORTS IN PERCENTAGE OF TOTAL EXPORTS

	1989	1991	1993	1995	1997
EU	43.17	43.10	40.10	45.83	41.48
Jordan	1.04	0.98	0.45	0.90	0.67
PNA	—	—	0.00	0.05	—
Israel	6.25	10.08	7.40	5.06	8.03
Other Arab countries	9.05	10.44	13.95	10.06	10.49
Others	40.49	35.39	38.10	38.15	39.33
Total	100.00	100.00	100.00	100.00	100.00

—. Not available.
Source: IMF 1996; for the PNA: Ministry of Economy and External Trade, Egypt.

Labor Mobility

While capital movements are generally assumed to be easier than labor movements, labor mobility in the region has been relatively more significant than capital transactions or intraregional trade. Table 2.4 shows the magnitude of labor remittances in absolute terms and as a percentage of GDP for the main suppliers of labor among Arab countries. The numbers are relatively stable, but their relative importance is greatest for Yemen, Jordan, and Egypt. The flows of remittances originate primarily in the oil-exporting economies. Although the region does not have the labor mobility enjoyed by Europeans, millions of workers—for example, from Egypt—work in the neighboring countries, and Palestinians rely heavily on employment in Israel.

Regional Integration and Economic and Political Incentives

The limited integration between Egypt and the region, including the triad, can arguably be attributed to the lack of adequate economic and political incentives to integrate. This argument may seem apparent and undeserving of further elaboration. However, most of the previous attempts at explaining the limited integration in the region have focused on the economic *or* political incentives, rather than on both simultaneously. Second, most attempts dealing with the economic incentives emphasized the issue of trade creation and diversion, with limited emphasis on the dynamic gains from integration. Finally, most attempts dealing with the political incentives to integrate tended to focus on the nature of governance, culture, religion, and historical events, rather than on the factors that create the political dynamics for integration. This section explores the role of economic and political incentives in explaining the limited regional integration so far.

TABLE 2.3. INFLOWS OF FOREIGN DIRECT INVESTMENT
(millions of dollars)

	1989	1991	1993	1995	1997[a]
Total inflows	200,162	158,936	217,559	331,189	400,486
EU	81,134	78,777	80,935	116,792	108,172
Percent	40.5	49.6	37.2	35.3	27.0
North America	72,754	25,539	48,302	69,596	98,994
Percent	36.3	16.1	22.2	21.0	24.7
North Africa[b]	1,642	886	1,579	1,262	1,811
Percent	0.8	0.6	0.7	0.4	0.5
Of which Egypt	1,250	253	493	598	834
Percent	0.6	0.2	0.2	0.2	0.2
West Asia[c]	−233	1,008	2,728	−1,751	1,105
Percent	−0.1	0.6	1.3	−0.5	0.3
Of which Jordan	−1	−12	−34	13	70
Percent	0.0	0.0	0.0	0.0	0.0
Israel	125	350	580	1,974	3,407
Percent	0.1	0.2	0.3	0.6	0.9
Others (percent)	22.4	32.7	38.1	43.0	46.4
Total (percent)	100.0	100.0	100.0	100.0	100.0

a. Estimated.
b. North Africa includes Algeria, Iran, Egypt, Morocco, Sudan, and Tunisia.
c. West Asia includes: Bahrain, Iran, Iraq, Jordan, Kuwait, Lebanon, Oman, Qatar, Saudi Arabia, Syria, the UAE, and Yemen.
Source: UNCTAD, *World Investment Report,* 1998

TABLE 2.4. WORKERS' REMITTANCES
(millions of dollars)

Labor-exporting countries	1989	1991	1993	1995	1997
Algeria	345	233	700	1,294	1,075
Egypt	3,323	3,723	3,835	3,279	3,256
Jordan	623	450	1,040	1,244	1,582
Morocco	1,337	1,990	1,959	1,970	1,893
Sudan	242	124	—	—	—
Syria	430	350	600	—	—
Tunisia	450	525	446	680	684
Rep. of Yemen	1,035	998	1,039	1,067	1,157

Country			Percent of GNP		
	1989	1991	1993	1995	1997
Algeria	1	1	1	3	2
Egypt	9	11	8	6	4
Jordan	16	12	20	19	23
Morocco	6	7	8	6	6
Sudan	2	1	—	—	—
Syria	5	3	5	—	—
Tunisia	5	4	3	4	4
Rep. of Yemen	—	21	23	31	23

— Not available.
Source: World Bank, *World Debt Tables, 1999.*

Economic Incentives

The economic incentives to integrate preferentially have evolved over time. In the period following World War II until a couple of decades ago, regional arrangements were initiated when developing countries were following import-substitution strategies, with the twin features of heavy protection and state, rather than market, allocation of resources. Under these conditions, preferential trade agreements (PTAs) can lead to significant trade diversion, albeit with some trade creation. As elaborated by Viner (1950), trade creation results from lowering trade barriers among the members of the PTA. Trade diversion occurs when members of the PTA import from other members whose products are produced less efficiently than in other parts of the world. Where the gains from trade creation outweigh the cost of trade diversion, there are economic incentives to integrate.

New regional arrangements, in contrast, are taking place among countries characterized by keen interest in participating in the world market (Lawrence 1996). These countries are more open, export- and market-oriented, and private sector–dominated (see Table 2.5 for details). The consequence of this development for the incentives to integrate regionally is increasing emphasis on the potential dynamic, rather than static, welfare gains from integration. The dynamic gains are associated with the flow of new investment, improved productivity, and low transaction costs. These benefits can outweigh the net loss in static welfare, provided that investors do not locate in the hub (rich countries) rather than the spoke (developing countries), productivity improves as competition increases and services are liberalized, and transaction costs are reduced following the adoption of more efficient regulatory schemes—for example, with respect to harmonization of procedures, standards, and certification. When countries are in the process of moving away from import substitution strategies toward more open economies, PTAs with large economies (for example, the United States) can serve as anchors that make the associated reforms more credible (Francois 1997).

Whether "traditional" or "new," the verdict on regionalism, with respect to the welfare implications for the trading partners, is ambiguous. Accordingly, the economic incentives to integrate have to be tested empirically on a case-by-case basis. This empirical analysis can be undertaken using sophisticated models (for example, gravity models) or by drawing on anecdotes. The shortcoming of sophisticated models is that they do not capture important effects of integration, especially those arising from investment and institutional changes. On the other hand, anecdotes do not permit generalizations. For both reasons, the approach followed here is somewhat eclectic. It is based on contrasting a number of insights drawn from both theories with some factual data for Egypt and the triad. Conclusions are then made as to whether or not Egypt has sufficient economic incentives to join the triad.

What, then, are the main insights that create economic incentives to integrate? The key ones can be articulated as follows:

- *Geographic proximity,* because proximity reduces transportation costs, and therefore encourages trade.

- *Openness,* because PTAs under heavy protection promote self-sufficiency and specialization among relatively inefficient producers, thus promoting trade diversion.

TABLE 2.5. REGIONALISM: OLD AND NEW

Old	New
Import substitution, withdrawal from world economy	Export orientation, integration into world economy
Planned and political allocation of resources	Market allocation of resources
Led by governments	Led by private firms
Mainly industrial products	All goods, services, and investment
Deal with border barriers	Deeper integration
Preferential treatment for less developed	Equal rules (different adjustment periods)

Source: Lawrence 1996.

- *Investment-friendly economies*, because such economies can use PTAs to offer location advantages to multinationals in the form of larger markets for output and various sources of inputs. They also allow domestic investors to specialize and take advantage of economies of scale in production and marketing.

- *Need for reform anchor*, because PTAs with large economies (such as the United States or Europe) can provide safeguards against policy reversal (Francois 1997).

The question is whether Egypt has sufficient economic incentives along these lines to join the triad in a customs union or a free trade area. The answer appears to be "no" in the short run. The possibilities for limited trade and specific projects are probably more appropriate at this stage. As Egypt and other neighboring countries move further in the direction of liberalization, as they conclude PTAs with the EU, and as they undertake more economic reforms domestically, the economic incentives to integrate with the triad and other neighboring countries will be higher.[2]

To elaborate the basis for this conclusion, clearly geographical proximity is an advantage. Yet transportation costs do not necessarily correlate with distance. The lack of adequate infrastructure and the sense of insecurity arising from the Arab-Israeli conflict are significant geographical barriers. These barriers are exacerbated when the goods being transported are bulky or perishable. Equally important, Egypt's economic incentives to join the triad at this time are limited because of the high level of protection accorded to several industries in the three countries and the PNA (Table 2.6). Although the Israeli economy is relatively more open, some commodities enjoy high effective rates of protection (for example, food, chemicals and chemical products, and rubber and plastic products). In Egypt and Jordan, the rates of effective protection are even more significant.[3] Under these conditions, attempts to integrate with the triad may amount to integration of industries which are relatively inefficient and highly protected from competition.

Members of the agreement may give each other access to their markets, but only in those products they import from the rest of the world. This will maximize trade diversion.[4]

Beside the need for further liberalization, especially in Egypt and Jordan, the limited inflow of FDI to the triad countries and Egypt relative to such fast-growing economies as Malaysia and Thailand suggests that more reforms are needed to make the business environment more hospitable to investment. Until such reforms are adopted, the merits of joining the triad to attract FDI are limited, in part because the size of the economies of the triad is relatively small. Finally, while Egypt can in fact use PTAs to anchor its ongoing structural reforms and gain investors' confidence, it can achieve this objective more credibly by joining the EU or the United States in a PTA.[5] Of course, joining the EU and the triad are not mutually exclusive—Israel

TABLE 2.6. AVERAGE NOMINAL TARIFF PROTECTION AND EFFECTIVE RATE OF
PROTECTION FOR SELECTED SECTORS

Sectors	Egypt		Jordan		Israel	
	Nominal	*ERP*	*Nominal*	*ERP*	*Nominal*	*ERP*
Mining	9.0	7.0	22.7	8.5	33.7	13.9
Food	36.0	72.0	41.1	22.5	9.5	114.3
Clothing	68.0	162.0	41.0	146.0	11.0	8.2
Leather	35.0	28.0	47.0	54.0	10.0	2.9
Wood and cork products	33.0	66.0	51.0	92.0	13.7	13.7
Paper and printing material	31.0	90.0	12.0	48.0		
Chemicals and products, excl. petroleum	15.0	21.0	26.7	20.1	7.4	43.8
Petroleum refineries	13.0	83.0	6.0	–3.0	—	n.a.
Metal products	28.0	14.0	17.0	14.0	27.9	14.8
Machinery	27.0	38.0	16.0	5.0	8.1	5.9
Transport equipment	40.0	90.0	31.0	102.0	–3.4	0.8
Rubber & plastic products	24.0	33.0	29.0	65.0	11.9	18.3
Average	29.9	58.7	28.4	47.8	10.8	19.7

— Not available.
Source: For Egypt and Jordan, Hoekman and Djankov (1997); for Israel, Halevi (1996).

has a free trade agreement with the EU and the United States. But trade diversion
and investment issues seem to suggest that Egypt may be better off waiting rather
than joining the triad now.

Political incentives
Even if countries have sufficient economic incentives to integrate with a few countries, they may not follow through because the leaders do not have the political
incentives to do so. PTAs can strengthen or erode the position of political leaders,
therefore, PTAs are pursued only when their political benefits outweigh their political costs. The leaders must consider PTAs politically *desirable, feasible,* and *credible* to sign them.[6]

Political desirability is met when the benefits of the agreement to the leaders
and their supporters outweigh the costs. It could come about if the current leadership and its constituencies face an external shock (for example., war) that changes
the political calculations of the costs and benefits in favor of a PTA. Alternatively,
desirability may come about if a country has a new leadership with new constituencies whose interest is more in line with a free trade agreement.

Political feasibility is met when the leaders are able to secure the approval of
and support for carrying out the agreement. It requires that the leadership is able to
secure the consent of other parts of government—legislatures, bureaucracies, and
the state or provincial governments. This is more difficult under democratic re-

gimes, especially where the leaders govern by minority in the legislature. Second, the leadership must be able to compensate the losers, at least partially, especially if they are a vocal minority prepared to destabilize weak coalitions and engage in civil disobedience.

Political credibility is met when the winners and losers believe that the promises to deliver the gains and compensations in the future are credible. In the present context, credibility depends in large part on the perception as to whether the agreement will be respected by all parties in the future, and whether the relationship between the parties is based on trust and irreversible peace. The leadership of the members of the PTA must be able to convince the losers that they will be compensated, and the winners that they will not be affected adversely.

Does a PTA encompassing the triad plus Egypt meet the conditions of desirability, feasibility, and credibility? In my view, it does not. Even if some countries meet all three conditions, the successful conclusion of the agreement requires that *all* political leaders involved find the agreement desirable, feasible, and credible. The foundations of this conclusion are elaborated below, with a particular focus on Egypt.

Consider *desirability*. For Egypt, the constituencies of the leadership are varied, as may be suggested by the government majority in parliament. The bureaucracy does not have a stake in an agreement with the triad. The private sector is more interested in trading in larger markets, especially the EU and the United States. There is a general sentiment, particularly among some in the intellectual community, that comprehensive peace is a precondition for full cooperation. Besides, Egypt is playing the role of a catalyst for peace in the region, and joining the triad may diminish its capacity to play that role. Overall, then, it does not appear that Egypt would consider joining the triad in a PTA desirable at this time.[7]

With respect to *feasibility*, Egypt is in a position to pass an agreement through the legislature if it is deemed politically desirable by the leadership. As already indicated, the government has a majority in parliament. The potential losers from such an agreement are likely to be too few and disbursed. The opposition of some intellectuals could not be stronger than when President Sadat signed a peace treaty with Israel. Therefore, Egypt meets the feasibility condition.[8]

Finally, even if the desirability and feasibility conditions are met, the credibility of the promises to be made in such an agreement may not be believable without external guarantees. Egypt has lived up to its commitments in the peace accord with Israel, but it cannot guarantee the actions of Israel and other parties. Reneging on previous commitments every time a new government is elected, or a disruptive act by opponents of the peace process, would not attract investors to the region, who need to be assured that tranquillity and free trade will be the order of the day. Therefore, that condition may not be attained without full peace and external guarantees of tranquillity, for example, by the United States and other members of the international community.

Interaction between Economic and Political Incentives

The economic and political incentives in favor of regional integration are not independent of each other. Moreover, the interaction between the two sets of incentives can be positive or negative. For example, the economic gains from regional integration may make a PTA politically desirable if the benefits accrue to the groups supporting the governing regime. Here the economic and political incentives work in the same direction. Conversely, where regional integration benefits the opponents of the ruling regime, it would be politically undesirable. In this case, the economic and political incentives are not aligned, and the agreement is not likely to come to fruition. This point may help explain, for example, why the EU is reluctant to liberalize its agriculture sector with Tunisia, Morocco, and now Egypt.

With respect to feasibility, comprehensive peace in the Middle East makes regional integration politically feasible, given that not all leaders can necessarily afford domestic or foreign opposition and stay in power. This opposition may diminish, however, if the economic incentives to integrate become strong enough for the supporters of the leaders to exert corresponding pressure on them to make peace. With respect to credibility, a peace guarantee by strong external forces will obviously reduce the risk facing investors. As a result, FDI may increase, contributing positively to the economic incentives to integrate.

In sum, Egypt does not seem to have sufficient economic or political incentives to join the triad in the short run. This should not necessarily be the case in the medium run.

Prospect of Integration in the Medium Run

The prospects for regional integration in the medium run depend on the changes in economic and political incentives the future brings. While the future is uncertain, it is not divorced from current and past events. Beside peace, two factors currently on the horizon seem to have the potential of influencing the prospects of regional integration in a significant way: PTAs with the EU and FDI. This section explores the role of these two factors on the economic and political incentives to liberalize and integrate in the medium run.

The Role of PTAs with the EU

Egypt is a full member of the WTO, and is soon to sign a partnership agreement with the EU. The government has also undertaken a series of economic reforms in the 1990s, the effect of which is to open the economy to foreign trade and investment. But Egypt is not the only country in the region moving in this direction. Israel has gone further. Beside liberalizing the economy and acceding to the WTO, Israel has PTAs with the EU and the United States. Jordan started a process of opening up its economy, is in the process of joining the WTO, and has also negotiated a PTA with the EU. The question is whether these agreements will speed or impede regional integration and further liberalization.[9]

The literature offers a number of reasons as to why the answer could be in favor of further liberalization and regional integration and a number of reasons to the contrary (Frankel 1995). On the one hand, major trading partners outside the PTA may demand accession or liberalization in the countries concluding a PTA, especially where the trade barriers facing them are relatively high. This will put pressure toward further liberalization. Operating in the same direction is the gradual phasing out of protection in the context of a PTA, as this gradualism diminishes domestic resistance to liberalization. Where the phasing out of protection is accompanied by some compensation and technical assistance, the resistance to liberalization is reduced even further. A final related point concerns the precedent that liberalization in the context of a PTA sets in motion. Subsequent to the agreement, domestic producers will understand that their government cannot easily provide them with protection, which may help further liberalization later.

PTAs may also promote regional integration through their potential influence on firm competitiveness. As indicated above, emerging arrangements are not only about trade but also about competition and investment. To the extent that PTAs remove tariffs and bring about reconciliation of divergent national practices with common rules and policies (for example, bringing standards up to mutual recognition), they pave the way for further trade with outsiders. While PTAs may divert trade, they could stimulate reforms that improve the business environment. Not only would this help domestic producers, but it may also make the country a more attractive location for foreign producers. All this will make firms more efficient, and therefore more open to further liberalization.

On the other hand, PTAs could make further liberalization and integration more difficult. They could entail new forms of protection by implementing rules of origin and administering antidumping and countervailing duties that have protectionist effects. Krueger (1993) and Hoekman (1993) argue that the new arrangements may include, for example, intricate rules of origin that represent a retreat from freer trade.

PTAs could also make further liberalization more difficult if the leaders invest much of their political capital into them rather than in multilateralism (Bhagwati 1992). Firms may, in addition, exert influence in designing new systems of rules that help insiders and hurt outsiders. For example, tariffs may be designed in such a way as to increase protection for certain interest groups, thereby diminishing the political support for multilateral and regional liberalization. Similarly, the way the gradual phasing out of protection is designed can also impede further liberalization, especially where tariffs are removed first on capital and intermediate goods (Hoekman and Djankov 1997). This is because this pattern of tariff reduction will increase effective rates of protection in the interim period, which makes liberalization of final goods more difficult.

All told then, it is an empirical question whether PTAs promote or reduce the possibility of further integration and liberalization. Liberalization in Europe coincided with the formation of the European Community and the European

Free Trade Area. In other regions, however, regional arrangements were associated with fragmentation of world markets and eventual failure of such arrangements.

The EU initiative in the Mediterranean region carries some promise in favor of liberalization in the future, but also some risks. The agreement Egypt is soon to conclude with the EU is expected to resemble those of Tunisia and Morocco. If so, it will require liberalization of manufactured imports from the EU over a 12-year period, and immediate duty-free access to the EU markets for Egyptian manufactured exports. It will require the adoption of competition policies as they relate to trade with the EU. In return, the EU will provide financial and technical assistance to help industries adjust to the new regime. The main shortcomings of the agreement are that it will provide little in improved access for agricultural products, require no liberalization of government procurement, does not ensure free movement of capital, and makes no commitments to liberalize services.

Because the PTA is fundamentally a move toward partial liberalization with a few trading partners, it can be beneficial if it boosts the sectors that are competitive and shrinks the sectors that are not. The danger is that while the agreement may succeed in reducing the size of the import-competing sector, it may do little to stimulate exports and FDI. In other words, it may contribute toward improving standards and policies, but with no significant impact on FDI. This is why Galal and Hoekman (1997) argue, in the case of the agreement under negotiation between Egypt and the EU, that Egypt should use the agreement to advance a growth strategy with liberalization as a critical component.[10] Otherwise, the agreement may generate small static welfare gains from trade creation over trade diversion, but leave the EU as the hub and Egypt as the spoke. This will be at the expense of further regional integration, given that countries like Egypt and Israel will prefer exporting to Europe rather than to countries in the region.

The Role of Foreign Direct Investment

The triad countries and Egypt are not capital-abundant countries. All of them are keen to attract FDI to grow rapidly and raise the standard of living of their populations. In Egypt, a sustained growth of 7 percent per year requires investment approximately equal to 27 percent of GDP, compared with national savings of 18 percent. This leaves a gap of about 10 percentage points of GDP, or about $12 billion. FDI can undoubtedly help, given the limited room for borrowing and the gestation period it takes to stimulate domestic private investment. The advantages of FDI go beyond providing capital, to include bringing knowledge about the latest technologies and access to major markets. Will this need for FDI promote regional integration and further liberalization in the future?

The answer depends in part on what policies Egypt—and other countries for that matter—adopt. FDI initially moved to developing countries to gain access to raw materials. It then moved to take advantage of import-substitution strategies by selling in internal markets behind high protection. Currently, many multinationals and governments pursue FDI to service external markets. To the extent that countries follow appropriate policies to promote exports, FDI can foster regional integration. Conversely, to the extent that FDI is attracted to produce for domestic markets under high protection, it may in fact discourage regional integration.

Another FDI-related factor in favor of improving the prospects of regional integration is the recent emphasis on privatization, deregulation, and financial liberalization. As these reforms intensify in the region, they will attract FDI, especially in such sectors as banking, communications, utilities, and transportation. As a result, domestic services will be produced more efficiently, capital movement will be easier, and the cost of conducting business will be smaller. All these factors will make the countries of the region more attractive locations for FDI, which will enhance the prospects of regional integration. Further reinforcing this is the possibility that countries will also undertake other reforms to attract FDI, including making credible commitments not to expropriate assets in the future, predictable and transparent rules of game, simplified regulatory regimes with respect to establishment and operation, and easy access to large foreign markets without complicated customs procedures.

On their part, multinational firms can also influence the tendency toward regional integration in the future. Because they are increasingly interested in producing complex products across borders, they often find it advantageous to source raw materials in one country, process labor-intensive components in a second, and technologically intensive processes in a third. They consider limited markets to be depriving them of the benefits of economies of scale in production. Accordingly, they can be expected to push for regional integration, to the extent that these arrangements make the movements of goods easier across locations. This is indeed what happened with respect to the regional trading blocks in Europe, North America, and Asia (Fishlow and Haggard 1992). The same can be expected to happen in the Middle East.

All told, the prospects of integration in the region are likely to be higher in the future, as countries adopt more investment-friendly environments, liberalize their economies, and harmonize their regulatory systems (standards and the like). These measures will attract FDI and multinationals and promote domestic investment, as well. Investors will in turn attempt to persuade politicians to integrate with other countries in the region to secure larger markets, capitalize on economies of scale, and optimize production across locations.

Concluding Remarks

This paper dealt with the economic and political incentives of regional integration, focusing, from an Egyptian perspective, on whether the PTAs with the EU will serve to promote trade within the region and with the Israeli-Palestinian-Jordanian triad, and the prospects for extending the incipient steps toward integration within the triad to Egypt. The key points can be summarized as follows:

- Future regional trade is a big challenge. The data on intraregional trade and factor movements continue to show that the region is remarkably unintegrated, accounting for less than 10 percent of total regional trade.

- The poor integration record can be attributed to the limited economic and political incentives to integrate. Economic incentives go beyond trade creation and diversion to cover the dynamic gains associated with investment and deeper integration reforms. Political incentives are not independent of economic incentives, but a regional agreement has to be politically desirable, feasible, and credible to take place.

- In the short run, Egypt has limited economic and political incentives to integrate with the triad. Geographical proximity is offset by the lack of infrastructure and lack of peace. The level of protection is high and may encourage trade diversion. The business environment is in need of improvement to permit FDI to take advantage of location and larger markets. And dynamic gains from regional integration will only come with investment, which is a medium run phenomenon.

- In the medium run, the prospects for regional integration are brighter. Egypt is about to sign a partnership agreement with the EU, and there is a keen interest in attracting FDI. Both factors are expected to bring about deeper reforms at home and create pressure for regional integration to allow firms secure access to larger markets, optimize locations across borders, and capitalize on economies of scale. With similar reforms in the triad and other neighboring countries, the prospects for regional integration will increase. Needless to say, peace is critical for all this to happen.

Before concluding, one question is in order: What could be done in the interim period until the prospects for deeper integration are present? Assuming satisfactory progress on the peace front, the countries of the triad may have strong economic and political incentives to integrate in an appropriate form. At the same time, effort should be focused on taking incremental steps that will bring about beneficial integration to all parties in the future. Reforms of national policies to make them hospitable to investment—domestic and foreign—and greater liberalization are key. These efforts can be supported and coordinated regionally. Simultaneously, it may be possible to work on joint regional projects, especially in infrastructure.

In short, regional integration, like other policy issues, can be beneficial, provided certain conditions are met. Perhaps the most important condition is that the parties to the exchange have both the economic and political incentives to carry it out. When both ingredients are present, a mutually beneficial integration will be forthcoming, otherwise the promise of integration will remain just that—a promise.

Notes

1. The author would like to thank Mona Aboulkheir and Francis Ng for helpful research assistance, Maha Philip for secretarial support and amiable trouble, and Patti Lord for copyediting. Thanks also go to Samiha Fawzi, Bernard Hoekman, and Mahmoud Mohieldin for useful discussions. The views expressed in this paper are those of the author and should not be attributed to the Egyptian Center for Economic Studies or its board of directors.

2. The prospects of regional integration in the medium run are discussed in "Prospect of Integration in the Medium Run" in this chapter.

3. This statement still holds although Egypt, under the reform program carried out in the 1990s, has unified and devalued its exchange rate, opened up the capital account, and reduced the maximum and dispersion of tariff rates.

4. Trade diversion will also be higher, the greater the share of imports from outside the PTA (Lipsey 1960) and the less similar the production structure of the members of the PTA (Viner 1950). The latter has been shown to hold in the case of Egypt and Israel (Fawzy 1994).

5. The evidence suggests that Mexico benefited from NAFTA as an anchor for its economic reform (Francois 1997).

6. These conditions were used in World Bank (1995) to explain why some countries reform their state-owned enterprises, while others lag behind.

7. Although it is difficult to ascertain for other countries, the Palestinians may be the key party in favor of an agreement. Mr. Arafat has just been elected, and he enjoys a broad-based support in favor of prosperity. Given that the Palestinian economy is dependent on Israel, not only for trade but also for employment, it seems reasonable to suggest that an agreement is desirable from a Palestinian perspective. On the Israeli front, it is more difficult to say. A new government has been elected, whose interest seems to lie more in security than in peace, trading in goods, or allowing labor movement. However, the government won by a very small margin, suggesting somewhat the contrary.

8. As for the members of the triad, the feasibility condition may not be fully satisfied. The Israeli government may not be able to push the agreement through parliament, because its constituency seems to favor security over peace. The gap in per capita income may also cause some opposition, given that Israeli's per capita income in 1994 was $11,363, compared with $1,521 for Jordan and $885 for Egypt. The Palestinians will also find it difficult to push for a trade agreement under limited progress on the peace front. Jordan seems to meet the feasibility condition.

9. Openness is key in helping countries begin a process of converging or catching up with richer countries, as shown by Sachs and Warner, 1995.

10. Galal and Hoekman (1997) detail that growth strategy for Egypt. The key reform areas emphasized are reforms to reduce the size of government (to promote domestic savings) and encourage investment, open the economy to trade and investment, and increase competition, mainly through privatization.

References

Bhagwati, Jagdish. 1992. *Trading Choices: The Americas or the World?* New York: Columbia University Press.

El Erian, Mohamed, and Stanley Fischer. 1996. "Is MENA a Region? The Scope for Regional Integration." IMF Working Paper. Washington, D.C.

Fawzy, Samiha. 1994. "The Egyptian-Israeli Trade Relations: A Future Perspective." In Hanaa Kheir Eldin, ed., *Economic Cooperation in the Middle East: Prospects and Challenges.* Cairo: Dar El-Mostaqbal Al-Arabi.

Fischer, Stanley, Dani Rodrik, and Elias Tuma. 1995. *The Economics of Middle East Peace.* Cambridge, Mass.: MIT Press.

Fishlow, Albert, and Stephan Haggard. 1992. *The United States and the Regionalisation of the World Economy.* Paris: OECD Development Center.

Francois, Joseph F. 1997. "Anchoring Policy Reform: External Bindings and the Credibility of Reform." In A. Galal and B. Hoekman, eds., *Regional Partners in Global Markets: Limits and Possibilities of the Euro-Med Agreements.* London: CEPR and ECES.

Frankel, Jeffrey A. 1995. "Does Regionalism Undermine Multilateral Trade Liberalization or Support It? A Survey of Recent Political Economy Arguments.", Institute for International Economics, Washington, D.C. Mimeo.

Galal, Ahmed, and Bernard Hoekman. 1997. "The Road to Maximum Benefits: Egypt and the Partnership Agreement with the EU." In A. Galal and B. Hoekman, eds., *Regional Partners in Global Markets: Limits and Possibilities of the Euro-Med Agreements.* London: CEPR and ECES.

Halevi, Nadav. 1996. "Trade Prospects in the Triad." Mimeo.

Hoekman, Bernard. 1993. "Rules of Origin for Goods and Services." *Journal of World Trade* 27:81–100.

Hoekman, Bernard, and Simion Djankov. 1997. "Effective Protection and Investment Incentives in Egypt and Jordan during the Transition to Free Trade with Europe." *World Development* 25(2):281–91.

International Monetary Fund. 1996. *Direction of Trade Statistics.* Washington, D.C.

Krueger, Anne O. 1993. "Free Trade Agreements as Protectionist Devices: Rules of Origin." Working Paper 4352. Boston: National Bureau of Economic Research.

Lawrence, Robert. 1996. "Preferential Trading Arrangements: The Traditional and the New." In A. Galal and B. Hoekman, eds., *Regional Partners in Global Markets: Limits and Possibilities of the Euro-Med Agreements.* London: CEPR and ECES.

Lipsey, R. G. 1960. "The Theory of Customs Union: A General Survey." *Economic Journal* 70:496–513.

Sachs, Jeffrey, and Andrew Warner. 1995. "Economic Reform and Global Economic Integration." Brookings Papers on Economic Activity, Vol. 1. Washington, D.C.: Brookings Institution, pp. 1–118.

Van den Boogaerde, Pierre. 1991. "Financial Assistance from Arab Countries and Arab Regional Institutions." Occasional Paper 87. International Monetary Fund, Washington, D.C.

Viner, Jacob. 1950. *The Customs Union Issue.* New York: Carnegie Endowment for International Peace.

UNCTAD. 1998. *World Investment Report.* New York: UNCTAD.

World Bank. 1995. *Bureaucrats in Business: The Economics and Politics of Government Ownership.* New York: Oxford University Press.

———. 1996. *World Debt Tables.* Washington, D.C.: World Bank.

Turkey, Tunisia, and Israel: A Comparison of Agreements with the European Union

Sübidey Togan
Bilkent University, Ankara

During the 1990s, the European Community (EC) set the objective of strengthening political, economic, and cultural links with Mediterranean countries. Political impetus to this process was given at the Barcelona Conference in November 1995. A new generation of Euro-Mediterranean Partnership Agreements is being negotiated. Agreements have already been concluded with Morocco, Tunisia, Jordan, the Palestinian National Authority, and Israel, and agreements are expected to be signed within the next few years with Egypt, Lebanon, Algeria, and Syria. Turkey established a customs union (CU) with the European Union (EU) starting on January 1, 1996.

This chapter studies the trade agreements Tunisia, Turkey, and Israel have signed with the EU, within a comparative framework, and highlights the differences as well as the common aspects in the three agreements. We concentrate on the comparison of Israeli, Tunisian, and Turkish agreements because these economies are quite representative of the region. Israel is a high-income, open economy. Turkey is a middle-income economy that has liberalized its economy considerably during the 1980s and 1990s. Tunisia is a middle-income economy that is in the process of opening up its economy, facing all the difficulties of adjustment.

Comparison of the Israeli, Tunisian, and Turkish Economies

Basic data on the Israeli, Tunisian, and Turkish economies are given in Table 3.1. Consideration of per capita GNP figures reveals that per capita income in Israel is 461 percent higher that in Turkey, which in turn is 46.6 percent higher than that in

Tunisia. Purchasing power parity (PPP) per capita income figures reveal that the ordering remains unchanged but that the gap between per capita income levels is narrowed. Consideration of foreign trade data shows that 1997 exports (imports) of Israel amount to $22.5 (30.8) billion, of Tunisia to $5.5 (7.9) billion, and of Turkey to $26.2 (48.7) billion, respectively. During the period 1995–97, output increased by the annual rate of 4.6 percent in Israel, 5.0 percent in Tunisia, and 6.8 percent in Turkey. During the same period, the annual inflation rate amounted to 10.4 percent in Israel, 4.6 percent in Tunisia, and 87.1 percent in Turkey.

Geographic distribution of foreign trade is shown in Table 3.2. The table reveals that the EU (EU-15) is the major trading partner of the countries under consideration. Thirty-two percent of Israeli, 85 percent of Tunisian, and 50 percent of Turkish exports are directed toward the EU, and the share of imports from the EU in total imports amounts to 52 percent in the case of Israel, 75 percent in the case of Tunisia, and 53 percent in Turkey. The table further reveals that the NAFTA countries account for 32 (21) percent of Israeli, 1 (5) percent of Tunisian, and 8 (9) percent of Turkish exports (imports). The share of Turkish imports (exports) from (to) Israel in total Turkish imports (exports) is 0.5 (2) percent, and the share of Turkish imports (exports) from (to) Tunisia is 0.1 (0.4) percent.

Table 3.3 shows the commodity composition of exports by Israel, Tunisia, Turkey, and the world as a whole. The table has been prepared using the four-digit Standard International Trade Classification (SITC) trade statistics from the United Nations Comtrade database, where the 1,167 commodities have been aggregated to 16 commodity groups using the aggregation procedure of the *Annual Report* of the World Trade Organization (WTO) (1997). A close consideration of the table reveals the following:

TABLE 3.1. BASIC DATA ON ISRAELI, TUNISIAN, AND TURKISH ECONOMIES

	Israel	Tunisia	Turkey
1996 population (million)	5.7	9.1	62.7
1996 GDP ($ billion)	95.2	19.5	181.5
Surface area (1000 km²)	21	164	779
GNP per capita, Atlas method (1996, $)	15,870	1,930	2,830
PPP estimate of income per capita (1995, $)	18,520	4,810	5,977
1997 exports ($ billion)	22.5	5.5	26.2
1997 imports ($ billion)	30.8	7.9	48.7
Real GDP growth rate 1995–97	4.6	5.0	6.8
Inflation rate 1995–97	10.4	4.6	87.1

Sources: World Development Indicators on CD-ROM 1998; IMF, *International Financial Statistics* on CD-ROM; IMF, *World Economic Outlook*, May 1998.

TABLE 3.2. GEOGRAPHIC DISTRIBUTION OF EXPORTS AND IMPORTS, 1996
(Percent)

	Israel		Tunisia	
	Exports	Imports	Exports	Imports
EU-15	32.1	51.8	85.1	75.0
NAFTA	31.6	20.6	1.4	5.2
Japan	5.9	3.7	0.3	2.1
Russia	1.3	0.6	0.1	1.1
Israel	—	—		
Tunisia			—	—
Turkey	1.0	0.9	0.9	1.2

Source: IMF, *Direction of Foreign Trade Statistics.*

TABLE 3.3. COMMODITY COMPOSITION OF ISRAELI, TUNISIAN, TURKISH, AND
WORLD EXPORTS, 1996
(Percent)

SITC code		Commodity	Israel	Tunisia	Turkey	World
0+1+4+22	1	Food	5.20	7.34	19.72	8.93
2-22-27-28	2	Agricultural raw materials	1.84	0.73	1.70	2.31
27+28+3+68	3	Mining products	1.25	12.09	3.60	9.99
67	4	Iron and steel	0.15	0.97	8.34	2.76
5	5	Chemicals	13.96	12.74	3.83	9.64
6-65-67-68	6	Other semimanufactures	34.83	4.00	6.92	7.93
71-713	7	Power-generating machinery	0.73	0.12	0.35	1.31
72+73+74	8	Other nonelectrical machinery	6.50	1.21	2.15	8.54
75+76+776	9	Office machines and telecommunications equipment	15.01	0.78	1.41	12.36
77-776-7783 78-785-786+	10	Electrical machinery and apparatus	4.40	6.87	4.14	4.67
7132+7783 79+785+786 +7131+7133	11	Automotive products	0.15	0.61	3.34	9.78
+7138+7139	12	Other transport equipment	2.52	0.17	1.22	3.64
65	13	Textiles	1.94	2.73	11.81	3.01
84	14	Clothing	3.15	43.43	26.32	3.01
8-84-86-891	15	Other consumer goods	8.10	6.13	3.87	8.86
9+891	16	Other products	0.20	0.00	1.21	3.16
Total exports (US$ billion)			20.4	5.5	23.0	4,810.0
First three sectors with highest shares			6, 9, 5	14, 5, 3	14, 1, 13	9, 3, 11

Source: UN Comtrade database.

- The three commodities with the highest export shares in Israel are "other semi-manufactures," "office machines and telecommunications equipment," and "chemicals."

- The three commodities with the highest export shares in Tunisia are "clothing," "chemicals," and "mining products."

- The three commodities with the highest export shares in Turkey are "clothing," "food," and "textiles."

- The three commodities with the highest export shares in the world are "office machines and telecommunications equipment," "mining products," and "automotive products."

It turns out that the share of "office machines and telecommunications equipment" in Israeli exports (15.0 percent) is higher than the corresponding share in world exports (12.4 percent). The shares of the same commodity in Tunisian and Turkish exports are 0.8 and 1.4 percent, respectively. Hence, Israel seems to have comparative advantage in this commodity, for which the world demand has been expanding rather rapidly. However, Tunisia seems to have comparative advantage in the production of "clothing," "chemicals," and "mining products." Similarly, Turkey seems to have comparative advantage in the production of "clothing," "food," and "textiles."

Table 3.4 is based on two-digit SITC foreign trade data obtained from Eurostat in Luxembourg. It shows the commodity composition of trade of Israel, Tunisia, and Turkey with the EU. A close consideration of the table reveals that

- The category of "machinery and transport equipment" is among the major export and import items of Israel, Tunisia, and Turkey to the EU.

- The category of "textiles and clothing" is among the major export items of Tunisia and Turkey to the EU, and it is also a major import item of Tunisia from the EU.

- The category of "chemicals and rubber products" is one of the major export items of Israel to the EU, and it is among the major import items of Israel, Tunisia, and Turkey from the EU.

- One of the major export items of Tunisia to the EU is "energy," and one of the major export items of Turkey to the EU is "food."

Table 3.5 shows the most dynamic exports of Israel, Tunisia, and Turkey defined as those commodities with highest average growth rate of exports over the

TABLE 3.4. COMMODITY COMPOSITION OF ISRAELI, TUNISIAN, AND TURKISH
EXPORTS TO AND IMPORTS FROM THE EU, 1997
(Percent)

SITC code	Commodity	Israeli exports to EU	Israeli imports from EU	Tunisian exports to EU	Tunisian imports from EU	Turkish exports to EU	Turkish imports from EU
0+1+4+22	1 Food	8.55	4.65	8.94	5.70	15.31	2.93
2-22-27-28	2 Agricultural raw materials	3.82	1.25	0.47	2.08	1.83	2.74
27+28	3 Crude fertilizers and ferrous ores	1.45	0.24	0.64	0.46	2.01	2.14
3	4 Energy	1.24	0.38	9.19	5.02	1.03	1.19
67+68	5 Iron , steel, and nonferrous metals	0.76	3.84	0.61	3.24	3.99	5.18
65+84	6 Textiles and clothing	7.66	4.45	53.13	28.28	47.48	5.40
61+83+85	7 Hides and leather	0.30	0.93	6.00	2.74	0.41	1.65
63+82+64	8 Wood manufactures, paper	1.04	4.48	0.45	1.61	1.08	2.79
66	9 Nonmetallic mineral manufactures	20.77	26.52	0.93	0.82	3.03	1.11
5+62	10 Chemicals and rubber products	18.08	12.30	5.40	8.62	3.66	15.38
69	11 Manufactures of metal	2.93	2.69	0.35	2.17	1.65	2.03
7	12 Machinery and transport equipment	22.23	29.99	11.89	32.69	15.78	51.24
81+86+89+9	13 Miscellaneous manufactures	10.31	6.32	1.88	5.61	2.68	6.17
Total trade (ECU billion)		6.3	11.4	4.0	5.3	11.8	22.3
First three sectors with highest shares		12, 9, 10	12, 9, 10	6, 12, 4	12, 6, 10	6, 12, 1	12, 10, 13

Source: Two-digit SITC trade data from Eurostat.

period 1990–97, for which the average share of the commodity over the 1996–97
period is not too small. The table reveals the following results:

- The dynamic sectors of Israel include telecommunications apparatus, non-metallic mineral manufactures (diamonds), medicinal and pharmaceutical products, electrical machinery, and office machines.

- Footwear, electrical machinery, clothing, textiles, and fertilizers are the major dynamic sectors of Tunisia.

- The dynamic sectors of Turkey include transport equipment, rubber manufactures, power generating machinery, manufactures of metal, tele-communications apparatus, electrical machinery, textiles, nonmetallic mineral manufactures (glassware, cement, and brick), vegetables and fruit, and clothing.

TABLE 3.5A. DYNAMIC EXPORTS, TURKEY

SITC code	Commodity	Share of commodity in exports, 1996–97	Average growth rate of exports, 1990–97
97	Gold, onmonetary	0.06	83.80
42	Fixed vegetable oils and fats	0.45	58.22
79	Other transport equipment	4.25	52.12
67	Iron and steel	2.72	37.63
58	Plastic materials	0.14	36.49
63	Cork and wood manufactures	0.09	35.55
61	Leather manufactures	0.11	32.81
78	Road vehicles	3.03	29.60
54	Pharmaceutical products	0.18	24.76
62	Rubber manufactures	1.45	24.18
71	Power-generating machinery	1.19	24.15
72	Specialized machinery	0.35	23.90
73	Metalworking machinery	0.17	19.84
69	Manufactures of metal	1.62	19.63
87	Scientific instruments	0.26	19.44
74	General industrial machinery	0.85	19.15
22	Oil seeds	0.11	17.96
03	Fish and fish preparations	0.72	17.31
76	Telecommunications apparatus	2.63	17.18
77	Electrical machinery	3.99	17.03
28	Metalliferrous ores and metal scrap	0.63	16.66
52	Inorganic chemicals	0.75	16.18
68	Nonferrous metals	0.89	14.65
09	Miscellaneous edible products	0.10	13.80
65	Textiles	11.56	13.51
26	Textile fibers and their wastes	1.15	13.41
55	Essential oils and perfumes	0.091	13.40
66	Nonmetallic mineral manufactures	3.03	12.76
64	Paper	0.14	12.74
11	Beverages	0.12	11.20
05	Vegetables and fruit	12.12	10.87
27	Crude fertilizers and crude minerals	1.39	10.73
51	Organic chemicals	0.49	9.58
07	Coffee, tea, cocoa, spices	0.20	8.18
84	Clothing	35.60	7.79
93	Special transactions	0.25	6.78
04	Cereals and cereal preparations	0.10	6.68
06	Sugar and sugar preparations	0.14	6.54

TABLE 3.5B. DYNAMIC EXPORTS, TUNISIA

SITC code	Commodity	Share of commodity in exports, 1996–97	Average growth rate of exports, 1990–97
54	Medicinal and pharmaceutical products	0.19	50.15
61	Leather manufactures	0.36	34.81
8	Feeding stuff for animals	0.16	29.69
87	Scientific instruments	0.80	29.21
72	Specialized machinery	0.44	24.94
71	Power-generating machinery	0.70	24.04
85	Footwear	5.24	19.86
63	Cork and wood manufactures	0.10	16.08
77	Electrical machinery	7.82	15.96
74	General industrial machinery	0.33	14.15
25	Pulp and waste paper	0.17	13.35
84	Clothing	51.26	10.96
65	Textiles	2.74	9.56
68	Nonferrous metals	0.05	9.18
52	Inorganic chemicals	1.26	8.61
83	Travel goods	0.37	8.56
89	Miscellaneous manufactured articles	0.55	7.60
26	Textile fibers and their wastes	0.15	7.29
56	Fertilizers, manufactured	4.07	7.18
82	Furniture	0.21	7.17
42	Fixed vegetable oils and fats	4.25	6.64

TABLE 3.5C. DYNAMIC EXPORTS, ISRAEL

SITC code	Commodity	Commodity in exports, 1996–97	Growth rate of exports, 1990–97
25	Pulp and waste paper	0.04	92.23
21	Hides, skins, and furskins, raw	0.08	39.13
76	Telecommunications apparatus	7.60	32.39
54	Pharmaceutical products	1.30	26.36
53	Dyeing, tanning, and coloring materials	0.21	25.65
79	Other transport equipment	0.71	24.39
55	Essential oils and perfume materials	0.50	21.02
6	Sugar and sugar preparations	0.24	19.06
74	General industrial machinery and equipment	3.54	18.29
66	Nonmetallic mineral manufactures	20.28	17.29
89	Miscellaneous manufactured articles	5.50	16.15
77	Electrical machinery	4.87	15.91
71	Power-generating machinery		

(Table continues on next page.)

TABLE 3.5C. *(continued)*

SITC code	Commodity	Commodity in exports, 1996–97	Growth rate of exports, 1990–97
	and equipment	1.06	15.42
69	Manufactures of metal	3.04	12.07
83	Travel goods	0.07	11.99
28	Metalliferrous ores and metal scrap	0.49	11.52
51	Organie chemicals	4.07	10.96
85	Footwear	0.21	9.87
93	Special transactions	0.46	9.54
57	Explosives	1.80	9.51
4	Cereals and cereal preparations	0.12	8.79
87	Scientific instruments and optical goods	2.95	8.77
75	Office machines	2.52	8.69
7	Coffee, tea, cocoa, spices	0.15	8.62
58	Plastic materials	2.11	8.57

Trade Liberalization

Turkey's application for association with the EC was made in 1959. The application ultimately resulted in the signing of the Association Agreement in 1963. According to the agreement, the association was to be implemented in three stages: a preparatory stage, a transitional stage, and a final stage. In 1967, Turkey lodged its application for negotiations on entering the transitional stage. The Additional Protocol to the Ankara Agreement, signed in 1970, allowed Turkey to benefit from duty-free access to EU markets for manufactured goods with certain exceptions. The basic aim of the Additional Protocol was the establishment of a customs union (CU). In 1995, it was agreed at the Association Council meeting that Turkey would create a CU between Turkey and the EU starting on January 1, 1996. Before the formation of the CU, the Turkish economy was still highly protected. According to Togan (1997), the average economy-wide nominal protection rate (NPR) during 1994 amounted to 10.2 percent in trade with the EU and 22.1 percent in trade with third countries.

The first trade agreement between the EC and Tunisia was signed in 1976. It allowed Tunisia to benefit from duty-free access to EU markets for manufactured goods. The agreement was not reciprocal. Tunisia continued to apply tariffs to goods of EC origin. As emphasized by Lahouel (1998), the import regime was based for a long time on licensing and tariff protection. Licensing had been very restrictive until the 1990s, when the country replaced the positive list with a negative one indicating the goods under restriction. Customs duties were relatively high, exceeding 40 percent on average, and widely dispersed, ranging between 5 and 236 percent. Under the reform program of 1987–90, average nominal protection rates fell to 29 percent for the whole economy and dispersion was also reduced. During the 1990s, the EC set the objective of strengthening political, economic, and cultural links with Mediterranean countries, in line with the objectives set at the Corfu European Council in 1994. In the context of the Euro-Mediterranean partnership, a new generation of Euro-Mediterranean Association Agreements were negotiated with Mediterranean countries, and Tunisia was the first country among these countries to sign a free trade agreement (FTA), with the EU in July 1995.

In the case of Israel, the first trade agreement with the EC was signed in 1964. With that agreement, the EC reduced the Common External Tariff (CET) on some industrial goods from Israel. The agreement was followed by a preferential trade agreement signed in June 1970. Through the latter agreement, the CET on imports from Israel by the EU was cut by 30 percent immediately and 5 percent on each January 1 until 1975. On certain products, the reduction was less than 30 percent. During 1972, the EC introduced the Global Mediterranean Policy. With that policy, the EC aimed at the creation of a free trade area in manufactured goods in the whole Mediterranean area. A new agreement was signed with Israel in May 1975. Under this agreement, Israeli manufactured exports, including some processed agricultural commodities, enjoyed duty-free access to the EC as of July 1, 1977. Certain sensitive imports from Israel continued to be subject to quotas and other restrictions for some time, but all these terminated at the end of 1979. Israel's agricultural exports were subject to tariffs and controls such as minimum prices, quotas, and voluntary restrictions. Tariff-free entry for EC exports of manufactured goods to Israel was achieved over a longer period. As emphasized by Pomfret and Toren (1980), Israeli tariffs on manufactured imports from the EC were abolished by January 1, 1980 on 60 percent of EC exports, and they were completely eliminated by January 1, 1985. Quantitative restrictions on imports from the EC were completely abolished during the period 1980–85. In December 1995, the 1975 Agreement with Israel was transformed to an FTA within the context of the Euro-Mediterranean partnership.

Liberalization of Trade in Industrial Commodities
According to the stipulations of the Additional Protocol to the Ankara Treaty signed on November 23, 1970, Turkish imports from the Community were divided into two lists. Those industrial products in which it was thought that Turkey could achieve international competitiveness relatively early were placed on the 12-year list. Other manufactured products were put on a 22-year list, for which a CU would not be achieved until 1995. With the formation of a CU with the EU, Turkey has reduced to zero the NPRs for all of the commodities belonging to the 12-year and 22-year lists. Besides these commodities, there are products within the province of the European Coal and Steel Community (ECSC). For these commodities, an FTA was signed in December 1995 between Turkey and the EU. The agreement envisions gradual liberalization of trade in ECSC products over a period of three years. Thus, by 1999, the NPRs for all industrial products will be zero in trade with the EU.

The EU-Turkey Customs Union Decision (CUD) of March 1995 required Turkey to adopt the Common Customs Tariff (CCT) against third-country imports by January 1, 1996, and to adopt all of the preferential agreements the EU has concluded with third countries by the year 2001. Trade with third countries by the EU can be studied under trade with countries to which the EU applies CCT, and trade with EFTA countries, the Mediterranean countries, the Central and Eastern European (CEE) countries, the Baltic countries, developing countries having GSP treatment, and the Lomé Convention countries. The EU has concluded preferential trade agreements with each of these country groups. Since Turkey, after the formation of the CU, will have to apply the Community's CCT and accept all of the preferential agreements the EU has concluded over time at the latest by 2001, Turkey in three years will be faced with different sets of tariff rates for different groups of countries. In the case of EFTA countries, CEE countries, Baltic countries, and Israel, which have FTAs with the EU, the nominal tariff rates that will be applied by Turkey in 2001 on imports from these countries will be identical to those applied on imports from the EU. Thus, as shown by Togan (1997), the economy-wide average NPRs for countries the EU has FTAs with will be reduced from 22.1 percent in 1994 to 1.3 percent in 2001. However, the economy-wide average NPRs for countries such as the United States, Japan, and Canada will be reduced from 22.1 percent in 1994 to 6.9 percent in 2001, and for GSP beneficiaries from 22.1 percent in 1994 to 2.7 percent in 2001.

According to the stipulations of the EU-Tunisia FTA, Tunisian quotas are to be abolished upon the entry into force of the agreement except as allowed by GATT rules. Tunisian tariffs on industrial products will be reduced to zero over a 12-year period. The agreement divides the industrial commodities into five groups, four of which are defined in the Annexes to the Agreement. Tariffs and surcharges on industrial commodities not mentioned in the annexes, accounting for 10.0 percent of imports and for which average tariffs are 21.6 percent, are to be abolished upon entry into force of the agreement. As emphasised by Hoekman and Djankov (1996), tariffs and surcharges on products listed in Annex 3 (Annex 4) accounting for 24.0 (29.0) percent of imports and for which average tariffs amounted to 26.7 (30.4) percent, will be eliminated over a five- (12-) year period. Tariffs and surcharges on products listed in Annex 5, accounting for 36.0 percent of imports and for which average tariffs amounted to 33.8 percent, will be eliminated over an eight-year period. But during the first four years after the agreement enters into force, the tariffs will remain unchanged and thereafter tariffs will be reduced in steps of 11–12 percent per year. Finally, the products contained in Annex 6, accounting for 1 percent of imports, are exempt from tariff reductions.

With the EU-Tunisia FTA, the parties agree to abolish mutual barriers to trade in industrial goods over a 12-year period while each party maintains its own policy relative to nonparticipating third countries. Thus, Tunisia will neither adopt the CCT of the EU nor accept any of the preferential trade agreements the EU has concluded over time, and it will keep the protection rates against third-country imports at the levels it considers appropriate. Article 23 of the EU-Tunisia FTA states that the agreement shall not preclude the maintenance or establishment of customs unions, free trade areas, or arrangements for frontier trade, except insofar as they alter the trade arrangements provided for in the EU-Tunisia FTA.

In the case of Israel, the 1995 EU-Israel FTA confirms the existence of free trade in manufactured goods achieved through the 1975 agreement. According to the stipulations of the agreement, customs duties on imports and exports of industrial commodities, and any charges having equivalent effect, are prohibited between the Community and Israel. Finally, we note that the EU and Israel will maintain their own commercial policies toward nonparticipating third countries. Thus, Israel keeps the protection rates against third-country imports at their previous levels, which, according to Razin and Sadka (1993), are relatively high. Article 17 of the EU-Israel FTA[1] states that the agreement will not preclude the maintenance or establishment of customs unions, free trade areas, or arrangements for frontier trade, except insofar as they alter the trade arrangements provided for in the EU-Israel FTA.

These considerations reveal that in the case of industrial products, free trade has already been established between the EU and Israel through the 1975 EU-Israel FTA, and that it will be established by January 1, 1999 between the EU and Turkey through the CUD and between the EU and Tunisia by 2010 through the EU-Tunisia FTA. If bilateral FTAs between Mediterranean countries can also be signed by 2010, the countries under consideration will establish a free trade area covering flows of industrial goods. There are some differences between the three trade agreements. The EU-Israel and EU-Tunisia trade agreements are FTAs, and the EU-Turkey trade agreement is a CUD. As such, the EU-Turkey CUD requires that Turkey adopt the CCT against third-country imports by January 1, 1996, and adopt all of the preferential agreements EU has concluded with third countries by the year 2001. Similar restrictions are not imposed on Tunisia and Israel. These countries are free to maintain their own policies toward nonparticipating third countries. Furthermore, there are no clauses on rules of origin in the CUD, whereas the EU-Tunisia FTA (EU-Israel FTA) discusses the issue of "originating products" in Article 29 and Protocol 4 (Article 24 and Protocol 4). As Mediterranean countries conclude bilateral FTAs among themselves, the introduction by the EC of diagonal cumulation of origin will become an essential tool to facilitate the establishment of the Euro-Mediterranean free trade zone through the development of South-South commercial ties.

Liberalization of Trade in Agricultural Commodities

According to Articles 22–25 of the CUD, to establish the freedom of movement of agricultural products, Turkey will have to adjust its agricultural policy in such a way as to adopt the Common Agricultural Policy (CAP) measures. How can Turkey adopt the CAP measures? Studies reveal that substantial resources would have to be channelled into Turkish agriculture. Since Turkey cannot devote substantial resources to agriculture from its own sources and since the EU would be unwilling to bear the cost, the idea of Turkey adopting the CAP has to be postponed. Thus, it seems that the freedom of movement of agricultural products between Turkey and the EU cannot be achieved in the near future. However, Articles 17–21 of the CUD on processed agricultural products are of importance for producers and exporters of processed agricultural goods in Turkey. The CUD determines the percentage of prices of processed agricultural commodities that are "agricultural" as contrasted with the percentage that are "industrial." Since the "industrial" component of processed agricultural products will enter European markets duty free and since European protection will apply to the "agricultural" component of these commodities, Turkish firms in the food industry will be faced with more competition, the higher the fraction of the "industrial" component is. Similar considerations will apply for European firms in the food industry.

In the case of Tunisia, the FTA emphasizes gradual implementation of greater liberalization of the reciprocal trade in agricultural and fishery products. According to the agreement, the situation will be reexamined in the year 2001. In the case of Israel, the FTA foresees progressive and reciprocal liberalization of trade in agricultural products and extension of precedent concessions on a reciprocal basis. Existing concessions are to be reexamined in the year 2000. In both FTAs, there are provisions dealing with processed agricultural products that are similar to the CUD. Table 3.6 reports the major agricultural exports for each country.

The arrangements regulating the importation of agricultural products from Israel, Tunisia, and Turkey into the EU are shown in Table 3.7. The table reveals that Israel has obtained duty-free access up to the quota limits from the EU for most of the commodities considered among the first 12 commodities of Table 3.6. None of these quotas were binding for Israel during 1996. Among the five commodities of the second set of commodities in Table 3.7, Tunisia has obtained duty-free access to the EU market for fish, crustaceans, molluscs, and dates. In the case of olive oil, which is the major agricultural export item of Tunisia, during each marketing year from January 1, 1996, to December 31, 1999, a customs duty of ECU 7.81 per 100 kilograms will be levied on imports into the Community within the limits of a quantity of 46,000 tonnes a year. The parties will reassess the situation during the second half of 1999 and determine the trade arrangements for olive oil for the period from January 1, 2000. Turkey has benefited from preferential treatment by the EU for most of the commodities considered in the third set of commodities in Table 3.7, which are the commodities with relatively high shares in total Turkish agricultural exports.

Table 3.8 shows the unit export values of the commodities considered in Table 3.6 in terms of U.S. dollars for Israel, Tunisia, and Turkey. Of the 34 commodities, for which unit export price figures for both Israel and Turkey exist, the Israeli unit export price is higher (lower) than the Turkish unit export price in the case of 26 (8) commodities. The figures reveal that on average, Israel has obtained more U.S. dollars per unit of quantity of agricultural commodities exported from Israel than Turkey was able to obtain. The high unit price of exports obtained by Israel is probably due to the quality difference of the products. In the case of Tunisia, the concessions obtained seem within a comparative framework to be relatively satisfactory.

TABLE 3.6. TRADE IN SELECTED AGRICULTURAL COMMODITIES

Product	1996 Israeli exports, metric ton	1996 Israeli exports $1,000	Share in total Israeli agr. exports (%)	1996 Tunisian exports, metric ton	1996 Tunisian exports, $1,000	Share in total Tunisian agr. exports (%)	1996 Turkish exports, metric ton	1996 Turkish exports, $1,000	Share in total Turkish agr. exports (%)
Cut flowers and foliage		194,767	13.54	—	996	0.22	—	12,678	0.26
Oranges	247,000	104,710	7.28	21,788	9,250	2.07	84,077	29,072	0.59
Grapefruit and pomelos	123,000	74,000	5.14	0	0	0	44,970	15,880	0.32
Cotton lint (263.1)	26,988	58,300	4.05	0	2	0.00	76,035	124,059	2.51
Bulbs, cuttings, live plants		49,904	3.47	—	1,266	0.28	—	4,565	0.09
Avocados	45,953	45,782	3.18	0	0	0	72	23	0.00
Orange juice, single strength	60,600	39,739	2.76	0	0	0	1,130	648	0.01
Grapefruit juice, single strength	65,000	37,580	2.61	0	0	0	0	0	0
Orange juice, concentrated	21,500	28,264	1.96	6	8	0.00	2,442	1,924	0.04
Grapefruit juice, concentrated	16,900	26,720	1.85	0	0	0	23	15	0.00
Potatoes (054.1)	74,057	22,297	1.55	3,079	1,188	0.26	240,702	29,857	0.60
Tomatoes (054.4)	10,197	21,761	1.51	1,078	333	0.07	110,763	38,950	0.79
Olive oil	20	60	0.00	28,907	120,258	26.96	23,277	74,354	1.50
Crustaceans & molluscs		15	0.00	—	66,151	14.83	—	22,223	0.45
Dates (057.96)	212	1,407	0.09	18,216	47,914	10.74	130	93	0.00
Cigarettes	53	1,314	0.09	2,244	24,645	5.52	21,057	88,932	1.80
Fish		10,199	0.70	—	22,165	4.96	—	26,762	0.54
Tobacco leaves	4	25	0.00	435	895	0.20	162,027	538,548	10.90
Hazelnuts, shelled			0	34	107	0.02	143,282	442,941	8.96
Pastry	4,000	11,000	0.76	1,252	4,648	1.04	171,714	236,759	4.79
Sugar confectionery	5,500	9,335	0.64	1,434	3,069	0.68	74,076	194,812	3.94
Raisins (057.52)			0	0	0	0	171,869	188,322	3.81
Flour, wheat (046.01,02)	1,000	300	0.02	32,564	9,986	2.23	570,577	175,366	3.55
Prepared nuts (excl. GRNUTS)	25	110	0.00	0	0	0	45,448	134,711	2.72
Margarine & shortening	180	240	0.01	0	0	0	130,599	122,993	2.49

(Table continues on next page.)

81

TABLE 3.6. (Continued)

Product	1996 Israeli exports, metric ton	1996 Israeli exports, $1,000	Share in total Israeli agr. exports (%)	1996 Tunisian exports, metric ton	1996 Tunisian exports, $1,000	Share in total Tunisian agr. exports (%)	1996 Turkish exports, metric ton	1996 Turkish exports, $1,000	Share in total Turkish agr. exports (%)
Tomato paste	6,900	4,300	0.29	7,179	7,374	1.65	148,848	122,912	2.48
Lentils	0	0	0	0	0	0	246,142	112,166	2.27
Chickpeas	50	60	0.00	51	59	0.01	192,710	112,104	2.27
Dry apricots	0	0	0	36	18	0.00	43,821	106,072	2.14
Sheep (head)	0	0	0	0	0	0	240,576	82,992	1.68
Figs, dried	7	34	0.00	5	2	0.00	35,367	68,575	1.38
Lemons & limes (057.21)	4,700	2,127	0.14	49	36	0.00	110,441	59,659	1.20
Tangerines, mandarins, clementines, and satsumas	0	0	0	3	1	0.00	125,956	53,066	1.07
Total			51.76			71.82			65.24

— Not available.
Sources: Food and Agricultural Organization of the United Nations; UN Comtrade data.

TABLE 3.7. TARIFF QUOTAS ON AND TRADE ARRANGEMENTS FOR SELECTED AGRICULTURAL COMMODITIES

CN code	Product	Reduction of the MFN customs duty (%), Israel	Tariff quota volume (tonnes), Israel	Reduction of the MFN customs duty (%), Tunisia	Tariff quota volume (tonnes), Tunisia	Reduction of the MFN customs duty (%), Turkey	Tariff quota volume (tonnes), Turkey
060310 and 060491	Cut flowers and foliage	100	19,500	100	750	100	—
ex 080510	Oranges	100	290,000	100	31,360	100	—
ex 080540	Grapefruit and pomelos	100	—	80	n.a.	100	—
5201	Cotton lint (263.1)	n.a.	n.a.	n.a.	n.a.	100	—
0601 and 0602	Bulbs, cuttings, live plants	100	—	100 (roses)	—	100	—
080440	Avocados	100	—	n.a.	n.a.	100	—
200911 and 200919	Orange juice, single strength and concentrate	100	92,600	70	—	100	—
200920	Grapefruit juice, single strength and concentrate	100	—	70	—	100	—
ex 07019051	Potatoes (054.1)	100	20,000	100 (Nov.–Apr.)	15,000	100	—
070200	Tomatoes (054.4)	100	1,000	100	n.a.	100	—
150910 and 1510	Olive oil	n.a.	n.a.	(ª)	(ª)	100	(ᵇ)
1605	Crustaceans and molluscs	n.a.	n.a.	100	—	100	—
ex 08041000	Dates (057.96)	100	—	100	—	100	—
240220	Cigarettes	n.a.	n.a.	n.a.	n.a.	100	—
1604	Fish	n.a.	n.a.	100	—	100	—
2401	Tobacco leaves	n.a.	n.a.	n.a.	n.a.	100	—
080221 and 080222	Hazelnuts, shelled	n.a.	n.a.	n.a.	n.a.	duty rate 3 %	—
1902	Pastry	n.a.	n.a.	n.a.	n.a.	100	—
	Sugar confectionery	n.a.	n.a.	n.a.	n.a.	100	—
08061029	Raisins (057.52)	100	—	60 (table grapes)	na	100	—
1101	Flour, wheat (046.01,.02)	n.a.	n.a.	n.a.	n.a.	100	—
	Prepared nuts (excl. GRNUTS)	n.a.	n.a.	n.a.	n.a.	100	—

(Table continues on next page.)

TABLE 3.7. (continued)

CN code	Product	Reduction of the MFN customs duty (%), Israel	Tariff quota volume (tonnes), Israel	Reduction of the MFN customs duty (%), Tunisia	Tariff quota volume (tonnes), Tunisia	Reduction of the MFN customs duty (%), Turkey	Tariff quota volume (tonnes), Turkey
1517	Margarine and shortening	—	—	—	—	100	n.a.
200290	Tomato paste	—	—	100	2,000	100	(c)
071340	Lentils	—	—	100	n.a.	100	n.a.
071320	Chickpeas	—	—	100	n.a.	100	n.a.
080910	Dry apricots	—	—	100	n.a.	100	n.a.
020410-020443	Sheep	—	—	100	n.a.	100	(d)
08042021-08042029	Figs, dried	—	—	—	—	100	n.a.
080530	Lemons & limes (057.21)	100	7,700 and 1,000	100	n.a.	100	n.a.
080520	Tangerines, mandarins, clementines, and satsumas	100	21,000	100	n.a.	100	n.a.

n.a. Not applicable.

— Not available.

a. Each marketing year until December 31, 1999, within the limits of a quantity of 46,000 tonnes per year, a customs duty of ECU 7.81 per 100 kg shall be levied on imports into the Community of untreated olive oil from Tunisia.

b. Specific duty is to be reduced by 5–10 percent.

c. Prepared tomatoes (whole or in pieces) are subject to a quota of 8,000 tonnes, other prepared tomatoes with a dry matter content of not less than 12 percent by weight are subject to a quota of 30,000 tonnes.

d. No tariff quota, but in terms of specific duty there is tariff quota.

Sources: EU-Israel FTA; EU-Tunisia FTA; and Decision 1/98 of the EC-Turkey Association Council of February 25, 1998.

TABLE 3.8. UNIT EXPORT PRICES OF SELECTED AGRICULTURAL COMMODITIES

Product	Israeli unit price	Tunisian unit price	Turkish unit price	Israeli over Tunisian price	Israeli over Turkish price	Tunisian over Turkish price
Oranges	0.42	0.42	0.34	0.99	1.22	1.22
Grapefruit and pomelos	0.60	—	0.35	—	1.70	—
Cotton lint (263.1)	2.16	—	1.63	—	1.32	—
Avocados	0.99	—	0.31	—	3.11	—
Orange juice, single strength	0.65	—	0.57	—	1.14	—
Orange juice, concentrated	1.31	1.33	0.78	0.98	1.66	1.69
Grapefruit juice, concentrated	1.58	—	0.65	—	2.42	—
Potatoes (054.1)	0.30	0.38	0.12	0.78	2.42	3.11
Tomatoes (054.4)	2.13	0.30	0.35	6.90	6.06	0.87
Olive oil	3	4.16	3.19	0.72	0.93	1.30
Dates (057.96)	6.63	2.63	0.71	2.52	9.27	3.67
Cigarettes	24.79	10.98	4.22	2.25	5.87	2.60
Tobacco leaves	6.25	2.05	3.32	3.03	1.88	0.61
Hazelnuts, shelled	—	3.14	3.09	—	—	1.01
Pastry	2.75	3.71	1.37	0.74	1.99	2.69
Sugar confectionery	1.69	2.14	2.62	0.79	0.64	0.81
Flour of wheat (046.01, .02)	0.3	0.30	0.30	0.97	0.97	0.99
Prepared nuts (excl. GRNUTS)	4.4	—	2.96	—	1.48	—
Margarine and shortening	1.33	—	0.94	—	1.41	—
Tomato paste	0.62	1.02	0.82	0.60	0.75	1.24
Chickpeas	1.2	1.15	0.58	1.03	2.06	1.98
Dry apricots	—	0.5	2.42	—	—	0.20
Figs, dried	4.85	0.4	1.93	12.14	2.50	0.20
Lemons and limes (057.21)	0.45	0.73	0.54	0.61	0.83	1.36
Tangerines, mandarins, clementines, and satsumas	—	0.33	0.42	—	—	0.79
Macaroni	2.02	0.65	0.52	3.07	3.85	1.25
Apple juice, concentrated	2.23	—	1.28	—	1.74	—
Beans, dried	—	0.83	0.72	—	—	1.14
Beer, barley(112.3 ex)	1.57	1.80	0.58	0.86	2.68	3.08
Apples (057.4)	—	1.26	0.60	—	—	2.09
Cotton waste	0.8	0.29	1.01	2.70	0.78	0.29
Hen eggs	1.29	4.95	1.09	0.26	1.17	4.51
Grapes (057.51)	1.42	1	0.61	1.42	2.30	1.61
Mushrooms	—	3.76	11.89	—	—	0.31
Wine	2.42	0.74	1.51	3.26	1.60	0.49
Sunflower seed (222.4)	0.09	0.21	1.97	0.46	0.04	0.10
Cantaloupes and other melons	0.93	—	0.33	—	2.79	—
Almonds, shelled	2.84	6.92	4.99	0.41	0.56	1.38
Bread	1.90	24.10	1.67	0.07	1.14	14.40
Chickens (units)	1.31	6.90	0.43	0.19	3.01	15.83

— Not available.
Source: Author's calculations.

Antidumping and Safeguard Measures

The EU-Turkey CUD offers rapid liberalization of trade. However, there are loopholes in the liberalization provided through antidumping procedures and safeguard measures, which are mentioned in Articles 36, 42, and 61 of the CUD. Article 36 specifies that as long as a particular practice is incompatible with the competition rules of the CU as specified in Articles 30–32 of the CUD and "in the absence of such rules if such practice causes or threatens to cause serious prejudice to the interest of the other Party or material injury to its domestic industry," the Community or Turkey may take the appropriate measures. Article 42 allows antidumping actions as long as Turkey fails to implement effectively the competition rules of the CU and other relevant parts of the *acquis communautaire*. In those cases, Article 47 of the Additional Protocol signed in 1970 between Turkey and the EC will remain in force. Finally, Article 61 is about safeguards that offer another loophole in the liberalization. The Article states that safeguard measures as specified in Article 60 of the Additional Protocol will remain valid. According to Article 60, the Community (Turkey) may take necessary protective measures if serious disturbances occur in a sector of the economy of the Community (Turkey) or prejudice the external financial stability of one or more member states (Turkey), or if difficulties arise that adversely affect the economic situation in a region of the Community (Turkey).

Similarly, the EU-Tunisia FTA aims for liberalization of trade. As in the case of the CUD, however, there are loopholes in the liberalization provided through antidumping procedures and safeguard measures, which are mentioned in Articles 24, 25, and 27 of the EU-Tunisia FTA. Article 24 allows antidumping actions. The agreement specifies that antidumping actions must accord with Article VI of GATT. Since most EU practice is GATT consistent, there is little comfort for Tunisian producers. The Association Council will be informed of a dumping case as soon as the importing party starts investigating. If no solution has been reached within 30 days, the importing party may adopt the appropriate measures. Safeguards offer another loophole in the liberalization. The general safeguard clause contained in the agreement ties in perfectly with GATT rules. The safeguard measures have to be notified to the Association Committee and are subject to periodic consultations to establish a timetable for their abolition. Another derogation in the agreement enables the parties to deal with balance of payments difficulties. According to Article 35, the EU-Tunisia FTA safeguard measures are permitted for limited duration if imports from Tunisia cause "serious balance of payments difficulties for Member Countries."

Articles 18, 19, and 21 of the EU-Israel FTA contain clauses about antidumping procedures and safeguards. These articles are similar to Articles 24, 25, and 27 of the EU-Tunisia FTA. Article 22 is about safeguard measures the parties may take when they face balance of payments difficulties. It is identical to Article 35 of the EU-Tunisia FTA.

Rules and Disciplines

The CUD, EU-Tunisia FTA, and EU-Israel FTA contain articles on the harmonization of commercial legislation as regards competition policy, state aids, intellectual and industrial property rights, and technical barriers.

Competition Policies

Within the Community, a strong common competition policy was seen, since the foundation of the Community, as important to ensure free and undistorted competition, as anticompetitive behavior and subsidies can distort trade in the same way as border measures do. Outside the Community, cooperation on competition policy matters has increasingly been regarded as necessary to prevent anticompetitive practices that could hurt EU companies. Therefore, the EU has introduced clauses on competition policy cooperation into the trade agreements.

The competition policy articles of the Treaty Establishing the European Community are Article 85, dealing with anticompetitive practices; Article 86, dealing with dominant market practices; Article 37, dealing with state monopolies; Article 90, dealing with the conduct of public enterprises;, and Articles 92–94, dealing with state aid. The issues are covered by Articles 30–36 of the CUD, Articles 36–38 of the EU-Tunisia FTA, and Articles 25–27 of the EU-Israel FTA. There is a major difference between the CUD and the FTAs. In the FTAs, competition rules are covered under the heading of "Trade Related Provisions" in the EU-Israel Agreement and under the heading of "Competition and Other Provisions" in the EU-Tunisia Agreement. In the CUD, the rules are discussed under the headings of "Competition Rules of the Customs Union" and "Approximation of Legislation."

Article 30 of the CUD, which is identical to Article 85 of the EC Treaty, explicitly states all of the agreements among firms that are considered as incompatible with a proper functioning of the CU. In addition, Article 30 allows agreements among firms that will promote efficiency in production and distribution, promote technical progress, and provide consumers with a fair share of the benefits. An immediate consequence of these negative and positive sides to the article is that each situation has to be studied by competition board on its own merits, and the task of the Turkish Competition Board is to build the appropriate body of case law. Article 31 of the CUD, which is identical to Article 86 of the EC Treaty, prohibits the abuse by one or more undertakings of a dominant position in the territories of the Community and/or of Turkey or in a substantial part thereof, but only insofar as the abuse may affect trade between the Community and Turkey. It covers, for example, restrictions on supply or technical development and unfair pricing. But unlike Article 30 of the CUD, there is no provision for granting an exemption.

According to Article 32 of the CUD, which is identical to Article 92 of the EC Treaty, any public aid that distorts competition is incompatible with the functioning of the CU. Exceptions are aid having a social character granted to individual consumers, aid promoting economic development of Turkey's less-developed regions for five years, aid aiming at accomplishing structural adjustment necessitated by the establishment of the CU for a period of five years, and aid promoting culture and heritage conservation. Aid to facilitate the development of certain economic activities or of certain economic areas may also be considered to be compatible with the functioning of the CU. Article 37 of the CUD states that Turkey shall ensure that its legislation in the field of competition rules is made compatible with that of the European Community, and is applied effectively. Turkey shall ensure that, within one year after the entry into force of the CU, the principles contained in block exemption regulations in force in the Community, as well as the principles contained in the case law developed by EC authorities, shall be applied in Turkey. Within two years after the entry into force of the CU, Turkey will adapt all aid schemes other than those granted to the textile and clothing sector to the rules laid down in Community frameworks and guidelines under Articles 92 and 93 of the EC Treaty. According to Article 39 of the CUD, Turkey shall ensure that public undertakings, and undertakings to which special or exclusive rights have been granted, by the end of first year following the entry into force of the CU uphold the principles in Article 90, as well as principles contained in the secondary legislation and the case law developed on this basis. Article 40 of the CUD states that Turkey shall adjust any state monopolies of a commercial character so as to ensure that, by the end of the second year following the entry into force of the CUD, no discrimination regarding the conditions under which goods are produced and marketed exist between nationals of the member states and of Turkey. Finally, Statements 1 and 2 of the CUD state that the Community will apply safeguard measures such as antidumping and countervailing duties until Turkey effectively implements the measures on competition, including the measures on public aid.

In the EU-Israel FTA, Article 25.1 states:

> The following are incompatible with the proper functioning of the Agreement, insofar as they may affect trade between the Community and Israel: (i) all agreements between undertakings, decisions by associations of undertakings and concerted practices between undertakings which have as their object or effect the prevention, restriction or distortion of competition; (ii) abuse by one or more undertakings of a dominant position in the territories of the Community or of Israel as a whole or in substantial part thereof; (iii) any public aid which distorts or threatens to distort competition by favouring certain undertakings or the production of certain goods.

Paragraph 3 of Article 25 is about transparency in the area of public aid, and Paragraph 4 excludes the application of paragraph 1(iii) to agricultural commodities. Paragraph 5 of Article 25 states that if a particular practice is incompatible with the terms of paragraph 1, the affected party may take appropriate measures after 30 days following consultation within the Cooperation Council. Such measures have to be GATT consistent. Finally, Article 26 concerns state monopolies, and Article 27 is about public enterprises.

The competition rules of the EU-Tunisia FTA, covered by Articles 36–38, are similar to the competition rules of the EU-Israel Agreement. The first part of Article 36.1 is identical to Article 25.1 of the EU-Israel FTA. The second part of Article 36.1 allows for derogation under the treaty establishing ECSC. Article 36.2 states that practices contrary to Article 36.1 shall be assessed on the basis of criteria arising from the application of the rules of Articles 85, 86, and 92 of the treaty establishing EC, and in the case of products falling within the scope of the ECSC, the rules of Articles 65 and 66 of the treaty establishing that Community, and the rules relating to state aid, including secondary legislation. Article 36.4 (a) states that for the purposes of applying the provisions of paragraph 1 (c), the parties recognize that during the first five years after the entry into force of this agreement, any public aid granted by Tunisia shall be assessed, taking into account the fact that Tunisia shall be regarded as an area identical to those areas of the Community described in Article 92.3 (a) of the treaty establishing the EC. During the same period, Tunisia may exceptionally, as regards ECSC steel products, grant state aid for restructuring purposes provided that (a) it leads to the viability of the recipient firms under normal market conditions at the end of the restructuring period; (b) the amount and intensity of such aid are strictly limited to what is absolutely necessary to restore such viability and are progressively reduced; and (c) the restructuring program is linked to a comprehensive plan for rationalizing capacity in Tunisia. The Association Council shall, taking into account the economic situation of Tunisia, decide whether the period of five years should be extended. The remaining competition policy articles of EU-Tunisia FTA are similar to the corresponding articles in the EU-Israel FTA.

The above considerations reveal that there are major differences between the competition policy rules in the three agreements. These differences can be summarized as follows:

- Whereas the competition rules of the CUD are identical to Articles 85, 86, and 92 of the EC Treaty, the rules in the EU-Tunisia and EU-Israel FTAs are not. In addition, while the EU-Tunisia FTA makes reference to Articles 85, 86, and 92 of the EC Treaty, the EU-Israel FTA does not. As such, the EU-Israel Agreement is better than the other trade agreements. Under the rules of the EU-Israel FTA, Israel has to develop its own competition policy. Israel will not be subject to rules contained in Articles 85, 86, and 92 of the EC Treaty, Community rules on state aids (including secondary legislation), the principles contained in relevant block exemption regulations in force in the Community, and the principles in the relevant case law developed by EC authorities. Turkey will apply the principles contained in the relevant block exemption regulations in force in the Community as well as the principles contained in the relevant case law developed by EC authorities in one year's time, and will adopt in two years' time all aid schemes other than those granted to the textile and clothing sector to the rules laid down in Community frameworks and guidelines under Articles 92 and 93 of the EC Treaty.

- The declaration by the EC relating to Article 25 annexed to the FTA states that the Community will assess any practice contrary to that article on the basis of the criteria resulting from the rules contained in Articles 85, 86, and 92 of the treaty establishing the European Community, and for products covered by the treaty establishing the ECSC, from those contained in Articles 65 and 66 of that treaty and the Community rules on state aids, including secondary legislation Although this is a one-sided declaration, it shows the intention of the EU to refer to Articles 85, 86, and 92 of the EC Treaty in case of disputes.

- Whereas the competition rules are covered under "Trade Related Provisions" in the EU-Israel FTA and under "Competition and Other Provisions" in the EU-Tunisia FTA, the rules are covered in the CUD under two headings: "Competition Rules of the Customs Union" and "Approximation of Legislation."

- Turkey can grant aid for a period of five years from the entry into force of the CUD to promote economic development of the country's less-developed regions and to accomplish structural adjustment necessitated by the establishment of the CU. Aid to facilitate the development of certain economic activities or of certain economic areas may also be considered to be compatible with the functioning of the CU. In the case of Tunisia, any state aid during the first five years after entry into force of the agreement shall be assessed, taking into account the fact that Tunisia shall be regarded as an area identical to those areas of the Community described in Article 92(3)(a) of the treaty establishing the EC. In addition, Tunisia, during the first five years, may grant state aid in the case of ECSC steel products for restructuring purposes.

- Competition rules on public undertakings will be applied in Turkey by the end of first year following the entry into force of the agreement, and in the cases of Israel and Tunisia, by the end of fifth year.

- Competition rules on state monopolies will be applied in Turkey by the end of second year following the entry into force of the agreement, and in the cases of Israel and Tunisia, by the end of fifth year.

Intellectual, Industrial, and Commercial Property Rights

Besides competition policies, the CUD has clauses on intellectual, industrial, and commercial property rights. Article 29 and Annex 8 of the CUD require Turkey to ensure adequate and effective protection and enforcement of intellectual property rights and to implement the Uruguay Round Agreement on Trade Related Aspects of Intellectual Property Rights (TRIPS) by 1999. Furthermore, by January 1, 1998, Turkey will have to adopt legislation to secure the patentability of pharmaceutical products and processes. Regarding copyright, the agreement requires that piracy such as counterfeiting or bootlegging be effectively banned and that the terms of protection in cases of translation should not be less than 50 years in those cases in which the term is calculated on a basis other than the life of the person. In addition, Turkey had to accede to various conventions shown in Table 3.9 before the formation of the CU and will have to accede to other conventions indicated in Table 3.9 three years after the formation of the CU.

Similar considerations apply in the context of the FTAs. Article 28 and Annex 7 of the EU-Israel FTA state that in three years' time, Israel will accede to major multilateral conventions on intellectual, industrial, and commercial property rights, and ratify in two years' time the Rome Convention of 1961. Finally, Article 39 and Annex 7 of the EU-Tunisia FTA state that in four years' time, Tunisia will accede to major multilateral conventions on intellectual, industrial, and commercial property rights shown in Table 3.9.

Technical Barriers

Technical barriers exist when countries impose certain standards as conditions for entry, sale, and use; have different legal regulations on health, safety, and environmental protection; and have different procedures for testing and certification to ensure conformity to existing regulations or standards. The Community's approach to removing technical barriers rests on the principle of harmonization of national legislation, where uniform standards are set for all member countries. There are basically two approaches to harmonization. The "old approach" incorporates all the technical details of the mandatory requirements in a directive. Under the "new approach," essential policy requirements for particular products are set out, while the development technical standards conforming to the requirements has been entrusted to EU standardizing bodies. Moreover, in 1989, the Community put in place the "global approach to testing and certification," which sets principles for conformity assessment. The global approach is based on mutually acceptable auditing procedures. Goods manufactured pursuant to the requirements of the global approach are permitted to display a generic mark of conformity—the "CE" mark. All goods displaying that mark are entitled to circulate freely within EU and are exempted from further conformity assessment by an importing nation.

In the case of trade with third countries, mutual recognition arrangements (MRAs) were developed to allow competent third-country assessment bodies to

TABLE 3.9. MAJOR INTERNATIONAL CONVENTIONS ON INTELLECTUAL PROPERTY

Agreement	Description	EU-Israel FTA	EU-Tunisia CUD	EU-Turkey FTA
Patents				
Paris Convention (1883; revised, 1967; amended, in 1979)	Protection of patents and trademarks Allows for compulsory licensing	(a)	(a)	Accede before CU
Patent Cooperation Treaty (1979; modified, 1984)		Accede in 3 years	Accede in 4 years	Accede before CU
Budapest Treaty (1977; amended 1980)	International recognition of the deposit of micro-organisms for the purposes of patent procedure	Accede in 3 years	Accede in 4 years	Accede in 3 years
Upov Convention (1961; revised, 1991)	Protection of new varieties of plants	(a)	Accede in 4 years	Accede in 3 years
Copyright				
Berne Convention (1886; revised, 1971; amended, 1979)	Protection of literary and artistic works Basic copyright treaty	Accede in 3 years	(a)	Accede before CU
Trade and service marks				
Madrid Agreement (1891; Stockholm Act 1967; amended, 1979)	International registration of marks	Accede in 3 years		
Protocol relating to Madrid Agreement (Madrid, 1989)	International registration of marks	Accede in 3 years		Accede in 3 years

Nice Agreement (Geneva, 1977; amended, 1979)	Classification of goods and services for purposes of the registration of marks	(a)	Accede in 4 years	Accede before CU
Other				
Rome Convention (1961)	Protection of performers, producers of phonograms and broadcasting organizations	Ratify in 2 years	Accede in 4 years	Accede before CU

a. Denotes the cases where parties confirm the importance they attach to the obligations arising from the conventions.
Sources: EU-Israel FTA; EU-Tunisia FTA; and EU-Turkey CUD.

take part in the EU's conformity assessment activities. Under an MRA, each party is given authority to test and certify products against the regulatory requirement of the other party, in its own territory and before export. MRAs do not require prior harmonization of each party's requirements.

According to the stipulations of the CUD, the EU rules and regulations in the standards area will become legally effective in Turkey by the year 2001. After 2001, free circulation of goods must be admitted on the basis of the EC accord. Article 8 of the CUD reads as follows: "Within five years from the date of entry into force of this decision, Turkey shall incorporate into its internal order the Community instruments relating to the removal of technical barriers to trade.... The Parties stress the importance of effective co-operation between them in the fields of standardisation, metrology and calibration, quality, accreditation, testing and certification." Article 9 of the CUD states, "When Turkey has put into force the provisions of the Community instrument or instruments necessary for the elimination of technical barriers to trade in a particular product, trade in that product between the Contracting Parties shall take place in accordance with the conditions laid down by those instruments, without prejudice to the application of the provisions of this decision." Decision 2/97 of the EC-Turkey Association Council establishes the list of Community instruments relating to the removal of technical barriers to trade and the conditions and arrangements governing their implementation by Turkey. According to this Decision, any instrument corresponding to an EC or EC Regulation will be made part of the internal legal order of Turkey. In the case of instruments corresponding to an EEC or EC Directive, Turkish authorities will be free to determine the form and methods of how to incorporate the Directive into the internal legal order of Turkey. Thus, Turkey over the next few years will have to reduce differences in the fields of standardization and conformity assessment. To this end, Turkey has to promote the use of Community technical regulations and European standards and conformity assessment procedures, and achieve where appropriate the conclusion of agreements on mutual recognition in these fields.

In the case of the EU-Tunisia FTA, Article 40 states that "the Parties shall take appropriate steps to promote the use by Tunisia of Community technical rules and European standards for industrial and agri-food products and certification procedures. The Parties shall, when the circumstances are right, conclude agreements for the mutual recognition of certification." Article 51 of the agreement states that "the parties shall co-operate in developing: (i) the use of Community rules in standardisation, metrology, quality control and conformity assessment, (ii) the updating of Tunisian laboratories, leading eventually to the conclusion of mutual recognition agreements for conformity assessment, and (iii) the bodies responsible for intellectual, industrial and commercial property and for standardisation and quality in Tunisia."

Public Procurements

Public purchasing is often used by governments as a policy instrument to support national or regional firms or industries for strategic reasons, to support employment in declining industries, and to support emerging high technology industries. Studies show that the degree of import penetration in public purchases is lower than for the economy as a whole.

Concerning public procurements, we note that neither the CUD nor the EU-Tunisia FTA has special arrangements. Article 46 of the CUD states that a date for the initiation of negotiations aiming at the mutual opening of the respective government procurement markets will be set. In the case of the EU-Tunisia FTA, Article 41 states that the parties shall take as their aim a reciprocal and gradual liberalization of public procurement contracts.

Israel is the only country that has signed two agreements with the EU on, respectively, procurement by telecommunications operators and government procurement. The agreements were signed on February 24, 1997. The agreement on telecommunications procurements provides for a mutual opening of procurement by telecommunications operators through granting an exchange of national treatment. Furthermore, it requires that the procurement procedures and practices comply with the principles of nondiscrimination, transparency, and fairness. In Israel, price preference provision in favor of Israeli products will not apply against EU bidders. In the EU, the provisions of the Utilities Directive (93/38 EEC) will not be applied against tenders comprising products of Israeli origin. The EU-Israel Government Procurement Agreement complements and broadens the scope of commitments under the WTO's new Government Procurement Agreement. Israel is committed to open its government procurement markets in urban transport, services, and medical equipment. The new rules will be extended to procurements by municipal and state agencies.

Cooperation

While the principal aim of completing the European market is the removal of barriers to free movement of goods and factors, a secondary aim is the enhancement of dynamic efficiency through cooperative R&D arrangements to be coupled with tough competition. The first such cooperative R&D arrangement was the European Strategic Programme for Research and Development in Information Technology (ESPRIT), which started in 1984. The success of ESPRIT helped to establish the climate for framework programs. The first framework program ran from 1987 to 1991 with a budget of ECU 5.4 billion. The fourth framework program ran from 1994 to 1998 with a budget of ECU 13 billion. Emphasis is placed on information and communication technologies, energy, industrial technologies, and life sciences and related technologies.

The Turkey-EU CUD is silent on the issue of Turkey's participation in the EU's cooperative R&D arrangements. Article 47 of the Tunisia-EU FTA states that the aim of co-operation is to (i) encourage the establishment of permanent links between the Parties' scientific communities, notably by means of providing Tunisia with access to Community research and technological development programmes in accordance with Community rules governing non-Community countries' involvement of such programmes, Tunisian participation in networks of decentralised cooperation and promoting synergy in training and research, (ii) improve Tunisia's research capabilities, (iii) stimulate technological innovation and the transfer of new technology and know-how, and (iv) encourage all activities aimed at establishing synergy at regional level.

Israel is the only country among the three that has signed an agreement for cooperative R&D arrangements. The Agreement on Scientific and Technical Cooperation between EC and the State of Israel, signed on March 25, 1996, allows Israeli research entities to participate in all the specific programs of the Fourth Framework Programme (except nuclear energy) and in the activities of the Joint Research Centre. According to the agreement, research entities include universities, research organizations, industrial companies (including small and medium-sized enterprises), or individuals, and Israel will contribute to the budgets of the programs adopted for the implementation of the Fourth Framework Programme on the basis of the ratio of Israel's GDP to that of the member states of the EU. The agreement foresees the establishment of an EC-Israel Research Committee, whose function will include regular discussions on orientations and priorities of research policy in Israel and the Community.

In the cases of Tunisia and Turkey, it is stressed that provisions will be made for Turkey to take part on a project-by-project basis in all the specific programs of the fifth R&TD framework program (1998–2002), but that Turkey will not be able to draw on the funds allocated to the framework program. In addition, Actions II of the framework program (International co-operation—INCO2) will include for the first time an activity targeting cooperation with Mediterranean countries. Tunisia and Turkey will be able to participate fully in INCO2, and will receive Community financing to do so. Furthermore, dialogue on Euro-Mediterranean science and technology policy will also take place within the Euro-Mediterranean Monitoring Committee for Science and Technology Co-operation.

Conclusion

The purpose of this chapter was to study within a comparative framework the trade agreements Tunisia, Turkey, and Israel have signed with the EU, highlighting the differences and as well as common aspects in the three agreements. The study revealed the following results:

The EU-Israel FTA, EU-Tunisia FTA, and EU-Turkey CUD aim for free trade in industrial products between the EU and the countries concerned. Free trade in industrial products is already established between the EU and Israel. It was completely established by January 1, 1999, between the EU and Turkey, and will emerge in 12 years' time between the EU and Tunisia. By the year 2010, the EU and the countries under consideration will establish a free trade area covering flows of industrial goods provided bilateral FTAs between Mediterranean countries can also be signed by then. There are some differences between the three trade agreements. Whereas the EU-Israel and EU-Tunisia Trade Agreements are FTAs, the EU-Turkey Trade Agreement is a Customs Union Decision. As such, the EU-Turkey CUD required that Turkey adopt the CCT against third-country imports by January 1, 1996, and adopt all of the preferential agreements the EU has concluded with third countries by the year 2001. Similar restrictions are not imposed on Tunisia and Israel. These countries are free to maintain their own policies toward nonparticipating third countries. Furthermore, there are no clauses on rules of origin in the CUD, whereas the EU-Tunisia FTA and the EU-Israel FTA contain lengthy discussions of the issue of "originating products." As Mediterranean countries conclude bilateral FTAs among themselves, the introduction by the EC of diagonal cumulation of origin will become an essential tool to facilitate the establishment of the Euro-Mediterranean free trade zone through the development of South-South commercial ties.

In the case of agricultural commodities, the agreements foresee progressive and reciprocal liberalization and extension of concessions on a reciprocal basis. Study of the prevailing concessions in agriculture reveal that Israel, Tunisia, and Turkey have obtained relatively satisfactory concessions from the EU. All of the three countries have obtained preferential treatment for most of the agricultural commodities with relatively high share in their total agricultural exports. Consideration of the unit export prices in terms of U.S. dollars for the three countries reveals that the Israeli unit export prices on average are higher than the Turkish unit export prices. Thus, Israel, compared with Turkey, has been able to receive more U.S. dollars per unit of quantity exported of those commodities. The result may be due to the quality difference in the exports of the two countries. In the case of Tunisia, the concessions obtained seem within a comparative framework to be relatively satisfactory.

The EU-Turkey CUD, EU-Tunisia FTA, and EU-Israel FTA offer liberalization of trade in industrial commodities. But there are loopholes in the liberalization provided through antidumping procedures and safeguard measures. In addition, the CUD allows antidumping actions as long as Turkey fails to implement effectively the competition rules of the CU and other relevant parts of the *acquis communautaire*.

Comparison of the articles on competition policy in the three agreements reveals that there are major differences between the agreements. Whereas the competition rules of the CUD are identical to Articles 85, 86, and 92 of the EC Treaty, the rules in the EU-Tunisia and EU-Israel FTAs are not. In addition, while the EU-Tunisia FTA makes reference to Articles 85, 86, and 92 of the EC Treaty, the EU-Israel FTA does not. As such, the EU-Israel Agreement is a better agreement than the CUD and the EU-Tunisia Agreement. Thus, Israel, unlike Turkey, will not be subject to rules contained in Articles 85, 86, and 92 of the EC Treaty, Community rules on state aids (including secondary legislation), the principles contained in relevant block exemption regulations in force in the Community, and the principles contained in the relevant case law developed by EC authorities. Furthermore, according to the CUD, Turkey can grant aid for a period of five years from the entry into force of the CUD to promote economic development of the country's less-developed regions and to accomplish structural adjustment necessitated by the establishment of the CU. Aid to facilitate the development of certain economic activities or of certain economic areas may also be considered to be compatible with the functioning of the CU. In the case of Tunisia, any state aid during the first five years after entry into force of the agreement will be assessed according to EU rules for disadvantaged regions (Article 92.3 (a), Treaty of Rome). In addition, Tunisia during the first five years may grant state aid in the case of ECSC steel products for restructuring purposes. Competition rules on public undertakings (state monopolies) will be applied in Turkey by the end of first (second) year after the entry into force of the agreement, and in the cases of Israel and Tunisia, by the end of fifth year.

Besides competition policies, the trade agreements have clauses on intellectual, industrial, and commercial property rights. The countries are expected to accede to major multilateral conventions on intellectual, industrial, and commercial property rights and ensure adequate and effective protection and enforcement of intellectual property rights.

In the case of technical barriers, Turkey decided to make EU rules and regulations in the standards area legally effective within the country by the year 2001. Thus, the Turkish approach to removing technical barriers rests on the principle of harmonization of Turkish legislation with EU legislation. For this purpose, over the next few years, Turkey will have to promote the use of Community technical regulations and European standards and conformity assessment procedures, and achieve where appropriate the conclusion of agreements on mutual recognition in these fields. In the cases of Tunisia and Israel, MRAs have to be developed to allow these countries' assessment bodies to take part in the EU's conformity assessment activities. Under such a scheme, Tunisia and Israel will test and certify products against the regulatory requirement of the other party, in their own territory and before export.

In the case of public procurements, two separate agreements were signed between the EU and Israel. With these agreements, the parties reaffirmed their commitments to mutually open their respective procurement markets. In the cases of Tunisia and Turkey, the countries have the option of signing separate bilateral agreements with the EU as long as they are willing to open their respective procurement markets and ratify the WTO's new Government Procurement Agreement.

Among the cooperation schemes, the cooperative R&D arrangements are of prime importance for increasing dynamic efficiency in the countries under consideration. Among these countries, Israel is the only country to be associated with the Fourth Framework Programme of scientific research and technical development. The special status of Israel seems to be the result of its high level of scientific competence and the dense network of long-standing relations in scientific and technical cooperation between Israel and the EU.

The above considerations reveal that the policy of further opening up the Israeli economy and integrating it into the EU will be successfully pursued with the EU-

Israel FTA together with the Agreement on Procurements by Telecommunications Operators, Agreement on Government Procurements, and Agreement on Scientific and Technical Co-operation between EC and the State of Israel. A major remaining issue is to develop mutual recognition arrangements for overcoming technical barriers to trade. In the case of Turkey, the major task lies in the approximation of laws and adoption of the *acquis communautaire*. Turkey could aim to take part in cooperative R&D arrangements. In addition, Turkey and the EU could commit themselves to mutually open their respective procurement markets. Tunisia is in the process of opening up its economy, and the adjustment is expected to take a few years. Financial and technical assistance, together with institutional and administrative cooperation by the EU, could help Tunisia to overcome the difficulties of adjustment.

Note

1. In this chapter, all references to the EU-Israel FTA refer to the Interim Agreement published in the *Official Journal of European Communities* on March 20, 1996.

References

Hoekman, B., and S. Djankov. 1996. "The European Union's Mediterranean Free Trade Initiative." *World Economy* 19:387–406.

Lahouel, M. H. 1998. "Competition Policies and Deregulation in Tunisia." In Nemat Shafik, ed., *Economic Challenges Facing Middle Eastern and North African Countries: Alternative Futures*. London: Macmillan.

Pomfret, R. W. T., and B. Toren. 1980. *Israel and the European Common Market: An Appraisal of the 1975 FTA*. Kieler Studien. Tübingen: J. C. B. Mohr.

Razin, A., and E. Sadka. 1993. *The Economy of Modern Israel: Malaise and Promise*. Chicago: University of Chicago Press.

Togan, S. 1997. "Opening up the Turkish Economy in the Context of the Customs Union with EU." *Journal of Economic Integration* 12:157–79.

World Trade Organization. 1997. *Annual Report*. Geneva.

Chapter 4

Agricultural Trade Around the Mediterranean

A. Halis Akder

Euro-Mediterranean relations revolve around bilateral cooperation and partnership agreements between 15 members of the EU and 11 Mediterranean countries and 1 autonomous region (Algeria, Morocco, Tunisia, Egypt, Jordan, Syria, Israel, Palestine, Cyprus, Malta, and Turkey). Of the countries in the Mediterranean region, only two, Albania and Libya, have never been involved in the so-called Euro-Mediterranean relationship. The former Yugoslavia is also an outlier. After its disintegration, Yugoslavia continues to remain outside the Euro-Mediterranean framework, with some of the newly independent states such as Slovenia signing Association Agreements and intending to become members of the EU.

The intensity of the economic relationship between each Mediterranean country and the EU is not uniform. The major common denominator is that the relationship is bilateral. Cyprus, Slovenia, and Malta are accepted applicants to full EU membership (although Malta has withdrawn its application). Turkey has established a customs union with the EU, which includes only manufactured goods, and has applied for full membership. Israel (1995), Tunisia (1995), Morocco (1996), Palestine (1997), and Jordan (1998) have renewed partnership agreements. Egypt, Lebanon, and Algeria are negotiating similar arrangements. In May 1998, Syria made a start in negotiating an Association Agreement. The far-reaching target of all these agreements is to establish a free trade area around the Mediterranean. As bilateral trade agreements with the EU are discouraging intraregional trade, recently an Arab Free Trade Agreement was formed to counterbalance this possibility. In 1997, 18 Arab states approved an executive program for establishing the Arab Free Trade

Area (FTA), which came into effect on January 1, 1998. The new agreement foresees the elimination of import duties and other barriers to trade on goods of Arab origin over a 10-year period. Turkey started a similar regional integration movement around the Black Sea and signed preferential trade agreements with Israel and with several Central and Eastern European countries.

Euro-Mediterranean Partnership: Interdependence

Nonmember Mediterranean countries provide the EU with a substantial external market, and the EU is the main outlet for exports from many of these countries (Table 4.1). Almost 20 percent of the EU's energy imports come from the Mediterranean region.

The need for a specific Euro-Mediterranean policy stems from the huge disparity between the north and south of the Mediterranean region. The problems of the South diffuse in one way or another into Europe: illegal migration, drug traffic, the threat of unrest in Algeria to oil imports. In a similar manner, the tensions between Israel and Arab countries have negative impact on the EU. All these problems may persist in the future, and largely explain the need for Euro-Mediterranean partnership.

Drawing upon its experience and on the basis of past performance, the World Bank suggests a challenging scenario for doubling the GDP of the region by 2010. Such a (modest) scenario assumes (a) a peaceful environment (reduced military expenditures), (b) implementation of a wide range of economic policies, (c) effective regional cooperation in all fields of common interest, and (d) appropriate finan-

TABLE 4.1. TRADE BETWEEN THE EU AND THE MEDITERRANEAN BASIN (1995)

	Share of Mediterranean countries in imports	Share of Mediterranean countries in exports		EU's share in imports	EU's share in exports
EU (15 member states)	5.7	8.2	Algeria	56.0	63.5
Belgium and Luxembourg	6.1	12.4	Morocco	53.1	61.3
Denmark	1.4	3.2	Tunisia	69.1	79.0
Germany	4.8	5.5	Egypt	38.9	45.8
Greece	10.2	24.8	Jordan	31.1	5.0
Spain	7.6	12.3	Lebanon	43.6	15.8
France	9.4	11.8	Syria	31.7	56.7
Ireland	1.5	4.7	Israel	52.4	32.3
Italy	9.2	11.5	Palestine		
Netherlands	4.0	6.9	Cyprus	51.7	34.7
Portugal	8.0	8.0	Malta	72.8	71.4
U.K.	2.6	5.8	Turkey	47.2	51.2

Source: Eurostat, Euro-Mediterranean Bulletin on Short Term Indicators.

cial flows (domestic savings, workers' remittances, foreign direct investment, and commercial loans). Even under such favorable assumptions, the wealth gap between the EU and the Maghreb and Mashreq countries would possibly widen. The expectation is that the dynamic created by the progressive opening up of the Middle Eastern and North African economies to the competitive EU (free trade area) will become an additional factor that will hinder further widening of the disparities.

Despite the weaknesses in the past, the EU is optimistic in strengthening the current Mediterranean policy by liberalizing trade in manufactured goods. The traditional cooperation area, agriculture, will enjoy only a weak liberalization.

Agricultural Trade between the EU and Mediterranean Countries: Market Similarity

To determine the extent to which the member and nonmember Mediterranean countries and Central and Eastern Europe compete in the EU for the agricultural markets, the similarity of the geographical composition of exports has been measured (Table 4.2). Such information is useful for discussing the prospective consequences of EU enlargement to the East. For each pair of countries i and j, the similarity of their export markets (Ms) is given by

$$Ms^{ij} = \Sigma(\min M^{ik}, M^{jk}),$$

where M^{ik} is the percentage share of market k in total (agricultural) exports from country i and M^{jk} is the share of the same market in exports from country j. This index can take on values between 0 and 100. Zero represents fully different, and 100 indicates identical export profiles. The markets covered here are the 15 member states of the EU.

Rather than interpret these 288 pair-wise coefficients separately, an attempt has been made to configure these data by a multidimensional scaling technique that uses approximate similarities among the data. The results can be given spatial representation consisting of geometric configuration of points as on a map (Figure 4.1), which makes the data much easier to comprehend. The larger the dissimilarity between two countries, the further apart they should be on the spatial map.

The structure of the configuration of points indicates the principal export markets of respective countries. For countries on the right side of the x-axis, the German market dominates, while on the left side we find a group of countries that have their principal market in Italy. The upper part of the y-axis indicates the combination of German and Italian markets, and the lower part indicates the combination of French, Spanish, and U.K. markets.

The cluster of countries close to the center (Egypt, Spain, Italy, Bulgaria, France, Turkey, Lebanon) have a diversified (balanced) market distribution. Among these countries, France, Italy, Spain, and Turkey are the main agricultural exporters. The market similarity index, even if it has the same value between two pair of countries,

TABLE 4.2. MARKET SIMILARITY COEFFICIENTS AMONG THE MEDITERRANEAN AND EASTERN EUROPEAN COUNTRIES (percentage)

	1	2	3	4	5	6	7	8	9	10	11	12	13	14	15	16	17	18	19	20	21	22	23	24	25
1 Turkey																									
2 France	71																								
3 Italy	82	56																							
4 Greece	64	69	52																						
5 Portugal	56	54	57	46																					
6 Spain	70	65	68	61	63																				
7 Malta	39	35	33	59	44	49																			
8 Albania	61	53	49	70	34	53	51																		
9 Yugoslavia	79	57	67	67	39	61	46	75																	
10 Morocco	53	50	53	49	72	65	45	41	43																
11 Algeria	34	31	34	31	56	44	37	30	29	76															
12 Tunisia	36	39	28	65	55	39	69	52	46	53	49														
13 Libya	26	36	15	53	23	25	56	57	39	23	20	62													
14 Egypt	66	69	55	60	54	58	36	56	49	53	36	37	30												
15 Cyprus	46	51	48	35	38	42	16	27	37	34	17	17	19	54											
16 Lebanon	81	57	79	59	55	72	43	62	72	55	42	42	27	56	37										
17 Syria	70	66	58	67	53	52	32	61	74	52	40	56	36	53	33	67									
18 Israel	55	51	60	39	64	60	55	33	36	56	37	32	20	59	33	51	34								
19 Jordan	55	54	44	74	48	57	68	59	60	47	29	66	56	56	59	49	44	57							
20 Poland	80	56	62	56	39	60	36	55	75	42	24	29	21	53	56	74	64	40	46						
21 Czech Rep.	65	43	63	44	28	45	17	41	63	33	14	16	13	39	53	55	54	31	30	71					
22 Slovak Rep.	76	58	60	51	32	54	33	53	76	35	21	25	24	48	48	65	65	38	40	81	72				
23 Hungary	78	55	66	58	39	60	33	59	79	45	28	33	26	50	50	73	68	37	47	81	75	84			
24 Romania	65	59	56	78	41	60	53	76	77	43	27	52	46	55	55	66	60	36	66	62	53	64	70		
25 Bulgaria	80	65	74	58	54	68	35	66	67	50	30	31	33	74	74	67	54	57	56	65	56	62	66	68	

Source: Author's calculations from two-digit EUROSTAT trade statistics.

requires different interpretation. For example, the similarity index between Italy and Spain is 68 percent. This means that both countries export 68 percent of their agricultural exports to the same markets (countries) in the EU. The market similarity index for Malta and Jordan is also 68 percent. It also means that both countries export 68 percent of their export to the same markets (countries) in the EU.

However, the similarity of the first pair is due to the diversification of exports to several markets, whereas the second pair's similarity is due to the concentration of exports virtually in a single market.

The cluster of countries, Hungary, Slovakia, the Czech Republic, and Poland, has high market similarity because of their high share in the German market. Conversely, Libya, Tunisia, Malta, and Jordan also have quite high market similarity among themselves because of the high concentration in the Italian market. The group of countries in between, Greece, Romania, Albania, Syria, and the former Yugoslavia, has significant shares in both the Italian and the German markets. Algeria,

FIGURE 4.1. MARKET SIMILARITIES: MEDITERRANEAN COUNTRIES AND EASTERN EUROPE

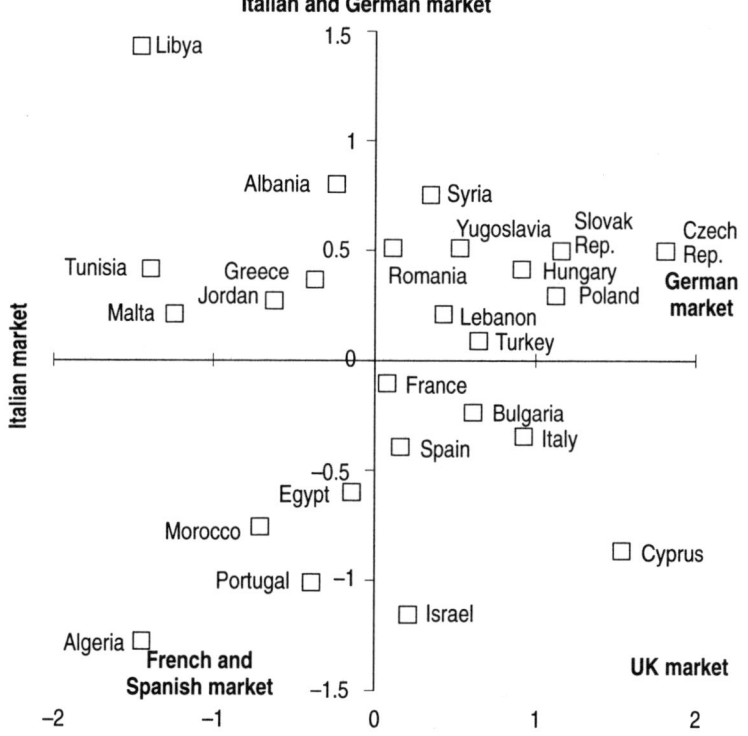

Morocco, and Portugal export mainly to the French and Spanish markets. The largest share of Israel's exports is actually directed to the Netherlands.

Other geographic characteristics can also be inferred from the configuration of data products. The line starting from the upper left—Libya, Tunisia, Malta, Morocco, Algeria—includes the Maghreb countries. The next line starting, from Jordan to Egypt, Israel, and Cyprus, includes many countries of the eastern Mediterranean region. Portugal, Spain, France, and Italy are the main northern Mediterranean countries. Bulgaria, Turkey, Greece, the former Yugoslavia, Albania, and Romania make up the Balkan countries. Hungary, Poland, Slovakia, and the Czech Republic are (Central) Eastern European countries. Thus, the movement along the horizontal axis from left to right corresponds to a movement from south to north.

The structure of the market-similarity matrix appears to indicate traditional (political) ties: France and Italy with the Maghreb, Germany with Turkey and Central Europe and the Balkans, the United Kingdom with Cyprus and Egypt.

Following the eastward expansion of the European Union, the northern Mediterranean countries will have greater competition for German and Italian markets. The southern Mediterranean countries will compete among themselves for the Italian, French, and Spanish markets. However, competition for the same broad market segments need not necessarily imply competition in the same products.

Agricultural Trade between the EU and Mediterranean Countries: Product Similarity

The similarities of product distribution among the same 25 countries have been calculated for agricultural products by using two-digit Nimexe categories 01-24 (Table 4.3). For each pair of countries i and j, the coefficient of product similarity (PS) is defined as

$$PS^{ij} = \Sigma \, (\min P^{it}, P^{it}),$$

where P^{it} is the percentage share of product t in i's exports to the EU and P^{jt} is the share of the same product in exports from j to the EU. The product similarities were again configured by a multidimensional scaling technique.

The structure of the product similarity seems to be quite different from market similarity. In general, market similarities are higher than product similarities. However, this is mainly due to the disaggregation level of the data: there are 15 market segments but 24 product categories. Further disaggregation of the product data would lead to even smaller indices.

The structure of this configuration reveals the most important export products of respective Mediterranean countries. These are fish and crustaceans, vegetables, fruits and nuts, olive oil, preparations of fruits and nuts, and beverages.

Countries on the left-hand side—Cyprus, Algeria, Spain, Israel, Turkey, Yugoslavia, and Morocco—export "specialty products," mainly fresh fruit and nuts and

TABLE 4.3. PRODUCT SIMILARITY COEFFICIENTS AMONG THE MEDITERRANEAN AND EASTERN EUROPEAN COUNTRIES (percentage)

	1	2	3	4	5	6	7	8	9	10	11	12	13	14	15	16	17	18	19	20	21	22	23	24	25
1 Turkey																									
2 France	25																								
3 Italy	52	61																							
4 Greece	53	34	55																						
5 Portugal	32	54	57	40																					
6 Spain	58	49	67	52	47																				
7 Malta	22	24	27	26	33	42																			
8 Albania	32	26	26	43	37	33	58																		
9 Yugoslavia	67	21	37	30	21	58	30	17																	
10 Morocco	62	23	50	46	48	68	47	41	57																
11 Algeria	54	33	40	32	38	50	34	33	55	48															
12 Tunisia	29	18	31	60	29	38	30	42	25	50	35														
13 Egypt	27	26	24	19	22	36	34	29	44	32	21	17													
14 Cyprus	50	29	46	35	30	68	34	16	70	54	45	23	59												
15 Lebanon	26	34	38	37	37	34	23	32	18	24	20	23	24	25											
16 Syria	23	27	23	38	18	32	23	37	22	26	10	30	33	21	60										
17 Israel	64	28	52	39	29	58	29	24	55	60	43	24	29	52	23	21									
18 Jordan	41	33	45	35	36	46	36	20	40	38	22	11	33	46	35	27	33								
190 Poland	51	51	58	48	43	57	32	39	40	55	33	33	34	38	28	23	51	36							
20 Czech Rep.	24	69	53	32	54	47	44	45	22	25	45	33	30	29	33	18	28	33	18						
21 Slovak Rep.	23	52	38	24	31	37	37	43	22	22	27	16	32	22	22	23	27	22	51	72					
22 Hungary	35	52	46	34	40	45	34	41	29	36	26	18	34	29	29	27	35	32	60	52	50				
23 Romania	37	55	55	37	45	54	34	33	38	39	36	22	38	45	33	33	37	46	61	58	54	54			
24 Bulgaria	41	54	58	40	60	49	39	39	31	36	39	17	32	38	35	21	40	43	55	59	45	59	55		
25 Libya	13	18	15	17	22	19	17	21	12	19	13	15	16	10	32	32	11	17	27	28	30	20	24	17	

Source: Author's calculations from two-digit EUROSTAT trade statistics.

preparations of these products (Figure 4.2). Turkey, Israel, and Morocco are the main non-EU-member exporters of these typical Mediterranean products. They stand out in terms of both the total value of their exports and the range of products covered in their exports. The EU was for a long time a net importer of these specialty products. The enlargement of the EU to include Greece and later Portugal, but especially Spain, has changed the traditional trends. EU imports of fruits and nuts from the nonmember Mediterranean countries are declining.

The upper part of the central axis of Figure 4.2 clusters those countries that export mainly beverages (wine) and animal products. Wine is another important export of the Mediterranean region to the EU. The lower left section of the central axis includes two countries—Tunisia and Greece—that have concentrated exports of olive oil and fish. Contrary to fruits, fish imports of the EU from the Mediterranean region are increasing quite rapidly. Vegetable exports have a large weight in Egypt's and Malta's agricultural exports to the EU and are increasing, too. Syria, Lebanon, and Libya, found on the right side of the axis, export nonfood products

FIGURE 4.2. PRODUCT SIMILARITIES: MEDITERRANEAN COUNTRIES AND EASTERN EUROPE

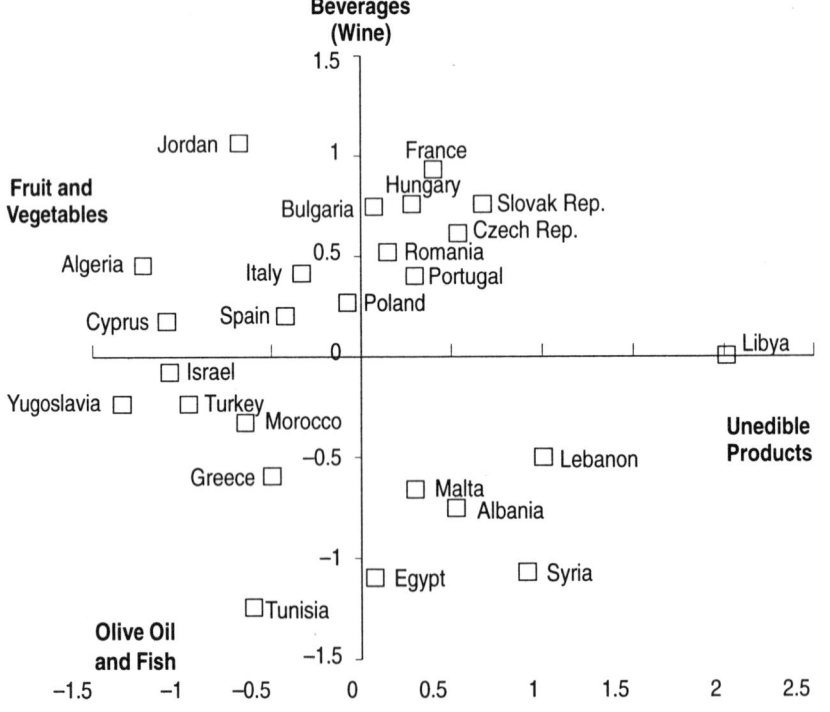

(inedible residuals). Considering the northeast-southwest diagonal, one can differentiate between plant production and animal products or southern and northern products. The hidden structure of this configuration, however, is (most probably) the preference hierarchy offered by the EU to the Mediterranean countries. One obvious indication is given by Tunisia. The generous preferences offered for olive oil make Tunisia's position almost an outlier.

Agricultural Policy Issues

The preference hierarchy offered by the EU will be affected mainly by (a) new free trade agreements with the Mediterranean countries, (b) adjustment to the Agreement on Agriculture of the World Trade Organization (WTO), and (c) eastward expansion of the EU.

After 1972, the so-called "Global Mediterranean Policy" offered the first major trade preferences to Mediterranean countries. Almost all association agreements offered free access to EU markets for all manufactures (except sensitive ones); however, preferential access for agriculture was granted for specific products only. Both the coverage of preference among countries and the preference margins among products differed considerably. However, before the Uruguay Round, the EU protected its own market against the main bulk of Mediterranean products by the so-called "reference price system." The reference price system, together with countervailing duties, usually resulted in a maximum quantity, as if a voluntary export quota had been applied. This made price competition among the Mediterranean countries almost impossible. The maximum quantity at a fixed reference price meant a loss in the market share if the share of the competitor increased. To obtain a larger market share, the exporting firm had to convince the importing EU firm to shift to its products rather than those of competitors. The sharing of the implicit quota rent was probably an important device for market sharing. Although the reference price system did not allow preferential treatment, tomatoes from Morocco and oranges and some citrus from Israel, Tunisia, and Morocco enjoyed exceptions after 1990.

The EU had to replace the reference price system after 1995 according to its commitments in the WTO Agreement on Agriculture. As the reference price system was a nontariff barrier, it was subject to tariffication. However, direct tariffication would have resulted in paradoxical outcomes. The end result may be considered as a modification of the old reference price system. There are now an entry price and two different tariffs. For imports respecting the entry price, the lower "normal" tariff is applied (tariffs that were already bound before the Uruguay Round). For imports coming in at a c.i.f. price lower than the entry price, "the maximum tariff" is applied. The new system has three important differences from the old one. First, the reference price system was administered on a country-by-country basis, while the entry price system is administered at a shipment-by-shipment level. Second, the new system will allow preferential treatment. The third new feature concerns protection (the so-called "special safeguard provisions") as the EU has undergone a tariffication for these products.

After 1993, trade relations between the EU and Mediterranean countries entered a new stage. The Euro-Mediterranean Agreements replaced the association agreements. The new agreements aim at the establishment of a free trade area for nonagricultural products and provide for close cooperation in several areas. However, agricultural trade will be organized on preferential terms. This sounds quite similar to the former association agreements, which offered free access to EU markets for all manufactures (except sensitive ones) and preferential access for agriculture. The main difference is now the EU's demand for reciprocity and the EU's new international commitments for sensitive products.

Another important development concerns the trading arrangements with Central and Eastern Europe. As indicated in Figure 4.2, the export products of the two regions differ quite considerably. Central and Eastern European countries are exporters of core products of Common Agricultural Policy (CAP), the so-called northern products. As these products are protected by relatively high tariffs, the preference margins offered to them are relatively higher than those offered to the Mediterranean countries, but the product coverage of preferential trade for Mediterranean countries seems to be more favorable.

However, an important indirect source of competition for Mediterranean countries may occur in the future. Central and Eastern European countries will become full members of the EU. It might be quite difficult to support their agricultural sector by including them in the existing EU CAP. The budgetary burden may become too high. If the adjustment on account of this expansion were to pose difficulties for southern member states, Mediterranean countries would probably be confronted with new offsetting decreases in preferences.

Conclusions

The CAP has been able to survive both internal and external criticism and international negotiations for decades. In spite of some reforms and modifications, the southern (Mediterranean) product component has changed little. The EU offer of free access in manufactured goods but preferential trade in agriculture is also an unchanging policy toward the Mediterranean basin.

If agricultural trade is not liberalized to the same degree as the manufacturing sector for a long period of time, several problems may arise and existing ones may persist. The question that necessarily follows is whether the liberalization efforts initiated by the WTO Agreement on Agriculture is sufficient to solve this imbalance problem between agriculture and industry. The Agreement on Agriculture has neglected important problems concerning the liberalization of agricultural markets (for example, export taxes) in developing countries, and in spite of considerable liberalization commitments by the EU for core CAP products, the reference price system for the fresh fruit and vegetable sector has prevailed.

Considering that many Mediterranean countries are net importers of basic food from the world and from the EU, they will also face problems concerning their imports. As the Agreement on Agriculture will be more effective on core CAP products, it is more likely that their imports will become more expensive, although no prospects for significant export increases exist. The prospects for an improved agricultural situation around the Mediterranean will therefore depend very much on the improvement of domestic agricultural policies.

Chapter 5

Egypt: An Assessment of Recent
Trade Policy Developments

Amal Refaat
Egyptian Center for Economic Studies, Cairo

After decades of protectionist theories and industrialization policies based on import substitution, in the 1980s, economists began advocating development strategies based on trade liberalization and export promotion. The debt crisis of 1982; the poor performance of the inward-oriented economies compared to the outward-oriented, rapidly growing East Asian countries; and the collapse of the communist system all played an important role in reshaping policy views (Edwards 1993). Since 1983, the pace of global trade in goods and services has accelerated and outpaced the expansion of the world GDP. In the early 1990s, the elasticity of trade to GDP jumped to above two, and the ratio of exports to GDP reached 25 percent in 1995 (European Commission 1997).

On the whole, developing countries followed this trend. They have become more open over time, and for most developing countries, trade liberalization has been a gradual process. It usually begins with exchange controls, followed by nontariff barriers (NTBs) and eventually tariffs (Andriamananjara and Nash 1997). In the case of Egypt, it was the first among the MENA countries to adopt a trade liberalization policy during the 1970s (Wilson 1986).[1] But how have liberalization trends evolved in the Egyptian economy since then?

This chapter surveys the reforms in Egypt's merchandise trade policy since 1980 to date, to evaluate their impact on the openness of the economy. The analysis also considers the future prospects for trade liberalization in Egypt in light of its current and future involvement in multilateral, regional, and bilateral trade agreements. The ultimate objective is to identify the upcoming challenges Egypt will face as it moves toward a more liberal foreign trade sector.

The Main Features of Egypt's Foreign Trade Sector

Egypt's trade balance has been continuously in deficit throughout the whole period of the study, from 1980 to 1998. The gap between exports and imports has been increasing since 1981 at an average annual growth rate of 18 percent. In 1997, the share of the trade deficit in GDP was 11 percent, and it has remained in this range since the beginning of the Economic Reform and Structural Adjustment Program (ERSAP) in 1991.

The developments in Egypt's trade balance have had different underlying factors over time. Before 1988, the gap between exports and imports widened mainly as a result of an upsurge in the volume of imports, especially that of raw materials and investment goods. This trend was reinforced toward the end of the study period by a deterioration in Egypt's terms of trade (Figure 5.1). Between 1988 and 1993, the trade deficit fluctuated. These fluctuations were closely linked to the changes in the quantities of Egypt's exports. From 1994 onward, the deficit has been steadily expanding because of increases in the quantities of imports that outweigh the improvements Egypt has witnessed in its terms of trade for some years.

The trade deficit is problematic not only because it is growing, but also because the way it is financed embodies risk, which could have a negative impact on Egypt's balance of payment as a whole. A considerable amount of the financing is closely related to foreign aid and to oil—mainly through the foreign direct investment concentrated in the oil sector and workers' remittances that are indexed to the oil revenues of the Gulf region (Petri 1997). Add to this that oil and its products account for about half of total export revenues. In 1996/97, the official transfers represented 33 percent of the trade deficit and the net private transfers formed another 9 percent. Export coverage of imports was only 33 percent, with petroleum exports accounting for 52 percent of the total merchandise exports.

Egypt's exports remained concentrated in a handful of categories for the whole period of the study. The most important export category was mineral products, accounting for 58 percent of total Egyptian exports in 1984 and 47 percent of exports in 1996. The second most important export was textiles and clothing (26 percent in 1984 and 23 percent in 1996), followed by vegetable products (7 percent in 1984 and 10 percent in 1996), base metals and related products (5 percent and 8 percent in the two respective years), and chemical products (2 percent in 1984 and 5 percent in 1996). Within these export categories, the importance of some products increased while that of others decreased.[2] These changes translated to an increase in the share of manufactured goods in total Egyptian exports from 20 percent in 1984 to 44 percent in 1996, with woven cotton, cotton yarn, aluminum ingots, and bleached rice on the top of the list. Nevertheless, the performance of manufactured exports and Egypt's merchandise exports in general have been disappointing, especially when compared with China, Southeast Asian countries, and the Central and Eastern European countries (Sachs 1996).

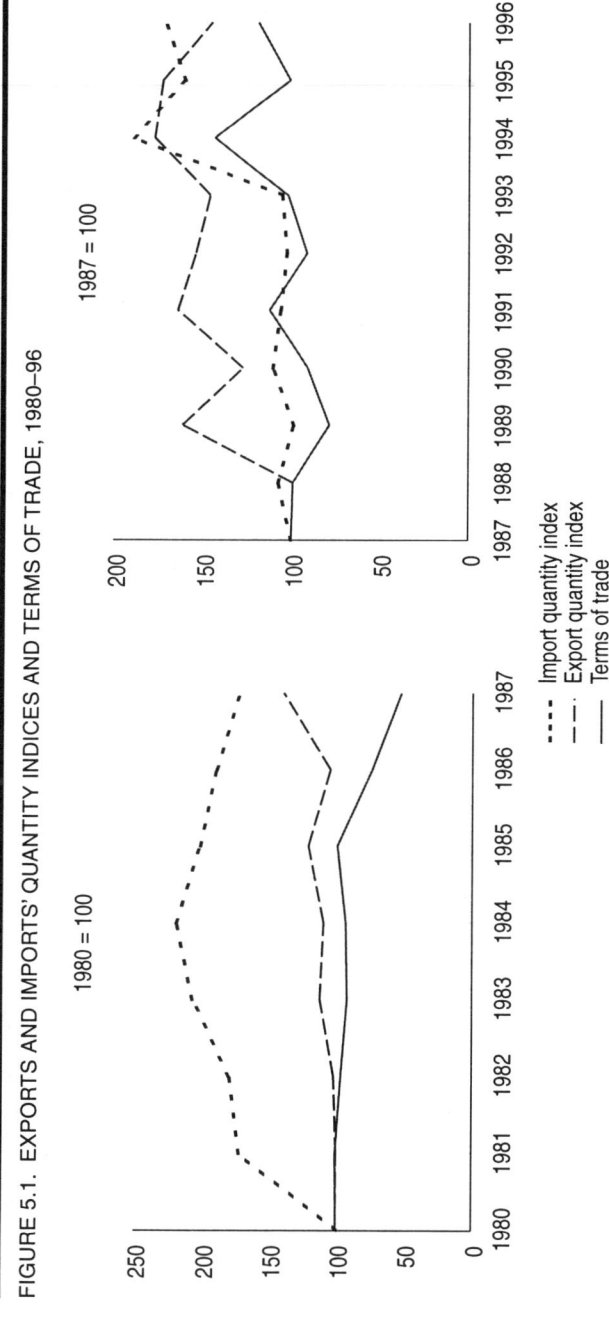

FIGURE 5.1. EXPORTS AND IMPORTS' QUANTITY INDICES AND TERMS OF TRADE, 1980–96

1980 = 100

1987 = 100

····· Import quantity index
–·–· Export quantity index
——— Terms of trade

Source: Calculated from CAPMAS, *Foreign Trade Indices*, different issues.

Egypt's imports are more diversified than its exports. In 1996, 94 percent of total imports were concentrated in 11 product categories, while 94 percent of total exports were concentrated in only 5 product categories. Machinery and vegetable products remained the most important imports between 1984 and 1996. Some import categories, as measured by their share of total imports, declined significantly, such as vehicles (from 12 percent in 1984 to 5 percent in 1996), mineral products (from 9 percent to 4 percent), and living animals and related products (from 7 percent to 4 percent). The share of other import categories in total imports increased, including paper, paper-making materials and related articles (from 2 percent to 4 percent); artificial resins, plastic materials, cellulose, and rubber (from 3 percent to 6 percent); and fats, oil, and related products (2 percent to 4 percent). The remaining import categories maintained their importance over time.

The direction of Egypt's trade changed significantly over the past 10 years. While the share of exports to the United States quadrupled between 1986 and 1996, the share of exports to Eastern Europe declined, as did the imports from this region. Currently, Egypt's major trading partners are the European Union (EU) and the United States. In 1996/97, they absorbed 66 percent of Egypt's exports and supplied Egypt with 65 percent of its import needs. Egypt's trade with the Arab countries is by far less significant. In the same year, only 10 percent of Egypt's exports were destined for Arab countries, and only 4 percent of Egypt's imports came from there (Table 5.1).

Changes in Egypt's Trade Policy and the Impact on Trade Openness

Egypt began the 1980s with a much less restrictive trade regime, compared to the period from 1958 to 1973, due to the trade liberalization policies implemented in the mid-1970s. Liberalization measures included eliminating the state monopoly on importation (by virtue of the Export-Import Law No.118/1975), introducing the

TABLE 5.1. DISTRIBUTION OF EGYPT'S EXPORTS, IMPORTS, AND TRADE DEFICIT BY TRADING PARTNER 1986/87 AND 1996/97
(Percentage)

	Exports		Imports		Trade Deficit	
	1986/87	1996/97	1986/87	1996/97	1986/87	1996/97
EU	39	34	40	41	–41	–45
United States	8	32	20	24	–24	–20
Arab countries	12	10	1	4	2	–1
Other African and Asian countries	11	16	11	14	–11	–13
Others	30	8	27	17	–26	–21

Source: Central Bank of Egypt, *Economic Review*, various issues.

Own Import System, phasing out bilateral trade agreements, and creating free trade zones (Wilson 1986).[3]

These measures focused mainly on liberalizing payments rather than reducing tariffs and NTBs to trade. This is why, at the beginning of the 1980s, the tariff rates were high and NTBs were used extensively.[4] The distortive effects of the trade policy were further aggravated by the prevalence of the multiple exchange rate. But how did trade reform proceed during the following years? Have there been significant shifts in the trade liberalization trends? Have the trade policy reforms led to greater or less openness of the Egyptian economy? This section attempts to answer these questions. First, the analysis focuses on the changes that occurred in the main trade policy instruments over the period of the study and then traces the impact of these changes on trade openness.

Trade Liberalization Trends: Changes in Trade Policy Instruments

In general, there are three main indicators of change toward trade liberalization: changes in tariffs and additional taxes and subsidies, changes in the NTBs to trade, and changes in the exchange rate system. Lowering the average level and dispersion of rates of protection and reducing the coverage and level of NTBs lead to more liberalization. A shift from multiple exchange rates to a uniform rate and a real devaluation also constitute a step toward liberalization. Unification of the exchange rate removes discrimination between tradable activities, and devaluation reduces the pressure of quantitative restrictions on rationing imports and reduces antiexport bias (Papageorgiou, Michaely, and Choksi 1991).

The changes in each of these indicators are discussed in detail next. It should be noted that these changes began with the tariff reforms in August 1986 and continued with the announcement of the ERSAP. The latter included a trade liberalization component that aimed at changing Egypt's inward-oriented import substitution strategy of the past decades.

CHANGES IN TARIFFS, TAXES, AND SUBSIDIES

Tariff-Based Protection

Over the period of this study, tariffs have undergone several changes that constitute a clear move toward liberalization and the beginning of an efficient use of tariffs as a policy instrument. First, the averages of both the nominal effective rate of protection (NRP) and effective rates of protection (ERPs) have declined over time, as shown in Table 5.2 below.[5] The collection rate—the ratio of import duties collected to the value of imports—has also been steadily declining, from 21 percent in 1991/92 to 17 percent in 1995/96 and further to almost 17 percent in 1996/97. It is expected that the collection rate will continue to decrease in the future to reach 15 percent in 1998/89 (International Monetary Fund 1998a).

Second, the tariff dispersion, as measured by the range of nominal tariffs and the standard deviation of the NRP and ERP, has been decreasing.[6] The maximum tariff rate declined from 110 percent in 1986 to 100 percent in 1992, 80 percent in 1993, 70 percent in 1994, 50 percent in 1997, and further to 40 percent in 1998. The standard deviation of the tariffs has also declined (Table 5.2). Yet, the existing pattern of protection discriminates against activities with a comparative advantage. The rank correlation coefficients between domestic resource cost (DRC) and between the NRP and ERP in 1997 were estimated at 0.44 and 0.45, respectively (Nathan Associates 1998). Inefficient sectors that are favored include beverages, furniture, and means of transportation, while efficient sectors that are not favored include cotton ginning. This pattern of protection has had its impact on resource allocation within the Egyptian economy. The most striking example is the cotton and ginning industry that has a comparative advantage but is effectively negatively protected. Discrimination against this industry was associated with a 50 percent decline in its share of total industrial output from the early 1980s to 1995/96.

Third, the extent of the economy-wide bias against exports decreased over the past few years from 25.7 percent in 1994 to 18.2 percent in 1997 (Table 5.3).[7] At the disaggregate level, the bias decreased in all economic activities except cotton ginning where it remained almost constant, and paper and printing and livestock, where there was a slight increase in the bias against their potential exports.

Despite these tariff reforms, more needs to be done. Egypt's tariff rates are still above the average tariffs prevailing in many other regions. In 1996, the weighted average tariff in Egypt (28 percent) was well above that of East Asia (21 percent), Eastern and Central Europe (9 percent), Latin America (14 percent), Sub-Saharan Africa (15 percent), and the average for developing countries (21 percent) (Alonso-Gamo, Fennell, and Sakr 1997). Also, the standard deviation of Egypt's tariffs is substantially higher than that of all countries represented in the World Bank, with only a few exceptions (Nathan Associates 1998).

Additional Taxes and Fees

Egypt's Law No. 87 of 1986 eliminated a series of taxes and fees that were formally levied on imports such as the statistical duty, subsidy tax, marine duty, and municipal tax. Currently, the Egyptian Customs Authority levies a 2–3 percent fee on imports, depending on the tariff applied. Items with tariffs of less than 30 percent are subject to service fees of 2 percent, and items subject to tariffs of more than 30 percent pay a service fee of 3 percent. A sales tax of 5–25 percent is added to the final customs value of imports (U.S. Dept. of State 1995/96).

In terms of exports, the Egyptian government levies charges on exports that are subject to quality inspection. Examples of these goods are citrus fruits, juices, and vegetables. All export taxes were eliminated in late 1992 (International Monetary Fund 1998b).

Changes in the NTBs

The importance of the different forms of NTBs in Egypt has varied over time. The significance of import bans, as measured by their production coverage, is declining

TABLE 5.2. NOMINAL AND EFFECTIVE PROTECTION
(Percentage)

	Nominal			Effective			
	1986[a]	1994	1996	1997	1986	1994	1996	1997
Agricultural food products	31.0	8.9	7.0	6.8	38.0	8.8	6.8	6.6
Agricultural nonfood products	—	15.7	9.5	9.5	—	16.4	9.6	9.6
Livestock products	12.0	5.0	5.1	5.1	113.0	3.3	4.1	4.2
Food processing	8.0	8.4	6.9	6.9	17.0	7.5	6.3	6.4
Cotton ginning	0	5.0	5.0	5.0	−68.0	−24.6	−10.9	−11.0
Spinning and weaving	34.0	37.6	29.0	28.0	788.0	68.2	49.8	47.6
Ready-made garments	109.0	69.6	50.8	46.6	348.0	87.3	61.8	55.9
Leather and leather products (excl. footwear)	16.0	46.6	33.7	33.1	35.0	79.6	52.7	47.6
Footwear	51.0	63.9	41.4	39.1	160.0	94.1	53.6	50.8
Wood and wood products (excl. furniture)	42.0	11.0	8.7	8.6	40.0	6.8	6.0	6.1
Furniture	110.0	69.8	54.9	49.9	296.0	128.8	95.2	83.8
Paper and printing	16.0	17.1	17.4	17.1	36.0	17.6	18.3	17.8
Chemicals	15.0	11.1	10.1	10.0	75.0	9.2	9.1	9.2
Rubber, plastic, and related products	28.0	33.0	29.8	28.5	563.0	50.0	45.6	43.1
Porcelain, china, and ceramics	75.0	52.5	37.9	35.0	214.0	90.8	60.9	56.0
Glass products	36.0	33.2	21.2	20.7	54.0	39.4	23.8	23.2
Nonmetal products	6.0	23.1	15.4	15.2	1.0	29.0	18.4	18.5
Steal, iron, and metal products	17.0	23.0	17.2	16.1	120.0	26.4	19.4	18.1
Machinery and equipment	28.0	22.5	16.0	15.3	39.0	22.5	15.0	14.5
Means of transportation	60.0	52.7	45.7	44.0	628.0	65.0	57.8	55.6
Unweighted average	36.5	30.5	23.1	21.9	184.1	41.3	30.2	28.2
Standard deviation	32.0	21.9	16.1	14.8	237.6	39.7	27.4	24.7

— Not availab.e.
Note: Calculations for 1986 are based on the 1983/84 input-output tables, the rest are based on the 1991/92 input-output tables. It should be noted that the 1986 ERP estimates are less reliable than the 1990s ERP estimates because calculations of ERP ignore the effects of price controls, indirect taxes and subsidies, multiple exchange rates, and overvaluation that were more severe in the 1980s compared to the 1990s.
   Industries with a high positive ERP or below −100 percent will attract resources to them. Those with an ERP between -100 percent and zero squeeze out resources.
a. After August 1986 tariff revisions.
Sources: For 1994, 1996, and 1997: Kheir-El-Din 1998; for 1986: Kheir-El-Din 1989.

(Table 5.4). The import ban list, instituted in 1986 as a replacement for the import licensing system abolished in the same year, now covers only poultry parts, certain textiles, and apparel items, down from 210 items in 1990. These account for less than 4 percent of domestic production. As part of the Uruguay Round (UR) Agreement, Egypt agreed to remove the import ban on clothing by January 1, 2001; however, products removed from the import ban list are sometimes subject to high duty rates. The tariff on whole poultry, removed from the ban in July 1997, was set at 80 percent. Also, Egypt imposed a tariff of 54 percent, plus a 10 percent sales tax and a 1 percent service fee, on textiles removed from the ban list on January 1, 1998.

TABLE 5.3. CHANGES IN TARIFF-INDUCED BIAS AGAINST EXPORTS
(Percentage)

	1994	1997
Agricultural food products	8.49	6.48
Agricultural nonfood products	15.40	9.25
Livestock	4.26	4.50
Food processing	5.26	4.45
Cotton ginning	4.99	5.00
Spinning and weaving	32.69	24.44
Ready-made garments	65.49	43.98
Leather products (excl. footwear)	42.72	28.12
Footwear	60.95	36.98
Wood products (excl. furniture)	5.06	4.15
Furniture	64.55	46.24
Paper and printing	7.54	7.59
Chemical products (excl. oil refining)	4.93	4.73
Rubber and plastic products	26.84	23.45
Porcelain products	51.67	34.38
Glass products	27.29	16.91
Nonmetallic products	22.75	14.96
Metals and iron products	21.68	15.16
Machinery and equipment	10.75	7.27
Means of ransportation	30.57	26.62
Unweighted average	25.69	18.23

Source: Author's calculation.

Other items that were removed from the ban list, including meat, fruits, vegetables, household appliances, and transformers, were added to the quality control list (Office of the U.S. Trade Representative 1998).

Quality control is increasingly gaining importance as an NTB to trade, as noted in Table 5.4. The quality control list now consists of 131 items including foodstuffs, spare parts, construction products, electronic devices, appliances, and many consumer goods. Egyptian standards on imports are considered a trade barrier by the EU—Egypt's primary trading partner. Product standards set by the General Organization for Export and Import Control are at variance with internationally recognized standards, thus causing problems with imports from the EU, such as processed food, ceramic tiles, sanitary ware, and cosmetics (Nathan Associates 1998). All other NTBs listed in Table 5.4 no longer exist. These include canceling the list of special conditions by Ministerial Decree No. 288/93, as well as canceling letters of credit and servicing requirements.

Quantitative restrictions on exports include mainly three measures: export quotas, export bans, and prior approvals on exports (Kheir-El-Din and El Dersh 1992). Ministerial Decree No. 266/93 eliminated the only remaining item on the list of export quotas. The remaining item on the list of banned exports is raw hides, down

TABLE 5.4. PRODUCTION COVERAGE OF NTBS ON EGYPTIAN IMPORTS
(Percent of domestic production)

	Before 1991			After 1991 trade reform			1997		
	Public sector	Private sector	Total	Public sector	Private sector	Total	Public sector	Private sector	Total
Import bans	47.5	64.0	52.9	43.7	32.9	40.7			< 4
Quality control	3.6	21.4	15.8	19.9	21.9	20.5			—
Prior approvals	12.4	9.5	11.5	0	0	0	0	0	0
Special conditions	8.4	2.6	6.8	0.56	0.51	0.55	0	0	0
Suspension letters of credit	9.2	7.9	8.8	0	0	0	0	0	0
Servicing requirements	6.8	1.5	5.4	0	0	0	0	0	0

— Not available.
Source: Before and after 1991 trade reform: Kheir-El-Din and El Dersh 1992.

from 20 items before 1991, six items in 1991, and two items in 1993. This NTB is scheduled to be removed in 1998 (International Monetary Fund 1998b). In 1991, the number of goods subject to prior approvals was reduced from 37 items to one.

Changes in the Exchange Rate
In 1980, Egypt had a multiple exchange rate in effect. There were three rates of foreign exchange. The first rate was that of the Central Bank, which remained fixed at 0.7£E/US$ from 1979 until 1989. The Central Bank's sources of foreign exchange were earnings from exports of petroleum, rice, and cotton; Suez Canal revenues; royalties from the SUMED pipeline; and foreign currency transferred to the government as foreign aid. These proceeds were used to service debt and finance the import of seven basic products: wheat, flour, tea, sugar, vegetables, pesticides, and fertilizers. The second rate was the commercial banks' rate, initially fixed at 0.83£E/US$. The commercial banks' pool included the proceeds from all other exports, tourist payments, and workers' remittances. In addition, foreign exchange was traded at a premium in the "own exchange pool."

At that time, Egypt faced pressures from its trade balance, in addition to current account imbalances, due to the sharp fall in revenues from the Suez Canal, tourism, and workers' remittances. The exchange rate was not actively used, however, to restore external equilibrium, and instead the government resorted to imposing restrictions. This was probably motivated by fear that currency devaluation would fuel inflation. As a partial result of this policy, the real effective exchange rate (REER) appreciated by 38 percent between 1982 and 1985, and nonoil exports were discouraged by the overvaluation of the exchange rate (GATT 1993).

By the mid-1980s, the exchange rate policy in Egypt had to change significantly. This was necessary to attract the remittances of the nearly 2 million Egyp-

tians then working abroad, and because development and industrialization requirements in Egypt were inconsistent with the overvalued exchange rate. Following
pressure from international organizations, Egypt embarked on a gradual reform of
the exchange rate. This included both devaluation and gradual simplification of the
exchange rate regime. In February 1991, the unification of the exchange rate versus
the dollar took place only a few months after limiting exchange markets to two—
the primary and secondary markets. The exchange premium effectively became zero
in 1991 (Figure 5.2). This was accompanied by currency devaluation between 1985
and 1991, when Egypt began its stabilization program. No significant devaluation
has occurred since then, and as a result, there was a real appreciation of the Egyptian pound, with the inflation rate in Egypt much higher than that of its trading
partners. As measured by the REER, the real appreciation between July 1991 and
December 1996 was 30 percent (Subramanian 1997).

Despite this real appreciation of the Egyptian pound, a recent International
Monetary Fund study concluded that although the REER was substantially overvalued before 1993, since then it has moved close to the equilibrium real exchange rate
(ERER). At the end of 1996, the REER was estimated to have appreciated only 7
percent compared to the ERER. The reason for this improvement is the significant
appreciation of the ERER during the period from 1991 to 1995, which can, to a
large extent, be attributed to the reduction in the debt service ratio over this period.
Other factors that positively contributed to the appreciation of the ERER were technical progress and, to a lesser extent, the Gulf War. Terms of trade, government
consumption, and the lagged capital account balance contributed negatively to the

FIGURE 5.2. EXCHANGE RATE PREMIUM, 1981–96

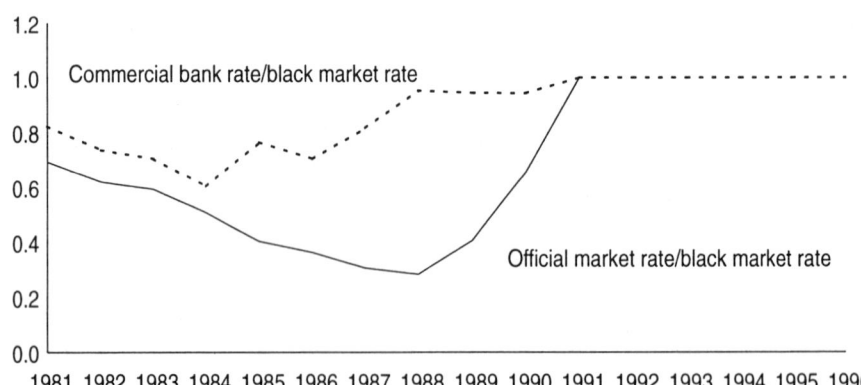

Source: Calculated from the International Monetary Fund, International Financial Statistics,
various issues.

appreciation of the ERER (Mongardini 1998). Sources of appreciation show that the appreciation of the ERER may not be sustainable in the future and that the Egyptian pound could be substantially overvalued if the exchange rate continues to be used as a policy anchor.

Changes in Trade Openness

Notwithstanding the trade reforms undertaken by the Egyptian government, measures of openness reveal two facts. First, Egypt exhibited a comparatively low trade profile over the period of the study. Second, its economy has become less open and less integrated in the world economy over time. This turn inward occurred in spite of the global trend to intensify international trade relationships. Table 5.5 compares a variety of trade performance indicators for Egypt along with selected fast-growing economies in two periods from 1983 to 1986 and 1993 to 1996. The indicators show that Egypt is the least open economy and is increasingly deviating from the averages of the fast-growing economies. The large public sector, the relatively high tariff barriers, the trade-distorting domestic regulations, and the overall institutional setting within which business is conducted in Egypt, can all be considered contributing factors to the development of Egypt's trade openness.

A more favorable business environment would undoubtedly enhance production and exports. Figure 5.3 illustrates the institutional constraints to business in Egypt as perceived by private firms.[8] Among the constraints, inefficient regulations on the ports and infrastructure sectors and the inefficiency of the banking system are widely acknowledged as trade barriers. It is estimated that the inefficiencies of the Egyptian port services add 10 percent to the cost of imported goods, and inefficient telecommunications services and financial services impose a tax on the manufacturing and agriculture sectors equivalent to 50 and 20 percent, respectively (Nathan Associates 1998).[9]

TABLE 5.5. DEVELOPMENT OF TRADE OPENNESS IN EGYPT AND SELECTED FAST-GROWING ECONOMIES

	Share in world exports		Share in world imports		Trade to GDP	
	1983–1986	*1993–1996*	*1983–1986*	*1993–1996*	*1983–1986*	*1993–1996*
Egypt	0.17	0.07	0.54	0.23	32	25
Thailand	0.41	1.05	0.52	1.31	43	71
Malaysia	0.83	1.40	0.67	1.39	89	160
Indonesia	1.08	0.94	0.69	0.77	42	42
Chile	0.21	0.28	0.15	0.3	44	48
Korea, Republic of	1.63	2.35	1.58	2.51	64	55
Average (excl. Egypt)	0.83	1.2	0.72	1.26	56.47	75.08

Source: Calculated from the International Monetary Fund, *International Financial Statistics*, various issues.

FIGURE 5.3. OVERALL RANKING OF INSTITUTIONAL CONSTRAINTS IN EGYPT

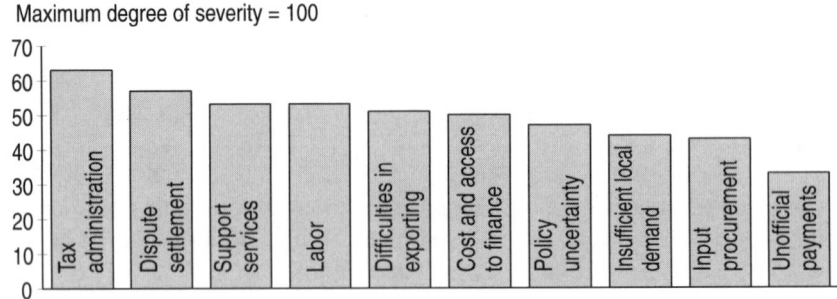

Source: Fawzy 1998b.

As Noll (1997) clearly indicates, in the case of a country like Egypt, where direct trade barriers—tariffs—are relatively high, the trade-distorting regulations should not be interpreted as motivated by the desire to impose indirect trade barriers. For Egypt, distorting regulations are the result of overall disadvantageous policies.[10]

EGYPT HAS GROWN LESS OPEN AND LESS INTEGRATED IN THE WORLD ECONOMY
The ratio of total trade imports and exports to GDP dropped by about 10 percentage points from 1980 to 1985 and from 1992 to 1996. Import penetration ratios, another important measure of openness, also reveal this unfavorable trend. The ratio of total imports to GDP declined over the period, as did the ratio of imports of consumption goods to total consumption.[11] Imports of investment goods declined between 1986 and 1991 but gained momentum in the following period (Figure 5.4).

FIGURE 5.4. OUTCOME-BASED MEASURES OF TRADE LIBERALIZATION

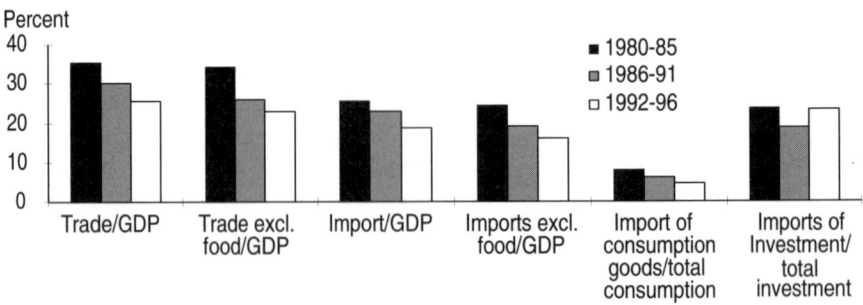

Sources: International Monetary Fund, *International Financial Statistics*, various issues; all other data from CAPMAS, *Statistical Yearbook*, various issues.

The declining significance of trade in the Egyptian economy can be partly attributed to the importance of oil in Egypt's trade and the volatility of its prices. During the 1970s and early 1980s, when there was a remarkable rise in oil prices, Egypt's share in world exports and imports and its trade share in GDP were higher than in the years that followed (Petri 1997). If the openness indicator of trade/GDP is calculated excluding Egypt's trade in fuel, Egypt's openness still declined over time but at a lower rate (Figure 5.5). Windfall gains to the economy from oil and other sources also contributed to Egypt's trade performance. They helped raise the price of nontradables versus tradables and thus attracted investment away from the tradable sectors. Egypt's structural adjustment program has also played a role by suppressing imports during its early stages (World Bank 1995a).

Future Directions for Egypt's Trade Liberalization

Liberalization trends in the Egyptian economy are expected to continue in the future, based on the trade agreements that Egypt has already signed and is currently negotiating. This section explores the impact of Egypt's multilateral, regional, and bilateral trade arrangements on the liberalization of the Egyptian economy, besides what they can offer Egypt in terms of market access.

Multilateral Liberalization
Egypt's unilateral liberalization efforts were essential for allowing its full participation in the UR negotiations, and the UR Agreement has in turn locked in these reforms. On the one hand, under the UR Agreement, Egypt binds 100 percent of its tariff lines in agriculture and 97 percent of its tariff lines in industry, thus approaching the commitments of the OECD countries and surpassing those of many other developing countries. After the full implementation of the UR Agreement commit-

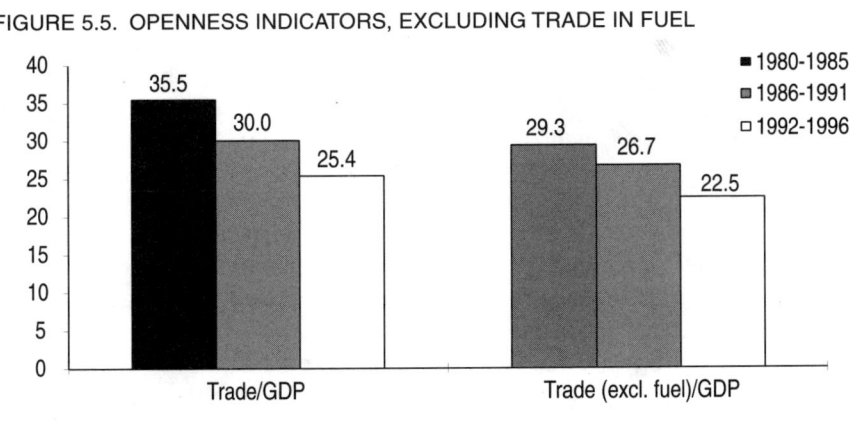

FIGURE 5.5. OPENNESS INDICATORS, EXCLUDING TRADE IN FUEL

Source: Author's calculations.

ments, however, Egypt's final bound tariffs to both agriculture and industry will be greater than the tariffs applied in December 1995 and the current applied tariff rates. Only 10 percent of all tariff lines will eventually have tariffs lower than the applied tariffs in December 1995. As regards quantitative restrictions on imports, it is expected that they will be eliminated at the end of 2005, except for those that are maintained for health or security reasons. Despite the fact that Egypt's commitments substantially exceed the developing countries' average in terms of bindings and the gap between bound rates and applied rates, the UR Agreement will have a limited impact on trade liberalization in Egypt (Hoekman and Subramanian 1996).

However, what market access does the UR Agreement offer Egypt? In terms of markets for Egyptian agricultural exports, the Agricultural Trade Liberalization Agreement in the UR Agreement represents one step forward and one backward. The tariffication and binding of all agricultural products is undoubtedly a step forward. But many of the newly established tariffs are so high in some countries that they effectively constrain trade. Binding tariffs to the base period of 1986 to 1988, when border protection was at a high point, diminishes liberalization. This is worsened in some cases by tariffication, since the new base tariffs offer even greater protection than the NTBs they replaced. The magnitude of extensive tariffication varied among countries and commodities. Among the industrial countries, tariffication was most extensive in the EU. Only Japan offered base tariff equivalents significantly lower than the nominal protection in the base year, except on rice. In addition, the high levels of bound tariffs fail to stabilize tariffs and improve market access by allowing countries to apply variable tariffs. Also, the UR Agreement did not address issues such as import subsidies, export taxes, and other domestic support measures (Ingco 1995).

If this is the case for agricultural products, what is awaiting Egypt's industrial exports? The proportion of industrial country tariffs on manufactured goods subject to bindings rose from 94 to 99 percent under the UR Agreement. About 18 percent of these countries' imports were already bound as duty-free tariff, reductions were applied to 64 percent of imports, and the remaining 18 percent were divided between bindings without reductions and no offers. In industrialized countries, the average tariff reduction on manufactured imports from developing countries is 30 percent, compared with 45 percent on imports from other industrial countries. This could have given Egypt a significant boost in market access, but the textile, clothing, and footwear sectors, which have the highest tariffs, experienced lower price reductions than many other sectors. These two labor-intensive sectors are considered sensitive and accordingly receive below-average tariff reductions. On one hand, it is often said that the phasing out of quotas and the multifiber agreement (MFA) compensate for this; but on the other hand, there is increased competition. In addition, the remaining tariff escalation in industrial markets is a concern to developing countries, including Egypt. As regards the industrial products in developing countries, only 60 percent of the tariffs are subject to bindings. Only 1 percent of their manufactured imports were initially bound as duty free, 32 percent bindings with tariff reductions, 26 percent bindings without reductions, and for the remaining 42 percent, no offers were made (World Bank 1995b).

The ultimate impact of the UR Agreement on Egypt's exports will be the outcome of three market-access effects. These effects arise from most favored nation (MFN) tariff cuts (a positive effect), the loss of preferential treatment due to MFN tariff cuts (a negative effect), and finally from liberalization of the MFA (a positive effect). Hoekman and Subramanian (1996) estimated the impact these three effects on Egypt's nonoil exports to the EU, the United States, and Japan. They concluded that the most significant impact would stem from the liberalization of textile and clothing quotas. The impacts of the other two effects are marginal and almost outweigh one another. These results should be taken with caution, since the estimation procedure does not take into consideration the impact of the expected increase of competition in textile and clothing due to the phasing out of the MFA. Egypt must reduce costs and increase efficiency to remain a viable exporter.

REGIONAL AND BILATERAL LIBERALIZATION

Egypt's regional and bilateral trade agreements include the free trade agreements (FTAs) with the EU, the United States, and some Arab countries, in addition to the Arab Free Trade Area (AFTA) and the Common Market for Eastern and Southern Africa (COMESA). It is worth noting that membership in an FTA is neither a necessary nor a sufficient condition for more liberal trade, according to empirical evidence.[12] It is a country's general acceptance of a liberal trade policy that can make the difference (Foroutan 1998).

AN FTA WITH THE EU

Egypt currently has preferential access to EU markets through the EU Generalized System of Preferences (GSP) and through the bilateral cooperation agreement of 1977. The latter grants Egypt duty-free access to the EU markets for industrial goods with some exceptions. A total of 32 textile products are excluded from duty-free entry into the EU.[13] Moreover, textiles and clothing imported from Egypt have been subject to antidumping regulations by the EU. The cooperation agreement also grants Egypt preferential access for agricultural goods. Processed agricultural products imported from Egypt are exempted from the ad valorem tariff the EU imposes on the industrial component but are subject to levies on their agricultural component. As for Egypt, it continues to impose tariffs on goods imported from the EU (Hoekman and Djankov 1997). In general, exporters in Egypt rely more on the bilateral cooperation agreement than on the GSP. Products not covered by the GSP or the cooperation agreement are subject to the regulations of the WTO.

Egypt is currently negotiating an FTA with the EU as part of the new EU-Mediterranean Strategy outlined in the 1995 Barcelona Declaration.[14] Implementation of the new strategy requires signing bilateral agreements with the Southern Mediterranean countries with the objective of creating free trade areas within a period of 12 to15 years and providing performance-linked financial assistance, among other requirements (Nsouli, Bisat, and Kanaan 1996). The association agreements that the EU has signed with other countries suggest that the EU agreement with Egypt will aim at achieving reciprocal free trade of most manufactured goods and will grant reciprocal preferential access for agricultural products.[15]

The Egypt-EU negotiations have been underway for more than three years, mainly because of the debate over agricultural and processed agricultural products. A number of key issues—oranges, rice, and potatoes—have been problematic. Egypt insists on acquiring the best market access for these three products, which it has a comparative advantage producing and which represent 61 percent of Egypt's aggregate vegetable product exports and more than 5 percent of Egypt's total exports. The levies the EU imposes on the agricultural component of processed food imports from Egypt have also been a point of conflict. The EU insists on an agricultural agreement that complies with its well-known Common Agricultural Policy (CAP), which provides for limits on production, a high level of external protection, and high support prices.

Critics maintain that the CAP could be an obstacle to Egypt achieving full market access for its agricultural products. Evidence for this is the UR Agreement on Agriculture. Negotiations for this agreement lasted for seven years because the EU insisted on ensuring the agreement's compatibility with the CAP. One of the reports by the EU shows the difficulties the Egyptian negotiators face: "The results of the UR give the EU enough room to maneuver to manage its own internal policies. Its market access commitments do not infringe on the principle of community preference and new possibilities have been opened up to European exporters.[16] Its export commitments are compatible with the 1992 CAP reform and the peace clause puts the EU out of danger of any attacks that non-EU countries may make on its agricultural policies"[17] (Directorate-General for Agriculture 1995). This indicates that Egypt and other Mediterranean countries should not have high expectations for the agreement; particularly because the EU considers Egypt's requests unrealistic based on agreements with the other countries, which trade more with the EU.

Nevertheless, the association agreement will be an important step toward trade liberalization, particularly because the EU is Egypt's major trading partner. The agreement with the EU also encourages liberalizing trade with third parties. For example, if Egypt enters into trade agreements with the other Mediterranean countries, it could benefit from the cumulation of origin allowed for in the agreements already signed with Tunisia and Morocco. An FTA with the EU, however, will not offer increased market access unless it improves the access of Egyptian agricultural exports to the EU markets. If the agreement is not signed, Egypt's access to the EU market will worsen, given that the cooperation agreement of 1977 will not be renewed and Egyptian exports will consequently face MFN tariff rates on the EU markets.

AN FTA WITH THE UNITED STATES

Egypt has preferential access to the U.S. markets through the American GSP regime that offers duty-free access to 3,666 tariff lines—about one-third of all U.S. tariff lines. Nearly 88 percent of the GSP applies to industrial products: two-thirds relate to machinery and mechanical appliances, chemical products, basic metals, and optical, photography, and cinematography products; 2 percent covers textiles and textile products to the United States; and the remaining 10 percent applies to agricultural products. Tariffs on other exports are set according to WTO regulations. Under the GSP regime, Egypt exported a total of $41.4 million in 1996, about 6 percent of Egypt's total exports to the United States that year. Egypt, in return, grants MFN status to imports from the United States according to its WTO obligations. Compared to the EU system of preferences, the American GSP is less favorable. The EU system is more reliable because of its contractual nature and because it provides Egypt with better market access, since the coverage of the American GSP is more limited.

Egypt and the United States agreed in May 1998 to begin talks on a Trade and Investment Framework Agreement (TIFA) (U.S. Embassy, Cairo 1998). The TIFA is typically a forum for discussing and monitoring trade and investment issues, identifying impediments to trade and investment, and working to remove these impediments. A TIFA is not a binding mechanism for resolving disputes. The TIFA is expected to be an intermediary step before beginning talks for a free trade area agreement at some time in the future.

When political and economic conditions are suitable to initiate an Egypt-U.S. free trade agreement, the agreement will likely be finalized more quickly than the Egypt-EU negotiations. This is mainly because the United States' agricultural sector is not as vulnerable as that of the EU with its CAP policy. Also, the prospects are better for offering Egypt more market access, if the NAFTA Agreement between the United States and Mexico is taken as a model for an agreement with Egypt. In addition to liberalizing trade in industrial products, NAFTA also managed to achieve this full liberalization in the agricultural sector (Office of the U.S. Trade Representative 1997). Table 5.6 shows the impact of NAFTA on tariffs in Mexico and the United States.

Given the relatively high tariffs applied in Egypt and the importance of the United States as a trading partner to Egypt, an FTA with the United States will entail a significant reduction of Egypt's average nominal protection. By eliminating all tariffs and NTBs on Egyptian exports to the United States, this FTA will increase access to U.S. markets. This is the case because in the absence of an FTA, the Egyptian exports will continue to face tariff barriers on the U.S. markets even after the full implementation of the UR Agreement, which commits the United States to reducing the trade-weighted average tariff on textiles from 17 percent to 15 percent. For specific textile imports, such as clothing, woven cotton fabrics, and textile yarn and thread, the U.S. tariff will be 11.0 percent, 19.0 percent, and 8.57 percent, respectively, after the UR Agreement. Also, important Egyptian agricultural exports, such as fresh vegetables, will continue to be subject to tariffs equal to 9.05 percent.

AFTA AND EGYPT-ARAB BILATERAL FTAS

The AFTA was launched on January 1, 1998. According to this agreement, an Arab free trade area will begin after 10 years, which means that tariff barriers will be

TABLE 5.6. TARIFF REDUCTIONS IN MEXICO AND THE UNITED STATES DUE TO NAFTA

Product groupings	Mexico 1992	Mexico 1996	United States 1992	United States 1996	End of transition period
Animals and products	6.5	4.4	0.7	0	Phasing out tariffs and
Vegetable products[a]	4.1	1.7	5.6	2.8	the immediate or
Waxes, fats, and oils	12.0	8.3	2.5	1.0	phased elimination of
Food, beverages, and tobacco	15.2	9.6	3.6	2.2	important NTBs
Mineral products	3.3	1.7	0.5	0	
Chemicals and related products	10.2	4.0	1.0	0.5	
Plastics, rubber, and related products	13.9	8.2	1.1	0.2	
Leather, travel goods, etc.	8.8	5.1	5.5	1.7	
Wood and related articles	14.4	5.0	0.3	0.1	
Pulp, paper, and related products	8.4	3.6	0.6	0.1	
Textiles and apparel[b]	16.0	5.3	9.1	1.3	
Shoes, headgear, and related products	18.8	0.6	7.8	4.1	
Ceramics, glass, and related products	16.0	6.2	4.3	2.6	
Jewelry, precious metals and stones	5.4	1.9	0.1	0	
Base metals and articles	12.4	6.7	2.0	1.3	
Electronic goods and appliances	13.4	4.4	2.6	0.4	
Transport equipment	15.1	4.9	1.6	0.6	
Scientific and other instruments	12.9	1.5	2.9	0.4	
Arms and ammunition	14.7	0	0.2	0	
Art and antiques	14.5	0	0	0	

a. NAFTA eliminated all NTBs and will eliminate all tariffs by the year 2008.
b. Tariffs will be phased out in 10 years for products that meet rules of origin requirements. Import quotas in the United States will be lifted immediately for originating goods. Barriers covering 80 percent of textiles and apparel trade between the United States and Mexico will be eliminated in six years or less.
Sources: Office of the U.S. Trade Representative 1997;U.S. Department of Commerce, Office of Textiles and Apparel 1997.

eliminated within these 10 years. Tariff reductions already began in January 1998 with a 10 percent reduction on tariffs, taxes, and duties with similar effects (Fawzy 1998a). As regards NTBs, a common list of goods prohibited for health, security, and religious reasons has been prepared. The elimination of the remaining NTBs will be negotiated with the concerned committee. In case some members do not remove unjustified NTBs, the other members can apply the principle of reciprocity. Each country is allowed to draw a list of manufactured goods to be exempted from tariff and nontariff reductions, so that local industries can restructure to withstand competition (Zarrouk 1998). Finally, the agreement allows agricultural products, during the harvest season, to be outside tariff reduction throughout the transition period. Each country is allowed to include a maximum of 10 products exempted during harvest, provided that exemptions do not exceed a total duration of more than 45 months. As of November 1998, almost a year from launching the AFTA, only 14 of 18 Arab countries signing the AFTA had begun implementation—Egypt being one of them.

Besides joining the AFTA, Egypt has been involved in bilateral trade agreements with a number of Arab countries.[18] The Arab League and the AFTA encourage other agreements that allow Arab countries to unilaterally, bilaterally, or multilaterally establish free trade areas as a step toward a comprehensive AFTA to be signed in 2008. The agreements Egypt has signed so far, or is currently negotiating, aim at establishing free trade areas, usually for a period of five years, as a more rapid approach to liberalizing intra-Arab trade, compared to the longer-term AFTA.

The AFTA and the Arab bilateral agreements are important in their own right because they can reduce the "hub-and-spokes effect" likely with the EU-Mediterranean agreements. They can also enhance border trade in bulky and short-lived goods and encourage Arab joint ventures. It is expected, however, that the AFTA will have limited impact on trade liberalization in Egypt. First, Egypt's trade with Arab states constitutes only a small portion of its total trade. Second, Egypt already exchanges goods at zero tariff with seven Arab countries and offers others preferential tariff treatment (*Al Ahram* 1998, April 28). The impact on Egypt's market access will depend on the readiness of Arab countries to abandon the restrictive NTBs they impose on imports of agricultural products and other imports, as well as on their ability to overcome the existing institutional and infrastructural constraints that could significantly limit trading opportunities among them.

COMESA

Egypt joined COMESA in June 1998 (US Embassy, Cairo 1998). This trade agreement establishes free trade between its 21 signatory countries by the year 2000. By 2004, these countries will introduce a common external tariff (CET) structure to deal with third parties.[19] The member countries agreed that the CET on capital goods will be zero and 5 percent on raw materials, 15 percent on intermediate goods, and 30 percent on final goods.

In 1996, Egypt's imports under COMESA constituted only 0.1 percent of its total imports, and exports to COMESA countries were only 0.8 percent of all Egyptian exports. Accordingly, COMESA will have only a limited impact on trade liberalization in Egypt. The most recent average tariff available to some COMESA countries indicates that the duty-free entry of Egyptian exports into this African market could significantly increase its market access.[20]

To conclude, if Egypt enters into FTAs with the United States and the EU, Egypt will enjoy a significantly more liberal trade regime in the 15 years from the signing date; however, this is not the whole story. Egypt faces major challenges to survive in this global environment and must withstand fierce competition in international and domestic markets. These challenges are discussed in detail in the next section.

Future Challenges

Export prospects are a major concern for Egypt, given the new international trade environment, which is becoming more liberal over time. The outcome of Egypt's trade liberalization will depend on the country's ability to compete in global markets. In the EU markets, for example, Egypt will face aggressive competition from the Central and Eastern European countries that share Egypt's advantage of relatively cheap labor and geographical proximity to the EU. In the U.S. market, there are the NAFTA member countries that also pose a competitive threat. To face this challenge, Egypt must be more engaged in subcontracting activities with its major trading partners, maintaining a responsive exchange rate, and improving the long-term indicators of competitiveness.

First, Egypt needs to be engaged to a much larger extent in subcontracting activities with the EU and the United States if it is to compete in today's global trading. Possible industries for cooperation are leather, garments, machinery, and furniture. The experiences of Central and Eastern Europe and Mexico with subcontracting have proven subcontracting to be a sound method for reducing the risks and costs of developing export markets while increasing exports. Subcontracting increased Central and Eastern European exports to the EU by 26 percent between 1989 and 1993 (Hoekman 1998). Since NAFTA began in 1994, Mexico's exports to the United States have more than tripled (U.S. International Trade Commission 1998). The increased imports of apparel from Mexico are primarily due to NAFTA provisions that enable duty-free and quota-free entry for apparel assembled wholly from fabrics that are formed and cut in the United States. Two-thirds of Mexico's textiles and apparel exports to the United States are currently manufactured using U.S. components, up from 42 percent in 1990.

Second, Egypt needs to maintain a responsive exchange rate. With the opening of the Egyptian economy, Egypt's imports are expected to rise, thus imposing pressures on the Egyptian pound, which is likely to appreciate. Furthermore, the significant currency devaluation in some Asian countries in relation to the dollar, a factor in the recent Asian financial crisis, puts additional pressure on the Egyptian pound.[21] The enhanced competitiveness in these countries could affect Egypt's export prospects. Maintaining a responsive exchange rate is also important because a steep real appreciation that undermines the current account generates expectations of reimposed trade controls. Also, a widely fluctuating real exchange rate implies uncertain profitability in many sectors. These two factors hamper the reallocation of resources toward more productive sectors.

Third, Egypt must acquire the long-run determinants of competitiveness. These include obtaining and using technology, developing human capital, promoting investment, making the institutions that influence trade efficient, and ensuring the overall efficiency of economic activity and reliable infrastructure (Rajapatirana 1997). Egypt has made significant progress in macroeconomic and structural reforms, yet more efforts are still required (Galal and Tohamy 1998). Structural reforms are an essential part of a more comprehensive reform agenda. A comprehensive reform agenda that extends beyond trade policies would help further Egypt's trade agenda and achieve the desired diversification that relies on the private sector initiative. Reform of labor markets, domestic regulation, and capital markets would allow adjustment to changes in world markets, thus preventing the buildup of opposition to liberalization.

Negotiating more than one FTA at a time is an additional challenge Egypt faces. Each FTA will have its own set of rules of origin that govern the duty-free entry of goods into the member countries. The Egyptian negotiating teams should coordinate to ensure that the various rules are consistent. Numerous sets of rules of origin will be an administrative complication and will cause confusion between exporters—virtually a new trade barrier.

For Egypt, the fear of the trade diversion due to FTAs is minimal, yet there remains the hub-and-spokes effect resulting from agreements with the EU and the United States.[22] As the EU is likely to expand before 2010 to include several countries from Central and Eastern Europe, the hub will become even bigger. Egypt, therefore, needs to be engaged simultaneously in FTAs with other Mediterranean countries, and Arab-Arab trade liberalization now has an additional incentive.

Concluding Remarks

Over the past two decades, Egypt's trade regime has become more liberal, as indicated by the decline in the average tariff; dispersion of tariff rates, trade taxes, and duties; reduced production coverage of NTBs; and finally by the unification and devaluation of the Egyptian pound. Yet indicators show that Egypt has consistently become less open than the fast-growing economies, over the period of the study, and has grown less open and less integrated with the global economy over time. Egypt's comparatively low trade profile can be attributed to the overall business environment, public sector dominance of economic activity, and relatively high tariff barriers. One possible reason for Egypt's turn inward is the importance of oil in the country's trade and the volatility of its price. High oil prices contributed to raising trade relative to GDP in the 1970s and early 1980s. In addition, falling prices in the mid-1980s negatively affected this measure of openness. Another possible reason for Egypt's decreasing openness is the windfall gains to the economy from the oil revenues and others that raised the prices of nontradables versus tradables and thus attracted investment away from tradable sectors. Economic reform can be considered a third reason, as it was accompanied in its early stages with import suppression.

Egypt's efforts to liberalize trade through different trade agreements must be reinforced with a strong conviction in the benefits of free trade. To maximize possible benefits from these agreements, Egypt should complement its eagerness to reach the best agreement terms by developing its ability to compete in the different markets. This is crucial considering that Egypt has had excellent access to the EU markets for the past 20 years but was unable to penetrate the markets sufficiently and continues to loose ground.

A key element in increasing exports should be subcontracting, as in the case of the Central and Eastern European countries to the European Union, and Mexico to the United States. Other challenges include encouraging the role of the private sector, facilitating domestic and foreign investment, and maintaining a responsive exchange rate. Competitiveness, Egypt's ultimate aim, is best achieved through a comprehensive reform agenda. Long-term determinants of competitiveness will include technology acquisition, openness to investment, human capital development, and efficient institutions that govern the economic activity in Egypt.

As Egypt plans to enter into a number of free trade agreements, each with its own rules of origin, it is necessary to guarantee the consistency of these rules across different agreements. Anything other than unified rules of origin will leave importers, exporters, and government administration in a state of confusion, thus adding yet another barrier to trade with Egypt.

Notes

1. Trade liberalization is defined as a reduction in trade restrictions and an increase in the use of prices instead of discretionary intervention.

2. There was an increase in the significance of refined petroleum in the minerals category (from 7 percent of mineral exports in 1984 to 32 percent in 1996) at the expense of crude petroleum (81 percent to 49 percent). In 1996, raw cotton accounted for no more than 11 percent of the textile exports compared with 50 percent in 1984, whereas ready-made garments and noncotton textile exports increased over time. Aluminum bars, which represented about 80 percent of total base metal exports, accounted for only 2 percent in 1996.

3. According to the Own Import System, the private sector is allowed to use its foreign exchange earnings to finance import purchases.

4. Over the period 1981 though 1985, the unweighted average Most Favored Nation (MFN) tariff in Egypt was 47.4 percent compared with 29.5 percent in Latin America, 26.3 percent in the Middle East and North Africa, and 20.3 percent in East Asia. Between 1984 and 1987, the percentage of tariff lines affected by nontariff barriers in Egypt was 48 percent compared with 40.1 percent in Latin America, 35.6 percent in the Middle East and North Africa, and 30 percent in East Asia.

5. The ERP takes into consideration tariffs on inputs and output. It may be defined as the excess of the domestic value added (value added under the prevailing tariff structure) over the international market value added (value added in absence of nominal protection). It thus reveals the incentive structure prevailing in the economy due to domestic policies.

6. Tariff dispersion in Egypt stems from the escalating nature of its tariff structure. A decline in this dispersion is a favorable development, given that a nonuniform tariff structure distorts production and investment incentives by making some sectors more attractive than others.

7. Export bias, B $_x$, against activity j, that is, (B $_{xj}$) occurs when domestic prices exceed export prices, thus making production for the domestic market more profitable. This is calculated as

$$B_{xj} = \{\frac{1 + tj}{1 + sj} - 1\} \times 100,$$

where tj = nominal tariff rate on activity j, and sj = export subsidy rate or the duty drawback per £E of exports and is calculated as

$\sum_i ti \times mij$, the technical coefficient of imported commodity i per unit value of activity j.

8. This is based on a survey of 154 firms. Split according to size, the sample had 31 percent large firms, 34 percent medium-size firms, and 35 percent small firms. According to type of ownership, the sample had 73 percent domestic firms and 27 percent foreign firms. According to economic activity, 64 percent of the firms were in the field of industry, 13 percent in trade, 9 percent in construction, 8 percent in tourism, and 6 percent in the oil sector.

9. For the financial sector, the real financial spread in Egypt and the EU were compared, and; accordingly, an implicit tariff of 20 percent was assumed for this sector. A 50 percent tariff equivalent was assumed for the telecommunications sector based on comparing the number of employees per line in Egypt with the world average.

10. See Noll (1997) for a discussion of trade opportunities in Egypt that are hindered by existing policies.

11. This version of the import penetration ratio is a useful indicator since it is the imports of consumption goods that are usually mostly restricted (Andriamananjara and Nash 1997).

12. Chile, the Republic of Korea, Mexico, Turkey, Argentina, Brazil, Peru, Uruguay, and Venezuela are examples of countries that have undertaken important liberalization steps before effectively joining any trade agreement, whereas the trade regime of the countries engaged in the Central American Common Market (CACM) and the Andean Pact remained highly protective for years after their establishment.

13. Among these products are woven cotton fabrics, knitted or crocheted fabrics, tulle lace embroidery, ribbons, traveling rugs and blankets, made-up articles wholly or chiefly of textile materials, articles of apparel and textile fabrics, and clothing accessories of textile fabrics.

14. The negotiations started in January 1995.

15. The EU already signed association agreements of this nature with Morocco, Tunisia, Israel, Jordan, and the Palestinian National Authority and is negotiating similar agreements with the Gulf States that should be completed by 1998. Negotiations with Syria, Algeria, and Lebanon have already started.

16. The principle of *community preference* means that preference is given to goods produced inside the community. This principle entails keeping the prices of the community below those of imports to the European market. This led to the institution of two basic mechanisms of the CAP: import levies and export refunds (subsidies for exported community products to make them more competitive on world markets).

17. The peace clause means that the CAP instruments will not be contested as long as the disciplines resulting from the UR Agreement are fully observed in domestic support, export subsidies, and market access.

18. Egypt has already signed free trade agreements with Jordan (1996), Tunisia (1997), and Morocco (1998) and is in the process of negotiating trade agreements with Lebanon, Kuwait, Syria, Yemen, Bahrain, and Saudi Arabia. Egypt has also signed economic cooperation agreements with Libya that may lead to eventual negotiations for a free trade area between them.

19. These countries are Angola, Burundi, the Comoros, Congo, Djibouti, Egypt, Eritrea, Ethiopia, Kenya, Madagascar, Malawi, Mauritius, Namibia, Rwanda, the Seychelles, Sudan, Swaziland, Tanzania, Uganda, Zambia, and Zimbabwe.

20. The tariff rates for some COMESA countries are Burundi, 37.0 percent; Ethiopia, 28.8 percent; Kenya, 19.9 percent; Malawi, 21.0 percent; Mauritius, 29.0 percent; Rwanda, 42.0 percent; Sudan, 50.0 percent; Tanzania, 27.5 percent; Uganda, 17.1 percent; and Zimbabwe, 21.8 percent.

21. Between January 1997 and January 1998, the nominal depreciation in the five most affected Asian countries (the Republic of Korea, Malaysia, Thailand, Indonesia, and the Philippines) ranged between 40 percent and 75 percent, and the real effective exchange rate depreciation ranged from 17 percent to 70 percent.

22. This is because Egypt will be engaged in these agreements with its major trading partners. The EU, the United States, and Arab countries together account for 76 percent of Egypt's exports and 69 percent of Egypt's imports. To minimize the diversion effect, Egypt should work to lower its MFN tariffs.

References

Alonso-Gamo, Patricia, Susan Fennell, and Khaled Sakr. 1997. "Adjusting to New Realities: MENA, The Uruguay Round, and the EU-Mediterranean Initiative." International Monetary Fund Working Paper 97/5. Washington, D.C.

Andriamananjara, Shuby, and John Nash. 1997. "Have Trade Policy Reforms Led to Greater Openness in Developing Countries? Evidence from Readily Available Trade Data." World Bank Policy Research Working Paper 1730 World Bank, Policy Research Department, Washington, D.C.

Edwards, Sebastian. 1993. "Openness, Trade Liberalization, and Growth in Developing Countries." *Journal of Economic Literature* 31:1358–93. Brussels.

European Commission Directorate-General for Agriculture. 1995. "GATT and European Agriculture." European Community, CAP Working Notes.

European Commission. 1997. *Annual Economic Report: Growth, Employment and Convergence on the Road to EMU.* http://europa.eu.int:80/en/record/aer97/chap2en.htm.

Fawzy, Samiha. 1998a. "The Arab Free Trade Area: Issues for Discussion." Working Paper presented to The Economic Research Forum for the Arab Countries, Iran and Turkey (ERF). Cairo: The Economic Research Forum.

1998b. "The Business Environment in Egypt." The Egyptian Center for Economic Studies Working Paper No. 34. Cairo.

Foroutan, Faezeh. 1998. "Does a Membership in a Regional Preferential Trade Agreement Make a Country More or Less Protectionist?" Working Paper 1898. http://www.worldbank.org/html/iecit/wp1898.htm.

Galal, Ahmed, and Sahar Tohamy. 1998. "Towards an Egypt-US Free Trade Agreement: An Egyptian Perspective." The Egyptian Center for Economic Studies Working Paper No. 21. Cairo.

GATT. 1993. *Trade Policy Review: Arab Republic of Egypt, 1992.* Vol. 1. Geneva: GATT.

Hoekman, Bernard. 1998. "The WTO and the Arab World: Trade Policy Priorities and Pitfalls," in N. Shaflik (ed). *Prospects for MENA Economies.* London: MacMillan.

Hoekman, Bernard, and Arvind Subramanian. 1996. "Egypt and the Uruguay Round." World Bank Policy Research Working Paper 1597. World Bank, Policy Research Department, Washington, D.C.

Hoekman, Bernard, and Simeon Djankov. 1997." Towards a Free Trade Agreement with the EU: Issues and Policy Options for Egypt." The Egyptian Center for Economic Studies Working Paper No. 10. Cairo.

Ingco, Merlinda D. 1995. "Agricultural Trade Liberalization in the Uruguay Round: One Step Forward, One Step Back?" Working Paper 1500. http://www.worldbank.org/html/iecit/wp1500.htm.

International Monetary Fund. 1995. *Arab Republic of Egypt: Recent Economic Developments.* Washington, D.C.

———. 1998a. "Egypt: Beyond Stabilization, Toward a Dynamic Market Economy." Occasional Paper No. 163. Washington, D.C.

———. 1998b. *Trade Liberalization in IMF-Supported Programs, World Economic and Financial Surveys.* Washington, D.C.

Kheir-El-Din, Hanaa. 1989. "Evaluation of Protection and Anti-export Bias in the 1986 Customs Tariffs in Egypt." *L'Egypte contemporaine* 417–18.

———. 1998. "Effective Protection in Egypt Due to the Tariff Structures in 1996 and 1997 Compared to 1994." Study prepared for USAID/DEPRA, Cairo.

Kheir-El-Din, Hanaa, and Ahmed El Dersh. 1992. "Trade Policies in Egypt." In Said El Naggar, ed., *Foreign and Intraregional Trade Policies of the Arab Countries.* (In Arabic.) Abu Dhabi: Arab Monetary Fund.

Mongardini, Joannes. 1998. "Estimating Egypt's Equilibrium Real Exchange Rate." International Monetary Fund Working Paper 98/5. Washington, D.C.

Nathan Associates. 1994. *New Directions in Egypt's Trade Policy and Customs Reforms.* Report submitted to USAID, Cairo.

———. 1998. *Enhancing Egypt's Exports.* Report submitted to USAID, Cairo.

Noll, Roger G. 1997. "The International Dimension of Regulation Reform: With Application to Egypt." The Egyptian Center for Economic Studies Distinguished Lecture Series No. 8. Cairo.

Nsouli, Saleh M., Amer Bisat, and Oussama Kanaan. 1996. "The European Union's New Mediterranean Strategy." http://www.worldbank.org/fandd/english 0996/ articles/010996.htm.

Office of the U.S. Trade Representative. 1997. *Operation and Effect of the North American Free Trade Agreement.* <http://www.ustr.gov/reports/index.html>.

Office of the U.S. Trade Representative. 1998. *National Trade Estimate Report on Foreign Trade Barriers: Egypt.* <http://www.ustr.gov/reports/nte/1998/ contents.html>.

Papageorgiou, Demetris, Michael Michaely, and Armeane M. Choksi, eds. 1991. *Liberalizing Trade Policy.* Vol. 2. Oxford: Oxford University Press.

Petri, Peter A. 1997. "Trade Strategies for the Southern Mediterranean." Technical Paper No. 127. Paris: Organisation for Economic Cooporation and Development, Development Center. http://www.oecd.org//dev/pub/tp/Tp127.pdf.

Rajapatirana, Sarath. 1997. *Trade Policies in Latin America and the Caribbean: Priorities, Progress and Prospects.* San Francisco: International Center for Economic Growth.

Sachs, Jeffrey. 1996. "Achieving Rapid Growth: The Road Ahead for Egypt." The Egyptian Center for Economic Studies Distinguished Lecture Series No. 3. Cairo.

Subramanian, Arvind. 1997. "The Egyptian Stabilization Experience: An Analytical Retrospective." The Egyptian Center for Economic Studies Working Paper No. 18. Cairo.

Thomas, Vinod, and John Nash . 1991. *Best Practices in Trade Policy Reform.* Washington, D.C.: World Bank.

U.S. Department of Commerce, Office of Textiles and Apparel. 1997. *Sector Summary for Textiles and Apparel in NAFTA.* http://otexa.ita.doc.gov/nafta/ execsum.htm.

U.S. Department of State. 1995/96. *Country Commercial Guide: Egypt.* gopher:// gopher.state.gov:7000ftp%ADOS...al%20Guides%3Aegypt20Commercial%20Guid April 5, 1998.

U.S. Embassy, Cairo. 1998. *Foreign Economic Trends and Their Implications for the United States: Report for the Arab Republic of Egypt.*

U.S. International Trade Commission. 1998. "Import Growth in Textiles and Apparel Sector Accelerates in 1997." News Release 98-028. http://www.usitc.gov/er/ER0428V1.HM.

Wilson, Rodney. 1986. "The Developmental Impact of Egypt's Import Liberalization." *Middle Eastern Studies* 22:481–504.

World Bank. 1995a. *Egypt into the Next Century* Vol. II: *Egypt in the Global Economy.* Manuscript. World Bank, Washington, D.C.

———. 1995b. "Widening and Deepening the World Trading System." *Policy Research Bulletin* 6(5) (November-December). http://www.worldbank.org/html/dec/Publications/Bulletins/pprb6,5.htm.

Yeats, Alexander. 1996. "Export Prospects of Middle Eastern Countries: A Post-Uruguay Round Analysis." Policy Research Working Paper 1571. World Bank, Policy Research Department, Washington, D.C.

Zarrouk, Jamel E. 1998. "Arab Free Trade Area: Potentialities and Effects." Paper presented at the workshop on Benefiting from Globalization, Mediterranean Development Forum II, Marrakesh.

Chapter 6

Trade Policies in Jordan, Lebanon, and Saudi Arabia

Riad al Khouri
Middle East Business Associates Ltd., Amman, Jordan

Almost all countries in the MENA region have been reforming and liberalizing their foreign trade regimes as part of a more general process of economic reform. Despite these efforts, the extent of integration of the region into the world economy remains relatively low (see Nabli and De Kleine in this volume). One dimension of this lag is reflected in the limited extent to which MENA countries have been able to eliminate or streamline administrative procedures related to trade. Another is that many countries in the region have yet to accede to the World Trade Organization (WTO). Algeria, Jordan, Lebanon, Oman, Saudi Arabia, and Yemen are in the process of acceding or have indicated an interest in doing so.

This chapter surveys the trade policy status quo in three of the *demandeur* countries: Jordan, Lebanon, and Saudi Arabia, focusing in particular on nontariff barriers and administrative "red tape." The intention is to document both what has been achieved and what remains to be done in making the trade regime more conducive to international trade. Some of the policies that are identified will need to be changed as part of the process of accession to the WTO; but many will be unaffected. The message of this chapter is that much remains to be done by governments to facilitate trade, and that attention must center on reducing the prevalence of nontariff barriers to trade. To maximize the benefits of WTO membership it is important that efforts are made to facilitate export-oriented production by eliminating to the greatest extent possible trade-related transactions costs.

Common to all three countries is continued prevalence of licensing requirements, to some extent reflecting the scope of exemptions granted to certain types of goods or importers, but more generally reflecting regulatory regimes. Conformity assessment procedures for goods subject to mandatory product standards and technical regulations are also becoming a more important barrier to trade (see the chapter by Kheir-El-Din in this volume). In Jordan and Lebanon, agricultural trade is subject to high barriers on a seasonal basis, with reliance on direct controls rather than price-based instruments such as tariffs. In all three countries, nontransparent customs practices continue to be a problem, despite recent efforts to streamline procedures.

Jordan

Since its inception as a state in the 1920s, Jordan has suffered from chronic trade deficits and a narrow export base. This has partly been due to the scarcity of natural resources, but a long-term crisis in agriculture, a small manufacturing sector, and the restrictive polices of the government, among other factors, also help to explain the country's continuing trade imbalance.

Because of these constraints, trade policy has traditionally tended to be mercantilist, and the government has depended on wide-range, high tariffs for revenue. However, Jordan's application to join the WTO has led to measures ensuring a more liberal and open foreign trade regime. By the mid-1990s, inputs for agricultural production and a large number of those required for local manufacturing had been exempted from customs duties. Higher tariff rates for manufacturing underscore the benefits that the industrial sector reaps from the relatively low tariffs on raw materials and intermediate goods. In a move to boost exports, the authorities continue to reduce tariffs on a multiple range of raw materials and intermediate goods used in the production of export-oriented finished products. By the mid-1990s, inputs for agricultural production had also been exempted from customs duties.

Most of Jordan's imports come from European Union (EU) countries, especially Germany, Italy, France, and the United Kingdom. Jordan has signed a Euro-Mediterranean Partnership Agreement with the EU that will further boost Jordanian-EU trade and create a Euro-Mediterranean free trade zone, including Jordan, by the year 2010. However, Iraq remains Jordan's major trading partner, as it supplies most of Jordan's oil needs.

Significant trade reforms have been undertaken in the last decade. The government has taken a number of measures to reduce the levels and variation in tariff rates, to simplify customs procedures, and to abolish quantitative restrictions on imports. As a result, Jordan now has six tariff bands (0, 5, 10, 20, 30, and 40 percent), and the maximum tariff rate is being set at 30 percent. Exceptions are manufactured tobacco and tobaccos substitutes (70–100 percent) and alcoholic drinks (180 percent). Tariff reductions have been complemented by efforts to apply a General Sales Tax (GST) to imports and domestically produced goods in order to maintain revenue.

Registration, Documentation, and Customs Procedures

Import licensing requirements for all products other than those maintained for national security, health, safety, environmental, and religious reasons have been abolished. Registration, documentation, and customs procedures in Jordan have undergone streamlining and simplification through the introduction of computerization and decentralization away from customs headquarters in the capital. Nevertheless, customs procedures remain cumbersome and are time consuming because of the inefficiency of customs personnel. This inevitably leads to a lack of transparency. Many traders perceive that the situation has actually become worse, despite the adoption of procedural reforms.

Import cards are required by an importing firm, which in turn must be registered with the Ministry of Industry and Trade (MIT). Such registration, as well as the annual issue of cards, is routine and subject only to a nominal fee. If the importer does not present an import card for goods not requiring an import license, then a fine of 5 percent of the value of the goods is added to the cost of clearance.

A customs declaration form must be filled in for all goods, including those exempt from duties and taxes. Every declaration form must be accompanied by original copies of the commercial invoice, which should also state in Arabic the classification of the goods according to the customs tariff and must be signed by the owner or his agent. Both the invoice and the certificate of origin must be certified by the Chamber of Commerce and the Jordanian diplomatic mission in the country where the commodity originated. If a Jordanian diplomatic mission does not exist there, certification from the Chamber of Commerce or other official bodies will suffice. Unsigned invoices or their copies can also be used on condition that they are certified by recognized chambers or Jordanian consulates.

Imported goods originating from Iraq, Lebanon, Syria, or Saudi Arabia must be accompanied by a customs declaration from these countries. This also applies to goods that are imported through the ports of these countries and enter Jordan by land. For goods entering country from other non-neighboring Arab countries, an Arab transit manifest is required.

If any necessary documentation cannot be submitted, the customs authority imposes a cash guarantee of 1 percent of the goods' value, refunded if the missing documents are presented within 60 days of payment of the guarantee.

The Jordanian Customs Department does not yet apply the Brussels Definition of Value or the GATT Valuation Code. Valuation is based on comments from the inspecting officer, invoice of the cargo, and a product price list complied by the Customs Department. The Customs Department has the right to reassess the value of the commodity if it is not satisfied with the figures on the declaration form. If the importer is not satisfied with the final value assessed by the customs official, then a claim may be submitted first to the Director of the Customs Center. A second appeal can be made to the Director General at customs headquarters. It must be noted, however, that the goods cannot be cleared on guarantee or otherwise until the dispute is settled.

Levies and Charges (Other than Import Duties)

The 1997 Duties and Taxes Consolidation Law No. 7 consolidated many additional fees, paratariffs, and surtaxes into the tariff. However, some fees and taxes are excluded from the consolidated tariff: the GST, the Sales Surtax, and an import and export surcharge of 5 percent imposed under Import and Export Regulation No. 74 of 1993. Import service fees are also applicable to imports from Morocco, Libya, and Lebanon (1 percent) and from Saudi Arabia (0.25 percent). Export service fees are also applicable to exports to Iraq (0.001–0.002 percent); Libya, Morocco, and Lebanon (1 percent); Yemen (0.50 percent); and Saudi Arabia (0.25 percent).

As stipulated in the Sales Tax Law No. 6 of 1994 and Amendment No. 15 of 1995, GST must be paid and collected by an importer, irrespective of the volume of imports. GST is due on imported goods at the rate prevailing on the date of the customs declaration and is collected before the goods are released. The standard rate is 10 percent. A higher tax rate of 20 percent of the value of the goods is levied on photographic film, air conditioning units, cosmetics, marble, tiles, cameras, dishwashers, microwaves, satellite transmission and reception systems, and video or voice recorders. Automobiles are subject to a GST ranging between 62 and 141 percent, depending on engine size. Specific taxes are levied on beverages (alcoholic and nonalcoholic), tobacco, certain construction materials, tires, and lubricants.

In addition to basic foodstuffs, pharmaceuticals and inputs used by the pharmaceutical industry, agricultural inputs (including machinery), materials to produce cement, paper and reading material, ambulances and fire trucks, and industrial machinery, the following are exempted from GST: (a) goods imported into free zones and duty free shops; (b) goods in transit; (c) purchases of arms, munitions, transportation means, spares parts, tires, and any other material the Council of Ministers agrees shall be imported or procured tax free by the armed forces, public security service, civil defense, intelligence services, and customs police for their own account; (d) imports exempted by virtue of the Investment Promotion Law No. 16 of 1995;[1] (e) any goods or persons the Council of Ministers decides to wholly or partially exempt in specific cases; (f) imports for mosques, churches, orphanages, and senior or handicapped citizens for their own use; (g) subject to reciprocity, and at the recommendation of the Foreign Minister, imports for embassies, legations, and regular consulates for their official use, as well as those for the personal use of foreign diplomatic and consular staff active in a nonhonorary capacity and accredited to the Jordan; (h) imports for international and regional organizations operating in Jordan and their foreign staff who enjoy diplomatic status; and (i) standard exemptions for specimens, items with no commercial value, personal effects of visitors, etc.

Import Bans and Licensing

The import of nuclear waste, salt, and vehicles more than five years old is prohibited. Import licenses used to be a significant nontariff barrier to trade with Jordan—the rule was that all imports required a license, unless exempted. This changed in

1997, and licenses are now required only for particular cases. According to MIT Regulation No. 1 of 1997, certain individuals or organizations importing goods into Jordan must apply for an import license with the ministry. Import licenses are issued for a period of one year and can be extended upon request for a period of one more year at the MIT. In fact, this requirement has become a mere formality in most cases and can no longer generally be considered a nontariff barrier. Nevertheless, should a severe balance of payments problem or other economic difficulties arise, the regulation, being in force, can be applied more stringently and could form a true barrier as the authorities seek to enforce it.

The following imports in particular require licenses:

- Goods imported from countries that have trade agreements and protocols with Jordan provided that these goods originate in those countries, namely: Bahrain, Egypt, Iraq, Israel, Kuwait, Lebanon, Libya, Morocco, Oman, the Palestinian National Authority, Saudi Arabia, Sudan, Syria, Tunisia, the United Arab Emirates, and Yemen.

- Goods and entities not subject to tariff in order to prove to customs that they are exempt. This pertains to goods imported in the name of banks, companies under establishment, farms, handicraft businesses, hospitals, hotels, ministries and other public institutions, newspapers, and religious, scientific and charitable organizations.

- Imports by individuals for personal, noncommercial use; goods brought into the country by passengers, of which the total value does not exceed JD2,000; companies, organizations, and individuals registered with official bodies to establish development projects in Jordan; foreign contractors and companies, including their branches, which are registered in Jordan as foreign entities; foreign entities permitted to operate a resident branch in Jordan to conduct business outside Jordan and non-Jordanian individuals working in media establishments; and foreign cigarettes. Failure to obtain a license may entail paying a customs fine of 5 percent of the assessed value of the imported goods.

Goods and agencies that are specifically exempt from import licenses include diplomatic and consular missions importing goods for official use; goods entering the country on a transit basis; goods entering the country for exhibitions or display, except for movies imported for commercial purposes; samples of goods brought into the country by traders within the limitations stipulated by the Customs Law; re-exported goods before customs clearance; goods imported directly into free zones and duty free shops; cattle; all goods imported according to the Investment Promotion Law; state universities; temporary admission goods, excluding goods cleared for local consumption and requiring import license; vehicles for use of the handicapped; goods stored in bonded areas; goods that customs authorities have agreed to place in their stores until customs clearance; and personal belongings and used furniture.

In some cases, approval to import certain goods is required from authorized bodies before the importers are able to apply for an import license. These goods currently include 45 categories. They are listed in Table 6.1 along with the authority responsible for issuing their approval to enter the country.

Only specific state-owned organizations may import certain items, that is, the Jordan Tanning Co. (raw hides), Jordan Petroleum Refinery Co. (oil and derivatives), Jordan Cement Factories Co. (Portland cement), Jordan Phosphate Mines Co. (explosives, ammonium nitrate, rock), and tire retreading companies (tires). These items accounted for 21 percent of the value of Jordanian imports in 1997.

Standards and Other Technical Requirements

Existing laws and regulations require that samples of certain imported items be examined to ensure that they meet state specifications before they enter the local market. All such products must be inspected by authorized analysts before being cleared by customs. Three samples of the goods are taken for analysis to ensure that the quality and the specifications of the goods are in conformity with regulations. Two of the samples are sent to a customs laboratory, and the third is kept at the Customs Center. The importer or the owner of the goods may object to the analysis results within five days from their release, in front of an arbitration committee. If the presence of the goods is not necessary for settlement of the dispute, then customs authorities may clear the goods before completion of the arbitration procedures against a guarantee from the importer. In certain circumstances, especially where perishable goods are concerned, the importer may request to immediately clear the consignment by posting a guarantee that the goods will not enter the local market until the results of the analysis have been released. In case goods are cleared prior to receiving laboratory approvals by authorized bodies, a letter of guarantee must be submitted promising that the goods will not be released in the local market until all approvals are obtained.

Goods failing to meet specifications must be re-exported if they do not conform to Jordanian standards or are deemed unfit for human consumption. In 1997, 51,000 customs transactions were received by the Control Department of the Jordan Institute of Standards and Meteorology. In only 65 cases were products re-exported because they did not comply with Jordanian mandatory standards. Most of these concerned foodstuffs (41) or electrical devices (18). Within three months from the date of re-export, the goods' beneficiary must present the documents to a refund of duties and other charges, except for storage fees, overtime fees, insurance fees, and fees for other services, which are not refundable.

Imports under the duty drawback scheme may not enter the local market until the results of the analysis are released. They may, however, be cleared immediately

TABLE 6.1. GOODS REQUIRING PERMISSION TO ENTER JORDAN

Rice	Ministry of Supply (MS)
Powdered milk	MS
Flour and derivatives	MS
Sugar	MS
Wheat, barley, corn	MS
Milk for industry	MS in coordination with MIT
Frozen animal sperm	Ministry of Agriculture (MA)
Live animals	MS in coordination with MA
Fresh, cold, and frozen meats	MA
Weapons and ammunition	Ministry of Interior/Public Security (MI/PS)
Explosives	MI/PS
Switchblades	MI/PS
Toy vehicles operating on fuel	MI/PS
Remote-control toy aircraft	MI/PS
Electric toys intended for commercial use	MI/PS
Electrical self-defense equipment	MI/PS
Uranium and other radioactive materials	Ministry of Energy and Mineral Resources
Wireless receivers and broadcast stations	Organizing Committee for the Telecommunications Sector (OCTS)
Wireless warning devices	OCTS
Remote-control devices	OCTS
Location-detecting devices	OCTS
Wireless receivers and broadcast devices	OCTS
Mobile telephones	OCTS
Decoders	TV and Radio Corporation (TVRC)
Satellite transmission receivers	TVRC
Color photocopiers	Central Bank of Jordan (CBJ)
Communication terminals	OCTS
Medicines and antibiotics	Ministry of Health (MH)
Nutritious ingredients for athletes	MH
Potassium pomate	MH
Foodstuff dyes	MH /Nutrition Department
Halogenous material	Ministry of Municipal and Rural Affairs
Postal clearing devices	Ministry of Communications
Potatoes, onions, and garlic	Agricultural Marketing Organization
Frozen ice cream in molds	MH
Asbestos boards and tubes	MH
Remote-control devices for aircraft toys	OCTS
Freon gas	General Corporation for Environmental Protection
Wireless telephones	OCTS
Wireless microphones	OCTS
Milk and other food for children	MH
Artesian wells drillers	Ministry of Water and Irrigation
Small and large used tires	MIT
New and secondhand military clothing	Jordan Armed Forces
Foreign cigarettes	MS

with a guarantee stating the goods will not be disposed of in any manner until the laboratory issues the results. For woven material, leather, or textiles, samples of these materials will need to be attached to the declaration form, so that at the time of export or re-export, a comparison can be made to confirm that the raw material was used in the manufacture of the end product. The samples are stamped and signed by a customs official and given a reference number.

Lebanon

Historically, Lebanon has relied on services exports and on remittances from abroad to support the balance of payments. The government has always depended on a wide range of relatively high tariffs for revenue. Since the early 1990s, measures have been adopted to reform the fiscal system, implement tariff and tax reforms, and dismantle trade barriers. Overall, tariff levels, the number of rates, and the degree of tariff dispersion and escalation have been reduced in an attempt to create an incentive regime conducive to outward-oriented growth. Tariff rates for agriculture are low, as trade in this sector is directly regulated.

Customs duties account for 44 percent of total government revenues, the largest contributor to the budget. The Lebanese government has regained control of customs after their domination by militias in 1975–91, and much has been done to rehabilitate and improve the administration. As of 1997, a new system, NAJM (an Arabic acronym for "Customs Information System"), based on ASYCUDA (Automated System for Customs Declaration), has reduced the number of steps in customs clearance. A Single Administrative Document was also introduced in the same year.

Other customs reforms have included a tariff reform as contained in Law No. 191 of 1993. The reform introduced a general reduction in tariff rates, with the exception of certain items. The following changes were also made:

- conversion from the Brussels Tariff nomenclature to the Harmonized System

- reduction in the number of tariff bands from 75 to 12 (0, 2, 4, 5, 10, 15, 20, 35, 40, 50, 80, and 100 percent)

- consolidation of the tariff schedule from 5,000 to 1,700 items

- application of ad valorem rates on 95 percent of import items.

Notwithstanding this progress, further reforms of the laws and official requirements need to be introduced. More also needs to be done to improve the efficiency of customs. Officials earn low salaries, and incentives and compensations are rarely linked to effort and productivity.

Registration, Documentation, and Customs Procedures

Registration, documentation, and customs procedures in Lebanon have undergone streamlining and simplification through computerization. Lebanese customs has launched a major rehabilitation program to modernize and streamline customs procedures. According to the new procedures, it normally takes only three or four steps and an average of four or five days for goods to be released from customs. (About 41 percent of goods now go through customs with no inspection at all, hence reducing the number of steps from four to three.)

NAJM has been implemented at the Port of Beirut and Beirut International Airport, covering close to 85 percent of customs volume. Remaining customs offices will be adopting this system by the second half of 2000. The adopted reforms have in fact reduced the discretion of officials greatly. Nevertheless, lack of incentives for employees and weak oversight measures have resulted in systemic corrupt behavior.[2] Once an importer has been assigned to a *Verificateur* and a Chief Inspector to inspect the goods and set the appropriate tariffs, it is impossible for an importer to request another *Verificateur* or a Chief Inspector in case of a dispute. This gives both the *Verificateur* and the Chief Inspector great power over the importer, and explains why both earn the larger portion of the bribes distributed to customs officials.

There is no effective channel to complain about the bureaucratic delay created by officials. In addition, a dispute between the Verificateur and the importer on the value of the goods imported is to be avoided, since otherwise an expert will be called upon to assess the goods. This will be very costly to the importer, since the expert, who is often a competitor, can do the following: request a fee of Lebanese pounds (L)50,000–150,000 (L1,500 = $1), or, although it is illegal, demand to check the actual price list of the goods, delay the release of the goods, or increase the value of the goods, hence forcing the importer to pay higher tariffs.

The interaction between grand corruption undertaken by high-level customs officials and petty corruption undertaken by low-level customs officials keeps the corrupt system intact. In fact, the low-level officials are left to their own devices within a certain margin to earn bribes and keep the customs running, whereas the high-level officials concentrate on the larger bribes of grand corruption. This consensual agreement between high and low levels officials is one of the main reasons for the persistence of the system.

Levies and Charges (Other than Import Duties)

As mentioned, the recent tariff reform resulted in the consolidation of import duties, municipality, and reconstruction fees into one tariff, as listed in the official tariff published by the Supreme Customs Council (SCC). The reform also specified that excise duties on certain items will be collected at the point of entry. Previously, excises were collected postentry, which rendered accounting and collection procedures more difficult. However, this consolidation may be reconsidered in the near future. In addition to the consolidated customs tariff fee, L50,000 is charged as a stamp duty on each customs transaction. "Unofficial" informal "facilitation" charges have been estimated at $500—1,150 per smaller shipment or per container.

Import Prohibitions and Licensing

All imports from Israel are prohibited. Government policies aimed at protecting the agricultural sector from competitive imports have been in place since the mid-1950s. These aimed at the protection of domestic production of fruits and vegetables from import competition through the Agricultural Calendar (AC). Under the AC, the import of many fresh fruits and vegetables, as well as processed foods (such as potato flour, frozen potatoes and fruits, olive oil, vinegar, and canned tomatoes) and animal products (milk, yogurt, eggs, and chickens) is banned.

It is up to the Cabinet, upon suggestion of the Minister of Agriculture, to ban or allow the import of any product, whether or not on the above list. The list is revised during the month of July of every year, upon the suggestions of the Minister of Agriculture and the Minister of Industry. Once ongoing studies and statistics concerning the imposition of customs duties for the benefit of local industry and for consumer protection are finalized, the ban on the above-mentioned items will be replaced by customs duties by cabinet decision upon the suggestion of the Minister of Agriculture.

Products of animal origin must be covered by a sanitary certificate issued by the appropriate health authorities of the country of origin saying that the products are free from disease. Live animals, whether intended for use in Lebanon or destined for transit shipment through Lebanon to another country, require sanitary certificates from the appropriate health authorities in the country of export, and should be legalized by Lebanese consular officials. A health certificate, as issued by the Department of Agriculture, must be presented to a consulate of Lebanon for legalization of all food products, frozen foods, live animals, and so forth. Finally, a "free sale" certificate must be issued for medical and pharmaceutical specialties and requires legalization by a consulate of Lebanon.

Import licenses and similar restrictions form significant nontariff barriers to trade. In fact, most of these apply annually to a limited value of traded items. Some exceptions are imports of certain agricultural products and of all seeds, which require a license, as do certain finished goods, such as sanitary ceramic ware, insulated electric and telephone wires, and cables made of copper. Also, medicines and surgical and dental instruments are admitted only under permit from the Ministry of Health in Lebanon. In total, 23 different types of import control permissions are issued by the state (Table 6.2).

A total of 42 government departments are involved in issuing import permissions, usually individually but sometimes with one or two other departments. In fact, the different permissions issued amount to 73, insofar as more than one government agency may issue the same type of permission, or the same agency may issue different permissions (Table 6.3). An example of more than one agency issuing the same type of permission would be the Ministries of Health and of Agriculture, respec-

TABLE 6.2. TYPES OF CONTROL MEASURES APPLIED

Control Code	
02	License
04	Advance License
05	Transport Permit
06	Transport Permit (Alcohol)
07	Certificate of Purity
08	Goods Subject to Monopoly
09	Invoice Certification
10	Visa
11	Permit
12	Advance Permit
14	Analysis and Production Certificate
15	Specialization Certificate
17	Alcohol Certificate
18	Sanitary certificate
19	Sanitary certificate or visa
20	Agricultural Sanitary Certificate
22	Laboratory Inspection Certificate
23	Certificate of origin
26	Agreement
27	Later Agreement
28	Advance Visa
29	Agricultural Calendar
30	Packing Requirements

tively, issuing an import license (control code 02). An example of one agency issuing more than one type of permission is the Ministry of Finance, issuing three different types of controls, Transport Permit (Alcohol), Goods Subject to Monopoly, and Alcohol Certificate. Over 1,250 commodities, ranging from the 4- to 8-digit level of the Harmonized System require import licenses or other special permission to enter Lebanon. In many instances, more than one authorization is needed.[3]

Standards and Other Technical Requirements
In Lebanon, sanitary and phytosanitary measures are established and administered by the Ministry of Agriculture's Direction of Plant Resources, in coordination with the Agricultural Research Institute of Lebanon. There are around 200 sanitary and phytosanitary measures in effect in the country. The institutional capabilities of the ministry are being upgraded to improve the control and the application of these measures. All imports of agricultural and animal products into Lebanon require the presentation of a sanitary certificate and a certificate of origin at the border. The Quarantine Department of the Ministry of Agriculture has the authority to forbid imports of any product not complying with the sanitary and phytosanitary regulations.

TABLE 6.3. CONTROL MEASURES BY GOVERNMENT ENTITY

Organization, department, etc.	Code
Council of Ministers—Industry Institute	10
Ministry of Interior	04
Ministry of Interior—Office for the Control of Printed Material	10
Ministry of Interior—Control of Narcotics	26, 27
Ministry of Finance	06, 08, 17
Ministry of Finance—Customs	17
Ministry of Finance—Indirect Taxes	05, 06
Ministry of Defense—General Directorate of the Army	04, 11
Ministry of Health	02, 10, 12
Ministry of Health—Office of the Minister	02, 12
Ministry of Health—Department of Sanitary Engineering	10
Ministry of Health—Department of Quarantine	07
Ministry of Health—Narcotics Unit	02
Ministry of Health—Department of Import/Export of Drugs	10, 11
Ministry of Health-—Department of Pharmaceutical Inspection	10
Ministry of Labor—Syndicate of Pharmacists	09
Ministry of Labor—Syndicates of Doctors	09
Ministry of Agriculture	02, 10, 18, 20, 29, 30
Ministry of Agriculture—Office of the Minister	02, 04, 12, 20, 23
Ministry of Agriculture—Office of the Minister/Inspection and Control	15
Ministry of Agriculture—Director General	02
Ministry of Agriculture—Department of Animal Resources	02, 10
Ministry of Agriculture—Animal Health Protection	18, 19, 23
Ministry of Agriculture—Health Protection	10, 14, 20, 22, 28
Ministry of Agriculture—Animal Breeding Unit	10
Ministry of Agriculture—Silk Office	12
Ministry of Economy and Trade	02
Ministry of Economy and Trade—Directorate for Price Policies	10
Ministry of Economy and Trade—Consumer Protection Department	10
Ministry of Economy and Trade—Anti-fraud Department	10
Ministry of Economy and Trade and Ministry of Posts/Telecommunications	11
Ministry of Economy and Trade, Ministry of Defense, and Council of Ministers	04
Ministry of Economy and Trade after approval of Ministry of Interior	02, 04
Ministry of Economy and Trade after approval of Ministry of Health	02
Ministry of Posts and Telecommunications	11, 12, 28
Ministry of Tourism—Directorate General for Antiquities	02
Ministry of Industry	02, 04, 10
Ministry of Industry—General Directorate of Industry	02
Ministry of Industry—General Directorate of Petroleum	02
Ministry of Environment	10

Standards and technical regulations in Lebanon are the responsibility of the Measures and Standards Organization (LIBNOR), which is the exclusive institution entrusted with the elaboration of standards and technical regulations. The Industrial Research Institute (IRI), an independent public institution, has the function of controlling the quality of goods to ensure that specifications conform to international export standards, and to control the conformity of imported products with national standards and technical regulations. Both LIBNOR and the IRI are currently in a process of rehabilitation and reinforcement. There are around 160 national standards in Lebanon, and the objective is to conform national regulations with Arab standards as provided by the relevant regional body in the context of the Arab League.

Lebanese customs regulations require that imported pharmaceutical products and foodstuffs bear specific labels containing the product's country of origin, and that labels on imported goods must not create any confusion with similar products or labels already protected in Lebanon. Violations of labeling requirements are sanctioned under Article 358 of the Lebanese Customs Code and can lead to the re-export of infringing products.

Technical controls for both imports and exports take about two to four days. Products subject to mandatory certification include canned vegetables, soups; jams, candies, honey, milk, and cheese; frozen or vacuum-packed meat or fish; canned meat; canned tuna; sardines; fats, oils, and butter; chocolate; pastas, and vermicelli; coffee and tea; sauces, dressings; flour, sugar, starch; prepared food, yeast, dough improver; food substitutes; canned fruits, powder for ice cream; juices; foodstuffs for human and animal consumption; disinfectants; soaps and detergents; hair spray, shampoo; diapers, napkins, sanitary towels; cosmetics, deodorants, perfumes; blades, shaving cream, toothpaste, and toothbrushes; mouth freshener, mouthwash products; and batteries for home use.

Saudi Arabia

The Kingdom of Saudi Arabia's efforts to join the WTO have led to the gradual adoption of a more liberal and open foreign trade regime. The kingdom has stated that it will remove all nontariff barriers that are against WTO rules. However, accession is not expected before the year 2000, and even then the removal of barriers may be slow. A tradition of state bureaucracy coupled with a rising trade deficit in recent years has sometimes complicated the dismantling of trade barriers and the introduction of other forms of liberalization. Although the trade balance is still in surplus, the excess of exports over imports will be too small to cover the deficit in the current account. From being in balance in 1997, the current account is projected to go into deficit in 1999 by $10 billion. In this context, Saudi Arabia will face a major challenge in opening its market widely to competition.

Saudi Arabia, along with Bahrain, Kuwait, Oman, Qatar, and the United Arab Emirates, is a member of the Gulf Cooperation Council (GCC), established for coordination and integration among its members in fields including economic and financial affairs, commerce, and customs. The GCC has made significant strides in efforts to rationalize and unify members' customs regimes and coordinate external trade policies. No customs duties exist on imports of domestic products from other GCC member states. Goods originating in GCC states are allowed duty-free entry, provided the producing firm is at least 51 percent owned by citizens of GCC member countries. Preferential duty treatment is also extended to some other members of the Arab League, including Egypt, Iraq, Jordan, Lebanon, Syria, and Yemen. This includes duty-free entry of certain nonindustrial goods and a 25 percent reduction in duty on some products. In addition, further duty reductions are accorded to imports from Arab states with which Saudi Arabia has concluded bilateral trade agreements: Jordan, Tunisia, Morocco, Lebanon, Syria, Yemen, and Egypt. Saudi Arabia also has a trade agreement with Canada aimed at promoting trade, and containing a most-favored-nation provision.

The National Industries Encouragement Act offers customs duty exemption on all imports for industrial establishments, including equipment, machinery, tools, spare parts, raw materials (primary or semimanufactured), and packing materials, including tins, bags, and cylinders. Concessions are awarded by the Ministry of Industry and Electricity (MoIE) on the recommendation of its Technical Industrial Bureau. The Foreign Capital Investment Act grants foreign capital the same concessions as national capital under the National Industries Encouragement Act. New and greatly changed investment laws are in the pipeline, and these should liberalize this process.

Registration, Documentation, and Customs Procedures

Although Saudi negotiations for WTO membership have resulted in changes in import procedures to bring them into line with WTO norms, customs procedures in Saudi Arabia are not transparent.

Every commercial establishment must register with the commercial registration office of the Ministry of Commerce (MoC) in one of the major cities in the kingdom. There are no substantive requirements to register with the MoC order to import. Any company, whether Saudi or foreign, that was commercially registered in the field of import trade could import goods without the need to get any further permission or authorization (except for items that require an import license).

Saudi Arabia has been implementing the Brussels Harmonized Commodity Description and Coding System since 1991. However, no facilities are available for advance rulings on customs classification. Commercial samples are subject to the payment of customs duty and surcharges either by a deposit equal to the duty at the time of import or by a bank guarantee. A refund is made if the goods are re-exported within 12 months. If the samples are sold, neither the deposit nor the guarantee will be refunded. Prior permission to import samples must be obtained from the director of customs. The request for permission to import must be accompanied by samples, prices, and catalogs. Advertising materials, excluding printed and illustrated calendars imported for display, may be imported duty free if the applicable duty is minimal. All catalogs and brochures for which no charge is made may be entered duty free. Goods may be entered temporarily for promotional purposes provided they include both an invoice with the value of the goods endorsed by the local chamber of commerce and a certificate of origin. Customs requires a refundable deposit of 12 or 20 percent, depending upon the type of goods.

Depending on the nature of exported goods to Saudi Arabia, or according to a request from the Saudi importer, certain special documents may be required. Importing arms for hunting and similar sports arms needs special permission. Books and publications are subject to inspection and approval by customs for entry. Agricultural seeds, live animals, fresh and frozen meat, periodicals, movies and tapes, religious literature and tapes, toxic chemicals and similar materials, pharmaceutical products, radio equipment, products containing alcohol (such as perfume), natural asphalt, and archaeological artifacts require special approval.

Requirements for labeling food and food products sold in Saudi Arabia are determined by the Saudi Arabian Standards Organization (SASO). Exporters of these products should comply with (among other SASO standards) Mandatory Standards SSA 1.1984, whether for sample demonstration or for commercial shipments, and must provide the following certificates:

- Food Manufacturer's Ingredients Certificate: The certificate should include a description of the exported food products (contents and percentage of each ingredient), chemical data, microbiological standards, storage, and life of product (date of manufacture and expiration). When products contain any animal fats, the certificate must confirm the kind of animal from which it is taken, or state that no pork is being used. This signed certificate must be obtained from the exporting country's Ministry of Health (MoH).

- Consumer Protection Certificate: The certificate confirms the healthiness of the various ingredients of food products imported into Saudi Arabia, and their safety and fitness for human consumption. The signed certificate must be obtained from an office of the exporting country's Ministry of Agriculture.

- Price list: The price list should be issued by the exporter on his letterhead, and it should indicate that the prices of the exported products to Saudi Arabia are the standard local market prices.

In addition to the general shipping documents, all meat or poultry shipments must be accompanied by a certificate of *Halal* meat, indicating that slaughtering has taken place in an officially licensed slaughterhouse according to Islamic procedures. The *Halal* meat certificate should be legalized by a recognized Islamic center in the exporting state.

An official health certificate is also required, indicating the date of slaughter, kind of animal, and average age of each shipment. The health certificate must also indicate that animals were examined within 12 hours of being slaughtered, and directly after, by a licensed veterinarian, and were found free from disease and suitable for human consumption. The health certificate is required for all exports to Saudi Arabia of all meats, (including poultry and seafood), meat products, livestock, vegetables, fruits, and human blood, attesting to the fact that they are free from pests and/or disease.

Imports of seed and grains must be accompanied by an authenticated certificate of inspection issued by a company specializing in seed inspection, a phytosanitary certificate (to verify that the seed or grain is free from agricultural disease), a seed analysis certificate (to prove the degree of purity of the seeds), and a certificate of weight.

Livestock imports require, in addition to general shipping documents, a certificate of weight, showing the average weight of the exported livestock; a health certificate from a Ministry of Agriculture verifying that the livestock are free from disease; a health certificate issued by a veterinarian; a pedigree certificate issued by a Ministry of Agriculture; production records; and a declaration of inspection and acceptance.

All shipments of vegetables and fruits to the kingdom require a radiation certificate certifying that shipments are free from pests, insects, and other agricultural diseases, and that they have not been exposed to ionizing radiation (but the shipments may have been treated with aluminum phosphide).

SASO certificates of conformity are required for electrical appliances, equipment, and accessories. There are two types of certificates: (a) the certificate of conformity for electrical appliances and equipment, and (b) the certificate of conformity for electrical accessories. The relevant certificate may be obtained from the Saudi consulate and must be issued by the manufacturer on their official letterhead, notarized by a notary public, certified by a local chamber of commerce, and then sent for verification to SASO in Riyadh at least two months before shipment date. Upon approval, the certificate will be returned to the manufacturing company, which must attach a stamped copy with each shipment to Saudi Arabia of the particular commodity. (Such premarket certification of consumer electronics and electrical appliances runs against international practice.)

At least three months before dispatching the first consignment of any type of motor vehicles in any year, the manufacturer must send to SASO a Motor Vehicles Conformity Certificate in English or Arabic for approval. Individuals must obtain the certificate from the manufacturer prior to shipment of any car for their personal use in the kingdom.

A certificate of free sale should accompany all shipments of pharmaceutical and medicinal products to Saudi Arabia and should be presented to a Saudi consulate with other documents. In addition, imports of pharmaceutical and medicinal products require a certificate issued by the exporter's MoH, stating that the medicines are actually used by the public in the exporting country under the same trade name and formula. The certificate must include the name of each product, the formula, and the date and number of the permit to manufacture them if one is required. No medicine or pharmaceutical products are admitted into the country unless a prior registration is made with the MoH. The ministry examines the applications, supported by the required certificates legalized by a Saudi consulate, and analyzes the samples to ensure that they conform to the specifications before granting a license.

Imports of plants, fruits, vegetables, seeds, live animals, and poultry must have the prior approval of the appropriate authorities and must be accompanied by a phytosanitary health certificate stating that they are free from pests and other diseases. All shipments of plants will be inspected upon arrival in Saudi Arabia.

Manufacturers and suppliers of carpets must indicate in Arabic the thickness or weight of each square meter, type, pile weight, and country of origin, to be applied on each five meters along the carpet roll length. All carpet manufacturers, suppliers, and distributors have to show the captioned data on the sales invoice. Importing used clothing requires an official disinfection certificate. These goods will be subject to inspection by quarantine officials.

The country of origin must be mentioned on all products imported, except when it is not feasible. All imports of "expensive" textile products are required to have the origin of the goods printed or stamped thereon indelibly. This requirement was introduced to protect consumers against deceptive practices. However, no precise Saudi definition of "expensive" exists, and this particular measure is nontransparent. A textile product is deemed to be expensive depending on an analysis of such factors as the quality, brand name, texture, design, and the price relative to other fabrics.

Levies and Charges (Other than Import Duties)
Imports are subject to a customs surcharge of 3.0 percent. Port fees per metric ton are levied on all goods exempt from import duty. There is also an inspection tax levied on all imports at the rate of up to 0.5 percent of the customs value of the goods, and the customs department collects a handling charge.

Import Prohibitions and Licensing
All imports from Israel are prohibited, as are imports of live pigs, pork meat and other pork products, frog legs, long-life pasteurized milk in packaging exceeding one liter (to be replaced with a tariff after accession to the WTO), nutmeg, opium and related drugs, alcoholic beverages, ethyl alcohol, and empty containers bearing marks or information on foodstuffs or cement or trademarks of the manufacturers, excluding those directly imported by companies for their own use. This last item is prohibited to ensure that it is not misused by packing deceptive goods, thus misleading the consumer. The restriction does not apply to state-owned firms.

Some items may be imported for legitimate purposes by government agencies for their own use and not for commercial sale. These include postage or revenue stamps, which can be imported only by government agencies, or parachutes, which can only be imported by the Ministry of Defense for its own use. The entry of some prohibited items may be allowed on a case-by-case basis, but information on goods permitted entry on this basis is not available.

The Ministry of Agriculture and Water (MoAW), MoC, Equestrian Club, MoH, Ministry of Interior (MoI), MoIE, and the Ministry of Posts, Telegraph and Telephone (MoPTT) are the main Saudi bodies with responsibilities concerning import license approval. Any individual or entity with a Commercial Registration may apply for an import license. There are no fees payable for obtaining an import license.

The MoC is responsible for issuance of import licenses for chemicals, petroleum, and asphalt imported by commercial importers, other than explosives and dangerous chemicals, which require approval from MoI and MoH. Chemicals imported by factories, as opposed to traders, require a license from the MoIE.

Each application requires three copies of the Commercial Registration of the importer, three copies of the invoice or pro forma invoice, and three copies of the form giving information about the place of storage and type of material, and explosive nature, if any. If the application is complete in all respects, an import license is issued the same day. A copy of the license is sent to the Customs Department at the port or airport of entry.

An importer wishing to import distillation equipment, used for producing distilled water by heating and condensation, is required to obtain an import license from the MoC. The importer is required to submit an application to the Deputy Minister of Commerce giving information on the technical specifications of the equipment, name and address of the manufacturer, necessity for the equipment in the field of activity, and place of installation of the equipment and the purpose of its use in detail. The application should be accompanied by a copy of the Commercial Registration of the importer, a copy of the purchase order, a copy of the invoice or pro forma invoice, and a detailed, printed catalog of the equipment. The application will be reviewed by the officials of the MoC, in particular the Director General of the Quality Control Department. If the ministry is satisfied that the import is for the stated use, it will be released. If the ministry is not satisfied, the importer will be so informed and given the reasons for refusal.

It takes on average two to three days to either issue the license or convey the refusal. In case of refusal, the importer can appeal to the Minister of Commerce. If the appeal is rejected by the Minister of Commerce, the importer can appeal to the Board of Grievances. There are no time frames fixed for the hearing of appeals or handing down of decisions. The Board of Grievances supplies written judgments to all parties to any appeal. Those judgments include the reasons for the decision. However, there is no legislation governing the appeal procedure of the Board of Grievances.

The MoIE has responsibility for issuing licenses for chemicals (other than explosives, dangerous chemicals, and chemicals requiring approval from the MoH) imported by factories. The import license requirement is to make sure the factory has satisfied the conditions of safe transport, handling, and storage of chemicals. The importing factory is required to submit an application to the MoIE giving information on the particulars of the factory, including its name, address, field of activity, and Commercial Registration; a copy of the invoice or pro forma invoice; detailed description of the chemicals to be imported, giving their name, specification, composition, quantity, and value (the quantity is limited to the requirement of the factory for one year).

If the chemicals to be imported by the factory are either explosives, dangerous, or those requiring approval from the MoH, the application is referred by the MoIE to the respective ministry. For other chemicals, if these are duty free they are cleared directly by the customs without an authorization from the MoIE. For dutiable chemicals, the MoIE issues a release order to the customs and gives a copy to the applicant. For chemicals falling in the last category above, the time taken by the MoIE is not more than two to three days. In many cases, the release order is issued the same day. All requests for import of chemicals, other than those requiring the approval of the MoI and MoH, are never rejected if all the documentation and information is complete.

Narcotics, psychotropics, and controlled substances for medical use; ethyl alcohol; chemicals the intermediary sales of which could lead to narcotics manufacturing; nonregistered medicines; biological and blood products; and other chemicals require a license from the MoH. The Directorate General of the MoH processes the application and issues a license.

An import license is required from the MoI for explosives and dangerous chemicals (Department of Weapons and Explosives of the ministry); radio and electronic equipment (Department of Public Security); TV-monitoring cameras and accessories, closed circuit television, and burglar or fire alarms (Department of Public Security); and high-quality photocopiers. To prevent misuse by criminals or terrorists, import licenses for these items are only issued to government enterprises and firms or individuals who have a contract with the government to supply such security devices from inside the kingdom or abroad. The MoI is the agency that determines whether the importer poses a security risk or not. The list of such items subject to import licensing is under review.

The MoPTT is responsible for authorizing imports of wireless sets and radio communication apparatus. The motivation for licensing is national security and rationalization of the use of frequencies. The importer is required to submit the name, address, and Commercial Registration of the importer; name and address of the ultimate user of the equipment; location and exact address of the place where the equipment will be used or installed; a copy of the purchase order; a copy of the invoice or pro forma invoice; a catalog of the equipment; and a detailed description of technical specifications of the equipment, including its conformity with International Telecommunications Union (ITU) and Saudi specifications.

Applications have to be made before effecting imports. The applications are processed by the Frequency Department and the Licensing Committee of the MoPTT. In the case of radio communication apparatus, it usually takes 1 to 2 months to decide on an application and to issue a license, while for network equipment it could take 6 to 12 months, depending on the peculiarities of each case and cooperation on the part of importers, end users, and suppliers.

Licenses are required for all agricultural machinery and equipment that is eligible for subsidies. Reasons for licensing are to ensure that the imports comply with the specifications approved by the MoAW, to determine the right subsidy, and provide the Saudi Agriculture Bank with the price and subsidy for each consignment. The import license is required even if the importer does not intend to apply for a subsidy payment. To get an import license, the importer must have a Commercial Registration; be an authorized dealer or agent; submit the catalog of the machinery, giving technical specifications, the price list, and the invoice price; have a certificate of origin for the machinery, specifying date of production; provide a report about the soils, crops, and climate that suits the use of such machinery; and have a one-year guarantee against any quality or production defect.

An import license will be issued to the importer for machinery and equipment that have been approved by the ministry, after the machinery has earlier undergone tests for its suitability. A committee consisting of agricultural and mechanical engineers tests the suitability of the imported machine. The period taken to issue the import license is between one to two weeks.

All varieties of seeds, transplants, chemical or organic fertilizers and soil enhancers, agricultural chemicals, pesticides, veterinary tests, and growth regulators require a license from the MoAW. The reason for requirement of import license is to ensure compliance with Saudi standards and specifications and to ensure that infected seeds and chemicals are not imported. To obtain an import license, the importer is required to submit an application including a copy of Commercial Registration; a copy of the invoice or pro forma invoice; exact description, specifications, and quantity to be imported; and literature on analyses or specifications of the goods. The application will be verified to ensure that the materials meet Saudi standards and specifications, and if so, a license will be issued. It takes one to two days to issue a license if all documentation is complete. The license is valid six months for fertilizers and soil improvers, seeds, and transplants, and three months for potato seeds. Imported pesticides must be registered with the MoAW, a process that takes one to two years.

The different average times to deliver a license are not determined by law or by a specific administrative order. Application review times, except for telecommunications, are under 30 days. Data on the proportion of Saudi imports subject to licensing are not available.

Standards and Other Technical Requirements

SASO is the sole body charged with the preparation, adoption, and application of standards for Saudi Arabia. Mandatory standards are applied to imports for the protection of health, safety, national security, public morals, and the environment and preventing deceptive practices. Procedures for assurance of import conformity to Saudi standards are enforced by the MoC.

SASO maintains an International Conformity Certification Program (ICCP) that relies on the private sector to inspect shipments for compliance verification in the exporting countries.[4] The ICCP is a *combined* conformity assessment, preshipment inspection, and certification scheme to regulate and monitor shipments of selected categories of products prior to their leaving their ports of exports before reaching Saudi Arabia (the program currently applies to 76 product categories divided into five groups: food and agriculture, electronics and electrical products, automobile and related products, chemical products, and others). A key element of the ICCP is that shipments are certified as being in conformity with SASO standards (or their approved equivalents) in their country of origin, ensuring both exporters and importers a streamlined customs process at the port of entry. An interesting aspect of the ICCP is that test data can be produced by nationally or internationally accredited laboratories approved by SASO, or by a manufacturer's declaration of conformity. At the conclusion of the SASO-approved laboratory testing, a Conformity Test and Evaluation Report is issued and submitted to the Regional Licensing Center for verification of conformity to SASO program requirements. SASO has contracted with an international firm to carry out certification of these activities. This firm is in turn assisted by a network of accredited testing laboratories and inspection bodies around the world.

Appropriate non-Saudi standards have been identified as the basis upon which products may be assessed, as well as the specific deviations that may apply. Saudi Arabia uses international standards except when they are found deficient because of the country's fundamental climatic and other factors. Examples are international standards that do not specify performance or testing of equipment apparatus or material at the high ambient temperatures prevalent in Saudi Arabia.

Saudi Arabia is a member of the International Organization for Standardization (ISO) and other international organizations. Certain Saudi standards have an ISO equivalent, which is indicated in the list of SASO standards. SASO refers most standards to technical committees; parties concerned with the subject matter of draft standards are normally represented on the relevant committees, including pertinent government, academic, industry, and trade sectors. Saudi-specific standards exist where the international ones would be an ineffective or not appropriate because of Saudi Arabian fundamental climatic, geographical, or technological problems, as allowed under international agreements. Shelf life standards for food products are developed by SASO. Saudi standards cover sanitary requirements for food products by means of measures following the standards and guidelines of *Codex Alimentarius* or, if not covered by the standards and guidelines of *Codex Alimentarius*, based upon scientific studies or other measures consistent with WTO practice.

All relevant international bodies are notified of all SASO standards. A high percentage of SASO standards uses international standards and other widely accepted national standards as references. About one-third of SASO standards cover food products predominantly using the *Codex Alimentarius* as a major reference.

A requirement for the marketing of food products is that at least half of shelf life validity remains on food products to allow for reasonable and adequate time for the distribution and marketing of these products throughout Saudi Arabia. Saudi shelf life for perishable food products is based on the assumption of a controlled storage temperature (by refrigeration or freezing) in accordance with internationally recognized norms. As for shelf-stable products, the main consideration for shelf life determination is the prevailing climatic conditions of Saudi Arabia. Saudi Arabia predominantly adopts the shelf life periods determined by the scientific studies of internationally recognized specialized institutes. In limited cases Saudi Arabia conducts the studies itself.

Shelf-stable products are normally stored under room or ambient temperature conditions. In the case of Saudi Arabia, shelf life determination for these products has to take into account the prevailing, high ambient temperatures in the country (averaging 33 degrees Celsius) and the wide temperature fluctuations between day and night and among seasons, not to mention the extreme variations in humidity. In contrast, shelf life for shelf-stable products determined by most food-exporting countries is based on an ambient storage temperature not exceeding 25 degrees Celsius. Thus, some of the time limits relating to shelf life in Saudi Arabia appear to be unduly short.

Sanitary and quarantine measures for animal health, living plants, and seeds, and measures for the prevention of epidemic diseases' spread and the control on the use of veterinary medicines and pesticides are administered by the MoAW, as well as the MoC and the Ministry of Municipalities (MoM). Standards for sanitary measures for food commodities (meat, meat products, and processed foods) are imposed by SASO but applied by the MoIE and MoC on locally made products, and by the MoC on imported products. The MoM participates in internal control of products in the markets that are mainly controlled by the MoC.

Saudi Arabian SPS measures conform to standard guidelines or recommendations issued by the bodies specifically designated by the WTO SPS Agreement, the *Codex Alimentarius* Commission, the International Office of Epizootics, and International Plant Protection Conventions. For SPS measures related to risk assessment and not covered by the above three international bodies (such as microbiological risks and shelf life of food products), Saudi Arabia relies on scientific studies, guidelines, and recommendations either carried out by itself in limited cases or by specialized, internationally accepted research institutes, universities, or scientific references.

There are no approved Saudi standards regarding maximum residue limits of hormones in food products. Most Saudi standards for meat and meat products only state that such products shall be free from synthetic hormones. Plant cuttings and seedlings imported into Saudi Arabia are subject to phytosanitary measures from the country of origin and visual inspection in the quarantine area. Saudi Arabia confirms that it will accept the certification of exporting countries, in accordance with the requirements under the WTO SPS Agreement. Where SPS measures are not found to be consistent with WTO practice, Saudi Arabia will ensure their consistency by the time of its accession.

Concluding Remarks

All three countries discussed above have made significant changes to their trade regimes in the 1990s. Tariffs have been consolidated with other fees and charges, the number of tariff bands has been reduced, and the average level of tariffs has fallen. The focus of discussion was on the nontariff dimensions of trade policy, reflecting the author's conviction that these are very important determinants of the incentive to engage in international trade. Much remains to be done by governments to reduce the administrative burdens encountered by traders in all three countries. Trade-related transactions costs remain high. Licensing requirements and related regulatory red tape, conformity assessment procedures for goods subject to mandatory product standards and technical regulations, direct controls on agricultural trade, and nontransparent and uncertain customs practices are all burdensome. Greater efforts to simplify and streamline procedures must be made. In Saudi Arabia in particular, although this is also true of Jordan, attempts have been made recently to enhance the image of the customs administration. Despite this, customs in both countries, as well as in Lebanon and part of the rest of the region, are basically nontransparent and inefficient.

Notes

1. Under the Investment Promotion Law No. 16 of 1995, projects in the following sectors may receive incentives, including customs and GST exemptions: industry, agriculture, hotels, hospitals, marine transport, railways, recreational resorts, convention and exhibition centers, or any other sector added by the Council of Ministers in accordance with the country's needs. The fixed assets of projects are exempted from taxes and fees within three years of their approval by the Investment Promotion Committee formed under this law. This period may be extended if the nature and size of the project require so. Spare parts imported for the project are exempted from taxes and fees, provided that their value does not exceed 15 percent of the value of the fixed assets that require these parts. The parts must be imported within 10 years from the production date after the Investment Promotion's Committee's approval of the spare parts to be imported The fixed assets needed to expand, develop, or modernize the project are exempted from fees and taxes, provided they increase the production capacity of the project by 25 percent or more. Hotel and hospital projects are granted extra exemptions from taxes and fees on their purchases of furniture and supplies for the purpose of renewal once every seven years. The furniture and supplies must be imported within four years of their being approved by the Investment Promotion Committee. Any increase in the value of imported fixed assets is exempted from taxes and fees if the increase results from the rise in prices, freight charges, or changes in exchange rates.

2. Corruption, while persistent in most other countries of the region, is more open in Lebanon, particularly in the lower echeslons of customs.

3. See al Khouri (1999) for a more detailed listing of licenses by issuing organization and commodity. Available on request from the author at MEBA@nets.com.jo.

4. This paragraph draws on Messerlin and Zarrouk (1999).

References

al Khouri, Riad. 1999. "A Survey of Non-Tariff Barriers in Selected Arab Countries." Middle East Business Associates, Amman. Unpublished paper.

Messerlin, Patrick, and Jamel Zarrouk. 1999 (forthcoming). "Trade Facilitation Technical Regulations and Customs Procedures." *The World Economy.*

Chapter 7

Para-Tariff Measures in Arab Countries[1]

Jamel Zarrouk
Arab Monetary Fund, Abu Dhabi, UAE
Economic Research Forum, Cairo

The purpose of this chapter is to shed some light on the general rules and principles for identifying para-tariffs and taxes with an effect equivalent to tariffs and to discuss collected information on the most common forms of para-tariff measures in Arab countries. The information on para-tariff measures used in this study has been derived from various sources, including the Arab Trade Information Network (IATIN) of the Program for Arab Trade Financing, the Trade Analysis and Information System (TRAINS) of the United Nations Conference on Trade and Development (UNCTAD), and various reports of the World Bank and World Trade Organization (WTO). In addition, the customs authorities in selected countries were also surveyed to verify the accuracy and maintenance of certain para-tariff measures. Last, in order to highlight the quantitative importance and incidence of para-tariffs on import costs in an Arab country, a questionnaire was filled out by a sample of importing firms in Egypt to indicate all import taxes and charges that they must frequently disburse.

Main GATT Rules and Practices in Identifying Para-Tariffs

In this section an attempt is made to define and describe para-tariffs in light of the GATT rules and the past discussions of the GATT Council involving the use of import surcharges by contracting parties.

The Nature of Tariffs and Other Taxes and Charges Applied to Imports

In general, taxes and charges levied on imported commodities may be classified into three main categories: tariffs, other taxes and charges on imports, and internal charges and taxes on Imports.

Tariffs are often calculated as ad valorem duties based on the CIF (cost, insurance, and freight) price. The CIF price coincides with the cost of the commodity at the port of entry. The applied ad valorem rates on imports are in general specified in the country's tariff schedule at the so-called tariff line corresponding to a specific commodity or group of commodities. National tariff schedules (statutory tariffs) are published in the Official Gazette, in accordance with the customs laws in force.

Other charges and taxes on imports are border charges and taxes complementing customs tariffs. These are collected in return for services rendered to importers and exporters. Examples include charges for legalizing certificates of origin and importation invoices, port services charges (unloading, storage, and so forth), and charges for inspection of goods.

Internal charges and taxes are levied on both domestic and imported products. Examples of internal taxes with a broad consumption base include the sales tax, the value-added tax (VAT), and the consumption tax. Nevertheless, as will be discussed later, internal taxes on imports may be collected in a discriminating fashion on domestic and imported goods. In this case, the internal tax is considered to have an effect equivalent to tariffs.

Definition of Para-tariffs on Imports

Para-tariffs fall within the category of import surcharges and taxes as well as internal charges and taxes. These are considered as additional charges and taxes not directly related to services rendered in import-export transactions. An Internal tax or charge may also be considered a para-tariff if it is collected on imported goods but not on goods locally produced, or is calculated in a discriminatory way compared with those applied to locally produced goods for the government to raise revenues, protect domestic producers from foreign competition, or other reasons. Para-tariffs are levied under various names through various laws and regulations issued by government agencies that are different in their activities, nature, and objectives. Methods of calculating para-tariffs vary according to the nature of goods imported and the purposes that the government concerned is striving to achieve.

Impact of Para-tariffs

Para-tariffs play a similar role to that of customs tariffs in that they aim at protecting products of national origin and generating revenues for the state treasury or addressing difficulties in its balance of payments. Para-tariffs have an effect similar to that of tariffs on import cost, but the magnitude of para-tariffs' impact is stronger. While ad valorem duties are calculated as a constant proportion of the value of the imported goods, many forms of para-tariffs tend to be much less transparent than tariffs. Para-tariff measures discriminate against imports and the customs valuation through decreed prices (which might be higher than the real value). In addition, para-tariffs raise the price of imports directly and restrict imports indirectly.

GATT Provisions for Para-tariffs

Despite the practical complexities of identifying the forms of para-tariffs in the import taxes structure of individual countries, general rules and principles for identifying such charges and ways of removing or reducing them in the context of a multilateral trade liberalization process have been established. The main GATT Articles and practices emanating from GATT Council decisions for applying the said rules are presented and briefly discussed below.

Article II (2c) and Article VIII (1-a) of the GATT stipulate that a

> State desiring to levy charges and taxes on imports or exports in addition to customs duties shall collect such charges or taxes [only] in return for specific services rendered and that these shall be computed on the basis of actual cost of services rendered in the conduct of a commercial transaction (be it an importation or exportation transaction). The GATT prohibits party-states from imposing additional charges or taxes on imports in any other form for the purpose of protecting national products or collecting additional revenues for the State treasury in an indirect manner.

Article VIII (a), (f), and (c) of the GATT call upon states to reduce the number of additional charges and taxes they impose, making them limited to the number of direct services rendered to importation or exportation activities. Among the examples on charges related to commercial transactions subject to the above-mentioned rules are charges for port services, inspection of goods, and certification.

Additional charges levied on imports on the basis of actual cost of services rendered entail abstaining from computing them as ad valorem, that is, in percentage of the import price. In this case, such surcharges will have an effect equivalent to tariffs and will consequently be considered an integral part of the customs duties.

Article III (2) of the GATT stipulates the application of the principle of national treatment in imposing internal charges and taxes on imports at rates and amounts applied to like domestic products. However, the existence of differences in the rates of internal taxes applied to domestic products and like imported products is considered a violation of the principle of national treatment. Moreover, the imposition of some internal charges and taxes on imports, while exempting like national products, is also considered a violation of the principle of national treatment.

The Executive Program for establishing the Pan-Arab Free Trade Area (PAFTA) calls in its Article 1 (4) for granting goods of Arab origin national treatment in respect of internal charges and taxes.

The GATT permits the use of para-tariffs and taxes on dumped imports that cause material injury to domestic industry or whenever it is proven that a foreign state is subsidizing its exporters and this damages producers in the importer state concerned. Finally, the GATT permits the use of para-tariffs justified on balance of payments grounds. In this case, temporary measures can be used to restrict imports, such as the imposition of additional surcharges on imports. The country concerned must specify the period in which import surcharges and taxes will be used, and is required to hold periodic consultations with the WTO and the International Monetary Fund (IMF) to gradually reduce such charges and taxes and eliminate them in line with the balance of payments improvement. It should be noted that countries that use para-tariffs under all the above situations may not simultaneously use quantitative restrictions. One or the other instrument must be chosen to address a deterioration in the balance of payments.

Classifying Para-tariffs

The most common forms of para-tariffs in Arab countries can be classified into three main categories: "service" charges affecting importers, "special" import taxes and charges complementing tariffs, and internal taxes on imports.

"Service" charges affecting importers: Although such charges are levied on imported goods in return for specific services, they become para-tariffs if the collected charges exceed the actual cost of such services. For example, computing the charges for the service rendered as an ad valorem rate (a percent of the value of imports) is a violation of GATT rules; consequently, a charge computed on this basis becomes part of customs duties. This category includes stamp taxes and consular fees calculated as a percentage of the invoice price of imported goods, or where the charges increase progressively with the import value. Other "service fees" may be maintained without having a direct relationship with the service provided to importers in as much as they are maintained in the general public interest. For example, importers are charged for veterinary fees and phytosanitary control fees, both of which serve the public health of consumers, and customs statistics fees, which also serve the general interest of the country.

"Special" import taxes complementing customs tariffs: These are import taxes collected without any services rendered in return. Included in this category are additional import taxes that may be imposed to support a country's economic and social development programs, to make up for shortfalls in revenues of the state treasury, or to address balance of payments difficulties, in addition to additional import taxes imposed as antidumping and countervailing duties. In general, "special" import taxes are temporarily levied and then removed when the situation calling for their imposition improves.

Internal taxes and charges violating national treatment: These are internal charges and taxes on imports, such as the sales tax or the VAT, that exceed those levied on domestic-like products, or an internal tax that is calculated in a manner different from that applied to the similar domestic products. Note that when a sales tax is levied on the basis of the value of an imported product inclusive of any tariffs, the sales tax accordingly increases the protective effect of tariffs.

Collected Data on Para-tariffs in Arab Countries

This section presents data on the most common para-tariffs maintained in Arab countries, using the previously described groups of charges and taxes to classify them. A brief discussion of the main characteristics of such charges and taxes follows. Four Arab countries (Saudi Arabia, Qatar, Bahrain, and Kuwait) were found not to levy para-tariffs.

Scope and Coverage of Para-tariffs by Surveyed Country

JORDAN

- "Service" charges affecting importers:
  - Fees for customs overtime wages are levied on all goods at 0.2 percent of the CIF value of imports and 0.1 percent of the value of exports.
  - Legalization charges of JD2 for certifying import invoices and certificates of origin and their attachments are levied on FOB value of imports ranging between JD1,000 and JD10,000. The certification fee is JD20 for FOB imports value exceeding JD10,000.
  - Additional specific duties are expressed as a fixed monetary amount per physical unit of the product imported, as shown in Table 7.1.

- "Special" import taxes complementing tariffs: none.

- Internal taxes or charges violating the national treatment of imports: Sales taxes of 10 and 20 percent of the CIF import value plus customs tariff and other customs duties are charged. Sales tax is levied on both locally manufactured and imported goods, except for staples (wheat, corn, sugar, gas, agricultural machines and equipment, and medications).

UNITED ARAB EMIRATES

- "Service" charges affecting importers: none.

- "Special" import taxes complementing tariffs: Surcharges are levied on imported tobacco and its derivatives, expressed as a fixed monetary amount per ton of the imported quantity. This is in addition to the high tariffs levied on tobacco and cigarettes at 80 percent of the CIF value (as of July 1, 1998).

- Internal taxes or charges violating the national treatment of imports: none.

TABLE 7.1. MAJOR SPECIFIC DUTIES AND TAXES APPLIED IN JORDAN

Specific duties and taxes	Method of calculation	Percentage or lump sum	Agency for whose account charge is collected	Nature of imported commodity subject to the surcharge
Surcharge on flammables	Percentage of CIF value	n.a.	Ministry of Municipal Affairs; Ministry of Finance	Gas and diesel oil
Surcharge on tobacco for farmers' assistance	Percentage of CIF value	n.a.	Ministry of Agriculture	Raw tobacco
Veterinary charges	Per head	20 fils	Ministry of Agriculture	Sheep
Customs duties on sheep[a]	Per head	JD5	Ministry of Finance	Sheep
Agricultural quarantine charge	Per ton	250 fils	Ministry of Agriculture	Vegetables and fruits
Head count tax	Per head	n.a.	Ministry of Agriculture	Sheep
Culture tax	Percentage of CIF value	n..a.	Ministry of Information	All audio and video tapes and magazines
Excess load charges	Per ton	n.a.	Ministry of Transport	Bulky goods transported by road
Traffic Department charges	Per period of stay	n.a.	Traffic Department	Foreign cars, by number of cylinders
Road passage charges	Per period of stay	n.a.	Ministry of Transport	Foreign trucks and lorries

a.   Imported sheep are subject to duties as a fixed amount per head. They are exempted from tariffs.
n.a. = not available
Source: Survey by author.

TUNISIA

- "Service" charges affecting importers:
  - "Services" charges (Redevance de Prestations Douanières) are levied at the rate of 3 percent of the total amount of collected tariffs and other import taxes or charges. If the good is exempted from tariffs, a fee of TD 5 per each section of the customs declaration is charged.
  - A computer data word-processing fee of TD2 per each page of customs declaration is charged.

- "Special" import taxes complementing tariffs: The FODEC tax (duty to assist the Fonds de Développement de la Compétitivité) is levied at the rate of 1 percent of the CIF value of imported goods that compete with similar local products.

- Internal taxes or charges violating the national treatment of imports:
    - Consumption tax is levied on imported goods and goods produced locally. This tax is computed only on the basis of CIF import value and ranges between 11 and 470 percent (luxurious passenger cars). However, the rate of 90 percent is applied to the majority of the goods subject to this tax.
    - VAT, which is levied on both imports and locally made products, consists of four different rates: 6 percent, 10 percent, 18 percent, and 29 percent. This tax is levied on the CIF import value plus the customs tariff and the FODEC tax, as well as the consumption tax, if applicable.

SUDAN

- "Service" charges affecting importers: not known.

- "Special" import taxes complementing tariffs:
    - Defense tax is collected at the rate of 4 percent of the CIF value of all goods except staples.
    - Business profit tax is collected at the rate of 5 percent of the CIF import value plus the customs tariff and other customs duties. This tax is levied on imported goods competing with locally produced ones.
    - Consumption tax is collected at the rate of 10 percent of the CIF import value plus the customs tariff and other customs duties. This tax is levied on consumer goods, including footwear, tobacco, soaps, and processed foodstuffs.

- Internal taxes or charges violating the national treatment of imports: not known.

IRAQ

- "Service" charges affecting importers: not known.

- "Special" import taxes complementing tariffs: Import charges to assist exports are collected at the rate of 0.5 percent of the CIF import value of capital goods and 0.75 percent of the CIF value of consumer goods.

- Internal taxes or charges violating the national treatment of imports: not known.

SYRIA

- "Service" charges affecting importers:
  - Import license fees are collected at the rate of 2 percent of the CIF value of all imported goods, except for imports by the public sector.
  - Consular fees for certifying all import invoices to Syria are collected. These fees are a function of the import value. They start with a minimum of 4 percent on the first S£1,000, then 3 percent on the next S£1,000 and 0.4 percent on all amounts exceeding the first S£2,000. The collected consular fees differ by country of shipment. For instance, consular fees for legalizing commercial documents by the Syrian Embassy in Washington, D.C., for shipments bound for Syria from the United States, start from a monetary amount of $5 for imports values ranging between $1 and $100, and rise to as much as $606 for CIF import values that exceed $150,000.

- "Special" import taxes complementing tariffs: Additional import taxes are levied on all imported goods. These are calculated as a percentage of the CIF value of imports. The rates are progressive with the ad valorem tariff rates. They range from 6 percent to 35 percent and comprise 24 band rates. For example, an additional import tax of 12 percent is collected on the CIF import value subject to tariff rates ranging between 3 percent and 6 percent. It increases to 14 percent for import values subject to ad valorem tariff rate ranging between 12 percent and 18 percent, and so forth. (The Syrian authorities have announced that the complementary import taxes and the ad valorem tariff rates were merged into unified ad valorem rates starting in 1999).

- Internal taxes or charges violating the national treatment of imports: not known.

LEBANON

- "Service" charges affecting importers:
  - Additional customs duties are levied on imported cars at 20 percent for the first L£25 million of the CIF value, and 35 percent for the balance of the CIF value of the imported car.
  - Specific duties are collected on alcoholic beverages and beer.
  - Stamp fees are levied on all imports at the rate of L£3 per each L£1,000 of the CIF imported value.

- "Special" import taxes complementing tariffs: not known.

- Internal taxes or charges violating the national treatment of imports: not known.

LIBYA

- "Service" charges affecting importers: not known.

- "Special" import taxes complementing tariffs:
    - An additional import tax, the "Artificial River Tax," is levied at the rate of 15 percent of the CIF import value. This tax is paid upon opening a letter of credit by the importer with his local bank. Imported products that are exempted from this tax are medications, staples, processed food products, and imports financed from the state treasury.

- Internal taxes or charges violating the national treatment of imports: not known.

EGYPT

- "Service" charges affecting importers:
    - The customs statistical tax, a flat fee of 1 percent of the FOB value of imports, is levied on all imports for services provided by customs.
    - The customs surcharge is collected at a rate of 2 or 3 percent of the import value of goods subject to ad valorem tariff rates between 5 percent and 29 percent or 30 percent and above, respectively.
    - X-ray (sic), health, and food control charges are levied on foodstuffs at the amount of $1 per ton.
    - Certification and stamp duties are collected progressively with the imported value.

- "Special" import taxes complementing tariffs: A specific surcharge to control standards and quality of exports is levied on imported goods and expressed as $7.30 per ton (25£E per ton).

- Internal taxes or charges violating the national treatment of imports:
    - The general sales tax (GST) levies two rates of 5 percent and 25 percent for imported and locally produced goods. The GST applies to the CIF import value plus tariffs and other customs charges.
    - Essential commodities such as basic foodstuffs are exempt from the sales tax, as are newsprint, papers, and magazines and some pharrmaceuticals.

–   "Income" tax of 1 percent on the CIF import value plus tariffs and other customs duties is levied. This tax is withheld as an advance deposit for income tax on the importer's income.

MOROCCO

- "Service" charges affecting importers: A para-fiscal tax (*taxe para-fiscale*) is collected at the rate of 0.25 percent of the CIF import value and levied on all imported goods, except those exempted from or subject to minimum customs tariffs. This tax is collected to assist standards and quality inspections of export-oriented goods, the Moroccan crafts industry, the Moroccan Center for Export Promotion, and the Industrial Development Council.

- "Special" import taxes complementing tariffs:
  - Fiscal withholding on imports (*prélèvement fiscale à l'importation*) is levied at the rate of 15 percent of the CIF import value plus the customs tariffs.
  - Specific import duties on timber (except wooden manufactured articles) are levied at the rate of 6 percent on the CIF import value plus tariffs and other customs duties as well as the fiscal withholding import tax.

- Internal taxes or charges violating the national treatment of imports:
  - VAT is levied on both imported and locally manufactured goods. This tax comprises five rates: 0 percent granted to certain foodstuffs; 7 percent levied on the consumption of electricity, water, medications, petroleum products, table oils, medical services, legal services, and bank and other financial services; 10 percent levied on imports of sugar and other derivatives; 14 percent levied on transport; and 20 percent levied on some other goods. The VAT levied on imports is calculated on the basis of the CIF value plus tariffs plus the fiscal withholding and other customs duties and charges.
  - Consumption tax is levied as a specific duty as follows:
    » surchages on imported alcoholic beverages, wines, and beer at the amount of Dh5 per 100 liters
    » surcharges on imported sugar and artificial sweetener (duty not known)
    » surcharges on imported rubber sheets, pneumatic tubes, and wheel tires (duty not known)
    » charges on the consumption of fuels and other energy products (duty not known)
    » charges for assaying and assuring gold, silver, an platinum con tents (duty not known).

Overall Assessment of Para-tariffs in Arab Countries

Virtually all the surveyed Arab countries have been found to use para-tariffs on imports, except for Bahrain, Saudi Arabia, Qatar, and Kuwait. Moreover, numerous para-tariffs lack transparency and are often disguised forms of trade tax, having an effect equivalent to tariffs. Detailed data on specific surcharges—that is, expressed as a monetary amount or a physical unit of the imported good—are not available in most of the surveyed countries. According to the aforementioned classification of para-tariffs, there are six countries that have been known to have used the first category of "'service' charges affecting importers." These surcharges vary widely in their forms and ad valorem incidence on import costs. Moreover, many of this form of para-tariffs are not directly related to import transactions—for example, the roadway passage fee and traffic administration fee in Jordan. In addition, numerous "service" charges affecting importers do not reflect the actual cost of services rendered to traders. In many cases, they are levied as ad valorem duties or expressed as progressive monetary amounts per the imported values. Illustrative examples are the consular certification fees and customs "services" statisitical fees.

The second category of para-tariffs is "'special' import taxes complementing tariffs." They are used by five countries for numerous purposes, either to address shortfalls in treasury revenues (fiscal withholding on imports in Morocco) or for assistance to economic and social development projects, such as the defense tax used in Sudan and the "Artificial River Tax" used in Libya (Table 7.2).

Finally, the third category of para-tariffs is "internal taxes or charges violating the national treatment of imports." Available information on this category indicates notable differences in the methods of determining the base for calculating internal taxes on imports. Table 7.3 shows that Arab countries that impose internal taxes—such as sales tax (Jordan and Egypt), the VAT (Tunisia and Morocco), or the consumption tax (Tunisia and Morocco)—levy such taxes on imported goods on the basis of import value plus tariffs and other surcharges and taxes. Note that when such internal taxes are levied on the basis of the value of an imported product inclu-

TABLE 7.2. "SPECIAL" IMPORT TAXES COMPLEMENTING TARIFFS AS KNOWN IN SOME ARAB COUNTRIES

Country	Nature of tax	Ad valorem rate (%)	Tax base
Tunisia	Fonds de Développement de la Compétitivité	1	CIF value
Sudan	Defense tax	4	CIF value
Syria[a]	General import tax	6–35	CIF value
Libya	Artificial River Tax	15	CIF value
Morocco	Prélèvement fiscal à l'importation	15	CIF value + customs tariff

a. This tax has been unified with the customs tariff rates as of early 1999.

TABLE 7.3. INTERNAL TAXES OR CHARGES ON IMPORTS IN SELECTED ARAB
COUNTRIES

Country	Nature of tax	Applied rates (%)	Tax base
Jordan	Sales	0, 10, 20	CIF value + customs tariff and other customs duties
Tunisia	VAT	0, 6, 10, 18, 29	CIF value + customs tariff + competitiveness promotion tax (if applied) + consumption tax
	Consumption	11–470	CIF value
Egypt	Sales	0, 5, 25	FOB value + customs tariffs + customs services charges + other customs duties
Morocco	VAT	0, 7, 10, 14, 20	CIF value + customs tariff + fiscal withholding tax + specific consumption tax
	Consumption	Variable according to the nature of imported goods	CIF value

sive of any tariffs or surcharges, this internal tax accordingly increases the protective effect of tariffs and weakens the national treatment principle.

Illustrative Examples of the Impact of Para-tariffs on Import Cost

To quantify the relative importance of para-tariffs on import cost in one Arab country, importers in Egypt were surveyed through a questionnaire on the taxes and charges that they must disburse for imports of selected prodcuts: a primary product (for example, apples), a semiprocessed good (for example, industrial chemicals [resins]), and a finished good (for example, silk ties).

Questionnaire returns (Table 7.4) indicate that the ad valorem incidence of para-tariffs on import cost is estimated between 5.5 percent and 5.7 percent of the FOB import value. The main forms of para-tariffs in Egypt are "service" charges affecting importers. These include X-rays, health, and food control fees and customs statistical fees. The GST as an internal tax is assessed on the basis of the final value of imports, which is the CIF value plus all the import taxes (that is, tariffs and para-tariffs). Such a valuation procedure increases the protective effect of tariffs against imported goods. Overall, this finding shows that the most binding constraints in import cost for Egyptian importers are high tariffs, which rank first, followed by freight and transportation costs.

Although the estimates on para-tariffs in Egypt show that they are relatively low as compared with the applied ad valoren tariff rates, para-tariffs increase the

TABLE 7.4. EGYPT: MAIN TAXES AND CHARGES LEVIED ON IMPORTS OF SELECTED PRODUCTS

	Agricultural products (apples)		Industrial chemicals (resins)		Finished products (ties)	
	Value (US$)	Rate (%)	Value (US$)	Rate (%)	Value (US$)	Rate (%)
Value (FOB) (=100)	100.00	([a])	100.00	n.a.	100.00	n.a.
Freight (on FOB value)	30.00	([b])	10.00	([b])	6.00	([b])
Insurance (on FOB value)	1.00	n.a.	1.00	n.a.	1.00	n.a.
CIF value (= items 1+2+3)	131.00	n.a.	111.00	n.a.	107.00	n.a.
Import duty (on CIF value)	52.40	40	11.10	10	57.78	54
Subtotal (items 4+5)	183.40	n.a.	122.10	n.a.	164.78	n.a.
Customs statistics charge (on FOB value)	1.00	1	1.00	1	1.00	1
Other customs surcharges (on FOB value)	3.00	3	3.00	3	3.00	3
X-rays, health, and food control charge (on FOB value)	0.20	([c])	n.a.	n.a.	n.a.	n.a.
Standards and quality control of exports charge (on FOB value)	1.50	([d])	1.50	([d])	1.50	([d])
Other (consular fees, cost of letter of credit) (on FOB value)	2.00	2	2.00	2	2.00	2
Port charges	2.00	([e])	2.00	([e])	2.00	([e])
Final value of imports	193.10		131.60	n.a.	174.28	n.a.
GST(on port charges)	0	Exempt	6.58	5	43.57	25
Whole sales cost	193.10	n.a.	138.18	n.a.	217.85	n.a.
Memorandum						
Ratio of para-tariffs (to FOB value)		5.7		5.5		5.5
Ratio of port charges (to FOB value)		2.0		2.0		2.0

n.a. Not applicable.
a. A single import shipment of 200 tons and (FOB) value of US$100,000 is assumed for imports of apples. The estimated (FOB) values were converted to 100 units for illustration purposes.
b. Freight via refrigerated trucks (for apples), via sea (for industrial chemicals), via air (for ties).
c. X-rays, health, and food control charges are levied for an amount of US$1 per ton.
d. Standards and quality control of exports charges are levied for the amount of $7.30 per ton (£E25 per ton).
e. Port charges are estimated for around US$ 10 per ton or 2 percent of FOB value.
Source: Survey by author.

effective rate of duty collection for Egypt to about 10 percent of the average tariff rate. Another element that may increase import cost through the imposition of para-tariff charges is the lack of transparency of these charges as well as their valuation procedures in numerous Arab countries.

Summary and Recommendations

Para-tariffs can be classified into three main categories: "service" charges affecting importers, "special" import taxes complementing tariffs, and internal taxes or charges violating the national treatment of imports.

A survey of 10 Arab countries was conducted to identify para-tariffs and their implications for import costs. The collected information indicates that with respect to "services" charges affecting importers, these are often higher than the actual cost of the service rendered. As far as import taxes complementing tariffs are concerned, these are found to be de facto customs duties in some countries but are kept separately via the procedural and legal bases on which they haved been imposed. Finally, internal taxes and charges that are violating the national treatment of imports have been tracked in the surveyed Arab countries in the form of stricter valuation procedures than those applied to domestically produced goods. Countries that apply broad-based consumption taxes (sales tax or VAT) calculate internal taxes on the basis of the CIF import value plus the other customs duties and surcharges, thereby increasing the protective effect of tariffs against imported goods.

In light of this, it can be said that liberalizing intraregional trade among Arab countries in the framework of the Executive Program establishing the Pan-Arab Free Trade Area (PAFTA) requires further efforts from the member countries to implement a number of measures:

- There is a need for Arab countries signatory to the PAFTA to disclose all para-tariffs and also their methods of calculation. Making information on all para-tariffs available to traders will help significantly to better predict trade cost and, overall, enhance the credibility of government trade policy reforms in the private sector.

- Arab countries that currently use service charges affecting importers should pledge to link the actual cost to service rendered. Other service charges levied without corresponding service directly related to import transactions should be removed.

- Special import taxes complementing tariffs, if any, should be consolidated and unified with national tariff schedules in order to be subjected to the tariff reductions.

- To grant full national treatment to intra-PAFTA imported goods, an agreement should be reached in the context of PAFTA on unifying the base for calculating internal taxes on imported goods. In this connection, a recommendation would be that internal taxes imposed on intra-PAFTA imports— for example, VAT or sales taxes—be calculated on the basis of the CIF import value only, that is, excluding tariffs and the other customs duties from the tax base of the imported value.

Note

1. The views expressed here and the included information are solely the responsibility of the author and should not be attributed to the Arab Monetary Fund or the Economic Research Forum.

Bibliography

Arab Trade Finance Program. 1998. IATIN database, iatinhq@emirates.net.ae.

GATT. 1965, May 25. "The Use of Import Surcharges by Contracting Parties." Note by the Secretariat, Document No. COM.TD/F/W/3. Geneva.

GATT. 1969, March. *The Text of the General Agreement on Tariffs and Trade 1947.* Geneva.

Hoekman, B. 1998. "The WTO, the EU, and the Arab World: Trade Policy Priorities and Pitfalls." In Nemaat Shafik, ed., *Prospects for Middle Eastern and North African Economies: From Boom to Bust and Back?* London: Macmillan.

Hoekman, B., and S. Djankov. 1997. "Effective Protection and Investment Incentives in Egypt and Jordan During the Transition to Free Trade with Europe." *World Development* 25(2):281–91.

Kostecki, M. M., and M. J. Tymowski. 1985. "Customs Duties versus Other Import Charges in the Developing Countries." *Journal of World Trade Law* 19(2):269–86.

League of Arab States. 1997. "Executive Programme of the Agreement on Facilitating and Developing Intra-Arab Trade for Establishing the Greater Arab Free Trade Area (GAFTA)." Secretariat of the Arab League, Directorate of Economic Affairs, Cairo.

UNCTAD. 1997. *Database on Trade Control Measures (TCMs).* Geneva.

World Trade Organization. 1995a. *The Results of the Uruguay Round of Multilateral Trade Negotiations, The Legal Texts.* Geneva.

———. 1995b. *Trade Policy Review: Tunisia.* Geneva.

————. 1996a. *Trade Policy Review: Kingdom of Morocco*. Geneva.

————. 1996b. *Working Parties' Memorandum on Saudi Arabia and Jordan*.

————. 1999. *Trade Policy Review: Egypt*. Geneva.

Zarrouk, Jamel. 1992. "Intra-trade: Determinants and Prospects for Expansion." In Said El-Naggar, ed., *Foreign and Intra-trade Policies of the Arab Countries*. Washington, D.C.: International Monetary Fund.

————. (Forthcoming). "Greater Arab Free Trade Area: Limits and Possibilities." In Bernard Hoekman and Jamel Zarrouk, eds., *Catching Up with the Competition: Trade and Global Integration in the Middle East and North Africa*. Studies in International Economics. Ann Arbor: University of Michigan Press.

Chapter 8

Trade Liberalization and Tax Reform in the Southern Mediterranean Region[1]

George T. Abed
International Monetary Fund

Association agreements have been signed with the European Union (EU) by Israel, Jordan, Morocco, and Tunisia, and are under discussion with Algeria, Egypt, and Lebanon. The agreements seek to establish, by the end of a 12-year transition period, a free trade area for industrial products. Detailed discussions of the broader Euro-Mediterranean Initiative under which the agreements have been negotiated have been presented by others (see, for example, Havrylyshyn 1997, August, Nsouli and others 1996, and Nabli 1996). This chapter adopts a narrower focus: it examines the impact of tariff reductions on budgetary revenue in the Southern Mediterranean Region (SMR) and assesses these countries' progress in implementing domestic tax reforms. These reforms are intended to help these countries compensate for the loss of tariff revenue and, more generally, to adjust to a more competitive environment of closer integration with the EU.

The principal economic provisions of the agreements include the elimination of any remaining restrictions maintained by the EU on the SMR countries' exports of industrial products, the gradual elimination (over a 12-year period) of all tariffs on industrial imports from the EU, the immediate removal of all quantitative restrictions, and the harmonization of policies and regulations concerning competition, intellectual property, and industrial standards. The agreements also grant marginally better access to the SMR countries' agricultural exports, and provide for a review of agricultural access no later than the year 2000. During the first four years under the agreements, tariffs on lightly taxed imports (for example, raw materials and capital goods) will be reduced or eliminated, followed by a gradual lifting of tariffs on other imports. The phasing of tariff elimination will take into account the extent to which such imports compete with domestic production. The signatory countries are also to receive financial assistance in the form of structural adjustment grants (from the EU) and loans (from the European Investment Bank).

Given the large share of the SMR countries' trade with the EU and the relatively high initial effective tariff rates (see below), the complete elimination of all tariffs (and other charges with equivalent effect) on all EU imports will represent a radical change in the trade regimes of these countries. The economic effects would probably be greater if the SMR countries were to pursue similar liberalization with non-EU countries in order to avoid the adverse effects of trade diversion.

Some SMR countries have pointed out some less desirable features of the agreements, such as the "hub-and-spoke" problem,[2] limited EU access for the SMR's agricultural exports, and the restricted application of the rules of origin. Nevertheless, the long-run, dynamic effects of this type of trade liberalization are widely recognized as important and generally positive, although any *quantitative* estimates of such benefits remains highly tentative. Given comparable experience elsewhere,[3] the SMR economies are likely to reap efficiency gains as they respond to the more Darwinian environment of global competition, from improved prospects for "deeper integration" with the EU (for example, harmonization of standards and market regulations, possible liberalization of financial and other services), and from improved opportunities for the transfer and development of new skills and technology. Under certain conditions, foreign direct investment in the SMR could also increase significantly; however, as is well known in such cases, the ability of a liberalizing, developing country to benefit from closer integration with a larger, more industrialized region depends on the developing country's own policy response. Specifically, benefits tend to be greater when liberalization in the developing country is accompanied, or preferably preceded, by policies aimed at stabilizing the macroeconomic environment, improving the flexibility of labor markets, and enhancing the adaptability of economic institutions.

For the SMR countries, *economic and financial costs* in the short to medium term could be significant, the magnitude of the costs being a function of (a) the degree of liberalization already achieved by SMR states (essentially rendering the adjustment less painful, the greater the progress achieved in reducing levels of protection); (b) the countries' macroeconomic performance as measured by such key indicators as the fiscal stance, the balance of payments, and the proximity of the exchange rate to its long-run equilibrium value; and (c) the international competitiveness of domestic industries. Specifically, the *immediate revenue impact* will depend on, among other things, the weight of import tariff receipts in total budgetary revenue and on the response of import demand to tariff reductions, whereas the *capacity of a particular SMR country to respond* to any revenue loss depends on the degree to which the structure and administration of the domestic tax system have been reformed, as well as the capacity to process and tax larger volumes of imports under a more liberal regime.

As important as the longer-term, dynamic benefits are, the primary focus of this chapter is on the more immediate fiscal implications of the agreements. Specifically, this chapter examines the *impact of the association agreements on SMR countries' budgetary revenues* and assesses these countries' capacity to reform their domestic tax systems to compensate for the loss of tariff receipts.[4] The EU, for its part, is providing financial assistance to SMR countries, partly to compensate for the loss of revenue but also to help these countries adjust to a more competitive environment. (The latter objective is being pursued in collaboration with the World Bank and other international organizations.)

It should be emphasized that in focusing on the agreements' impact on budgetary revenue and on the search for compensatory measures, one should not lose sight of the more interesting, and potentially more important, long-run issues of economic policy. Given the current worldwide tendency toward trade liberalization and globalization, the focus must surely be on the opportunities the agreements provide SMR countries to reform their tax systems (and other key aspects of their economies) so as to benefit more fully from trade liberalization and economic integration. In this broader context, a reformed tax system would not only help generate the budgetary revenue needed to meet the exigencies of tariff reductions, but also, by reducing distortions in production and exchange, it could serve to improve resource allocation and potentially contribute to the achievement of higher rates of sustainable growth over the long term.

Revenue Impact of the Agreements

The revenue impact of the elimination of tariffs on SMR countries' trade with the EU depends on (a) the initial share of import taxes in total tax revenue, (b) the import demand response to tariff reductions, (c) the share of imports from the EU in total imports, and (d) the elasticities of substitution between imports from the EU and from third countries (as an indication of the potential for trade diversion) as well as between all imports and import-competing goods and services produced domestically (an indicator of the potential for erosion of the domestic tax base). To help gauge at least the initial magnitude of the problem faced by these countries, the ratios given in Table 8.1 may be instructive.

As a first-order approximation and taking into account the shares of tariff receipts from EU imports in total tax receipts,[5] the revenue impact, measured in relation to total tax revenue, is likely to be the most adverse for Lebanon and Algeria. The potential revenue losses are smaller for Tunisia, Jordan, and Morocco.[6] A country's heavy dependence on trade tax revenue from EU imports may be due either to a relatively higher share of EU imports (for example, Tunisia, Algeria, and Morocco) or to higher tariff rates in general, even when the EU share in imports is not exceptionally high (for example, Egypt and Jordan). Israel (and, to some extent, the West Bank and Gaza Strip [WBGS]), which has already adjusted to its free trade association with the EU and which had been liberalizing its trade regime for many

TABLE 8.1. SOUTHERN MEDITERRANEAN REGION COUNTRIES: TARIFF REVENUE
FROM TRADE WITH THE EU
(Averages 1994–96)

	Import duties		*EU share in total imports*	*Import duties from EU trade*	
	In percent of total tax revenue	*In percent of GDP*	*In percent*	*In percent of total tax revenue*	*In percent of GDP*
Algeria	29.96	3.45	64.12	19.21	2.21
Egypt	19.74	3.37	39.84	7.87	1.34
Israel	1.26	0.40	52.40	0.66	0.21
Jordan	34.63	5.77	35.02	12.13	2.02
Lebanon	59.28	6.83	48.59	28.80	3.32
Libya	—	—	67.27	—	—
Morocco	17.55	4.30	58.78	10.32	2.53
Syria	21.81	2.43	33.11	7.22	0.80
Tunisia	22.18	4.45	71.49	15.86	3.18

— Not available.
Sources: Country authorities; IMF staff estimates; and IMF, *Direction of Trade Statistics Yearbook* (various years).

years before signing the agreement, has not had to face a particularly difficult task in compensating for the revenue loss, especially in light of its highly developed and efficient domestic tax system, which helps generate budgetary revenue equivalent to about 38 percent of GDP.

However, going beyond this simple view, one can distinguish several direct and indirect revenue effects.[7] The most obvious, and initially the largest, is the loss of revenue from tariff reductions on EU imports. A second effect arises from the substitution, by consumers in the SMR countries, of EU imports (made cheaper by tariff removal) for non-EU imports, thereby reducing tariff revenue collected on the latter. Indirect effects are more difficult to assess, as they are related to the possible switch by consumers in the SMR countries from domestic nontradables to imports (or to import-competing domestic products). This would reduce the tax base associated with the former, whereas the possible relative decline in the prices of domestically produced tradables as a result of competition from lower-priced imports could induce a shift toward export markets (thereby possibly affecting both direct and indirect tax bases). The restructuring of domestic industries and the resulting unemployment during the transition could have an adverse impact on direct and indirect taxes as profits, wage incomes, and turnover are reduced. However, this effect may be offset to some degree by the decline in the prices of imported raw materials and capital goods, nearly fully liberalized in the earlier phase of the 12-year period, which could lower production costs and hence stimulate domestic output. A negative revenue impact could also be directly felt if this restructuring were to affect the public and quasi-public enterprise sector, causing a decline in profit transfers to the budget while raising the possibility of higher budgetary outlays. Over the medium to long term, these budgetary costs would, of course, be expected to be more than offset by the positive effects of higher investment and growth. As indicated earlier, such benefits will materialize only if the liberalizing country succeeds in achieving the needed macroeconomic and structural reforms.

Some attempts have been made to estimate the size of the direct and indirect effects. A study by Rutherford, Rutström, and Tarr (1993) for Morocco used a computable general equilibrium model to estimate the longer-term growth and welfare gains from trade liberalization. The model calculated potential revenue losses at the equivalent of 3.3 percent of long-run equilibrium GDP.[8] Devarajan and others (1997) dealt more explicitly with some of the key direct and indirect revenue effects and, by assuming certain values for the relevant parameters, calculated the revenue losses for six of the SMR countries (Algeria, Egypt, Jordan, Lebanon, Morocco, and Tunisia). The direct effects as a percentage decline in total budgetary revenue ranged from 8.6 percent for Egypt to 31.4 percent for Lebanon. In terms of ratios to GDP (not calculated by Devarajan and others), the corresponding ratios would be 1.5 percent for the former and 3.6 percent for the latter. (Not surprisingly, these estimates are quite similar to those given in Table 8.1.) The indirect effects depended essentially on the assumed values for the elasticities of substitution between imports from the EU and those from third countries (that is, the extent of trade diversion). On the assumption of an elasticity of substitution of 2 for both cases, the indirect effects ranged from negligible for Morocco to an additional loss of 4.5 percent of total revenue for Algeria.

A simpler and more direct approach was developed in IMF staff studies on Morocco and Tunisia. This approach relied on more disaggregated data on trade and tariff revenue and took into account the phasing of the different tariff reductions over the 12-year transition period. Appendix Tables 8.A.1 and 8.A.2 show the results for Tunisia. These assume a static relationship between imports and GDP,[9] and no trade diversion. The revenue losses derive from simply applying the reduced tariff rates to the remaining categories of taxed imports from the EU in each of the 12 years. According to this calculation, revenue losses are estimated to rise gradually from about 0.3 percent of GDP in the first year to about 2.6 percent of GDP by the end of the 12th year of the transition period. This estimate is higher than the 1.82 percent of GDP estimated by Rutherford, Rutström, and Tarr (1993). The difference may be attributed to the positive dynamic effects of increased trade incorporated in the model of Rutherford and his colleagues that help mitigate the adverse revenue effects. In the case of Morocco, two alternative assumptions of no diversion and total diversion of imports from third countries were made (Appendix Tables 8.A.3 and 8.A.4). On the assumption of no trade diversion, revenue losses would rise from 0.3 percent of GDP in the first year to 1.8 percent of GDP in the 12th year; whereas, if total diversion were assumed, the comparable ratios would be 0.4 percent of GDP and 2.4 percent of GDP, respectively.

To put these estimates in perspective, it is worth noting that both Morocco and Tunisia are relatively "high tax effort" countries, collecting tax revenue equivalent to about 25 percent of GDP and 20 percent of GDP, respectively. Both countries have for some time been liberalizing their trade regimes and strengthening their domestic tax systems. As a result, trade taxes account for about one-fifth of total tax receipts. An increase in domestic tax revenue to compensate for the elimination of tariffs on imports from the EU in Morocco and Tunisia would, therefore, require an improvement in the productivity of their domestic tax systems of about 12–15 percent over the 12-year transition period.

For Lebanon, preliminary analyses reveal more serious revenue losses. Although Lebanon's imports from the EU constitute only 49 percent of its total imports, the country's heavy reliance on trade taxes as a source of revenue (about 59.3 percent of tax revenue is derived from import tariffs), together with its relatively less developed domestic tax system (Lebanon's tax ratio was only 11.4 percent in 1995), reduces its capacity to compensate for the loss of trade tax receipts in comparison with either Morocco or Tunisia.[10] Available estimates of the loss of trade tax receipts from the association agreement range up to 4.2 percent of GDP in the final year of the transition period (Appendix Table 8.A.5). This implies that to maintain the same ratio of tax revenue to GDP, Lebanon would have to increase revenue collection from its domestic tax system by nearly 60 percent, and by more if the tax ratio is to rise to levels that would be required to meet essential public expenditures. Given Lebanon's undeveloped tax system and weak administrative capacity, the task would be quite difficult to accomplish.

In summary, the revenue impact of eliminating tariffs on EU imports, even when taking into account likely trade diversion, is projected to be in the range of 1 percent to 4 percent of the terminal year GDP, with losses for most SMR countries being less than 3 percent of GDP, if no offsetting improvements in collection are made elsewhere in the tax system.

Tax and Tariff Reforms in the SMR

Since the mid-1980s, most SMR countries have undertaken tariff and tax reforms with the primary goal of addressing fiscal imbalances, often in the context of macroeconomic and structural adjustment programs. Progress, however, has been slow and uneven. To place these reforms in perspective, it may be instructive to recall the key features of what constitutes "good practices" in a reformed tax system in developing countries. These features may be summarized as follows:

- There should be increased reliance on a *broad-based consumption tax*, such as a VAT, preferably with a single rate and minimal exemptions, and a threshold to exclude the smaller enterprises. Excise taxes should be levied at ad valorem rates, or, if specific, adjusted for inflation in order to protect real revenue, and should be restricted to a limited set of products, principally petroleum products, alcohol, tobacco, and some luxury items (for example, private automobiles). The VAT and excises, where applicable, would be applied equally to imports and domestic products.

- *Import tariffs* should have a moderate to low average rate and, most important, a limited dispersion of rates—perhaps three nonzero rates ranging up to 20 percent. *Export duties* are to be avoided.

- A *personal income tax* should be characterized by (a) limited personal exemptions and deductions, (b) a moderate top marginal rate and few brackets, (c) an overall exemption limit that would exclude persons with modest incomes from paying taxes, and (d) extensive use of final withholding at source. A corporate income tax should be levied at one moderate rate, preferably the same rate as the top marginal rate under the personal income tax. Provisions, such as depreciation allowances, should be uniform across sectors and recourse to tax incentive schemes minimal.

- *Nontax revenue*, to the extent it reflects the extraction of surpluses from parastatals or profits from central banks, should decline with the development of the economy and, especially, with the devolution of the state's role in productive activities.[11]

- *Tax administration* reforms should be designed to enhance the accuracy and fairness of assessment, increase the efficiency of collection, reorganize the tax and customs administrations along functional lines, and improve taxpayer registration procedures as well as collection enforcement and audit. Computerization is generally required for more effective management of taxpayer databases, while pay incentive programs and greater autonomy for the tax authority, supported by the development of specialized skills among tax officials, are intended to promote honesty and efficiency in tax administration.

Among the SMR countries, considerable progress has been achieved, notably in Egypt, Jordan, Morocco, and Tunisia. Nevertheless, tax and tariff systems in most SMR countries remain complex, inefficient, and difficult to administer. Three of the SMR countries (Lebanon, Libya, and Syria) do not have a broad-based consumption tax, whereas the VAT systems in the other countries do not fully conform to "good practices" because of numerous exemptions and multiplicity of rates (Table 8.2). In general, business profits taxes have been reformed and rates are reasonable, although a few countries apply more than one rate. Five of the nine countries have maximum personal income tax rates in excess of 40 percent, and in all but one (Tunisia), these rates differ from the corporate tax rates. Special tax incentives are common. The impact of domestic tax reforms can be observed in those countries that, in line with long-term trends and good international practice, have shifted more of their revenue generation to broad-based consumption taxes. This has been achieved through the introduction of a VAT in Morocco (1986), Tunisia (1988), Algeria (1992), and the WBGS (1994), and a generalized sales tax (GST) in Egypt (1991) and Jordan (1994). Because of the slow pace of tariff reforms, these countries have not significantly reduced their reliance on trade taxes. However, the introduction of a VAT has triggered more comprehensive reform of domestic indirect taxes in general, thereby further improving revenue performance. Many excises have been transformed to ad valorem rates in the reforming countries, but several others remain specific and are inadequately adjusted for inflation.

Income tax systems have been simplified. Most SMR countries apply one or two rates to business profits and several rates to personal income. Personal income tax rates remain high and, in most of the SMR countries, large differences exist between statutory rates and effective rates due to weak tax administration and widespread exemptions. Even some of the reforming countries maintain special investment incentives that exempt businesses not only from the corporate income tax and from customs duties but also from the VAT (Algeria and Tunisia), while in some cases reducing or eliminating personal income taxes for employees (Egypt) or taxes on interest income from corporate bonds (Jordan). In addition, a number of the SMR countries have established free economic zones (Egypt, Jordan, Morocco, Syria, and Tunisia) and provided other exemptions and tax relief that could lead to tax evasion and abuse. In Morocco, however, a major step toward reforming tax incentives was taken recently with the promulgation of an Investment Charter to replace the various investment codes. Finally, several of the SMR countries rely heavily on nontax revenue, which, in most cases, reflects the collection of rents from the exploitation of a natural resource (Algeria, Egypt, Libya, and Syria) or from extensive public sector ownership of enterprises (Egypt, Jordan, and Syria). As these countries liberalize their trade regimes and, more generally, their economies—and therefore privatize public sector enterprises—economic rents in the form of nontax revenue are likely to come under pressure, thus increasing the urgency of domestic tax reforms.

As indicated earlier, tariffs have been undergoing simplification and rationalization in most countries of the region. In Morocco, the number of rates was reduced from 47 in 1980 to 6 nonzero rates in 1996, and the dispersion was narrowed by reducing the maximum rate to 45 percent. However, an additional fiscal levy of 15 percent still applies to most imports, while numerous commodities remain subject to notional pricing that renders tariff rates on some commodities as high as 300 percent.[12] The effective tariff rate, about 14.9 percent in 1995, was about average for the SMR but relatively high for the Middle Eastern region as a whole. More important, numerous exemptions are granted, leading to loss of revenue and creating opportunities for evasion and fraud. Reform of the customs administration is currently underway; systems and procedures have been simplified, selective and targeted controls have been introduced, and changes in organization and personnel have been

TABLE 8.2. SMR COUNTRIES: STATUS OF TAX AND TARIFF REFORMS, 1997

	Algeria	Egypt	Jordan	Lebanon	Libya	Morocco	Syria	Tunisia	WBGS[a]
1. Broad-based consumption tax:									
• Rates (in percent)	VAT 7,13,21	GST 10	GST 10	—	—	VAT 7,10,14,20	—	VAT 6,17,29	VAT 17
2. Excises									
• Ad valorem/specific	Mixed	Mixed	Mostly specific	Mixed	Mixed	Mixed	Mostly specific	Mostly ad valorem	Mostly ad valorem
• Coverage	Broad	Narrow	Broad[b]	Narrow	Broad	Narrow	Narrow	Narrow	Narrow
3. Tariffs									
• Quantitative restrictions	None	Very few	3 Commodities	Yes (on specified commodities, import bans)	Yes (specified imports)	Yes (specific agricultural products and few others)	Yes (numerous and complex)	Yes (8% of domestic products)	Yes (agricultural commodities)
• Maximum rate	50%	50%	40%	100%	100%	45%	200%	43%	100%
• Number of rates	6	8	5	12	n.a.	7	n.a.	26	85
• Surcharges	0%–6%	3%–2%	Numerous	None	Numerous	15% fiscal levy + 0.25% parafiscal	Numerous	2% + other	2% port fee 1.5% other
• Effective tariff	16.98%	16.72%	12.31%	16.72%	n.a.	14.9%	9.93%	19.62%	n.a.
4. Business profits tax									
• Maximum rate	38%	40.55%	35%	10%	20%–60%	39.5%	11%–66%	35%	37.5%
• Number of rates	2	3	3	1	Numerous	2	Numerous	1	1
5. Personal income tax									
• Maximum rate	50%	32%	30%	10%	90%	44%	17.25%	35%	48%
• Number of rates	6	2	6	1	8	5	5	6	5
6. Special tax incentives	Limited	Numerous	Numerous	Numerous	Numerous	Limited[c]	Numerous	Limited	Limited

(*Table continues on next page.*)

TABLE 8.2. (continued)

	Algeria	Egypt	Jordan	Lebanon	Libya	Morocco	Syria	Tunisia	WBGS[a]
7. Total revenue/GDP [d,e]	31.02	24.88	30.24	16.26	24.75	24.52	25.92	25.48	17.24
• Tax revenue	11.52	17.05	16.65	11.52	7.32	24.52	11.12	20.06	14.87
• Other revenue	19.49	7.83	13.59	4.74	17.43	—	14.17	5.42	2.37

a. The tariff structure for the WBGS is, for the most part, that of Israel; customs duties on import shipments are collected by Israeli customs.
b. Included in GST.
c. Incorporated in an Investment Charter and applicable to all investments.
d. See Table 8.
e. Averages 1994–96.
Source: IMF, *Government Finance Statistics* (various years); IMF, *World Economic Outlook, May 1997*; Alonso-Gamo, Fennell, and Sakr 1997; country documents; and IMF staff estimates.

effected. As a result, at the port of Casablanca, for example, customs officials no longer perform examinations on all shipments, and the *average* period of stay of goods in the port has thereby been reduced from 16 days to 3. (It is 1–2 days in most industrial countries.)

Tunisia, starting from even higher protection rates, has also been implementing reforms since 1988. However, the system contains inefficiencies, including quantitative restrictions on about 8 percent of the value of imports. The number of rates has been reduced to 26 and the maximum rate to 43 percent; but both remain relatively high, as does the effective tariff rate—about 19.6 percent (1995). Although customs administration has been undergoing significant structural reform in recent years, the prevalence of exemptions continues to lead to revenue losses, due to evasion and fraud; revenue losses due to exemptions were estimated at about 25 percent of total customs receipts in 1994.[13]

In Jordan, tariff reforms have reduced the number of rates to five, but several surcharges, special taxes, and fees still apply. Although the maximum tariff rate is set at 40 percent, in effect, duties range from 0 to 320 percent. Exemptions are widely applied, including generous incentives granted under the Investment Law and other discretionary exemptions. Petroleum imports are not subject to import duties, but to price markups of 10 to 15 percent—implying an implicit tax of equal magnitude as domestic distribution is controlled by a public authority. The tariff system remains poorly coordinated with the domestic tax system, particularly the GST.

In Lebanon, the tariff system has been undergoing reform since the end of the civil war (1992). In 1995, the tariff structure was simplified by consolidating the numerous supplementary charges into the standard tariff rates, reducing the number of rates to 12, and eliminating all quantitative restrictions. Rates, however, remain high—a maximum of 100 percent and an effective tariff rate of 16.7 percent. Algeria's tariff reforms, implemented in recent years in the context of an IMF-supported adjustment program, started from a high level of protection and included reducing the maximum rate to 50 percent, consolidating the number of rates to six, and removing all quantitative restrictions.

Tax administration reform has progressed even more slowly than tax policy reform. However, the introduction of a VAT in the late 1980s in Algeria, Morocco, and Tunisia, and the GST more recently in Egypt and Jordan, have provided important incentives for modernizing tax administration. Progress is now being made; for example, in these countries, tax administrations are being reorganized along functional lines, computerization is being introduced (at the level of subnational units in Algeria, Egypt, Morocco, and the WBGS), and taxpayer registration (including the use of unique tax identification numbers) is expanding steadily. However, even in countries with relatively more developed tax systems and improved tax administrations, performance can be strengthened. Assessment and collection of business profits taxes poses a particular challenge. In Tunisia, a relatively high tax effort country, fewer than half the businesses declare a taxable profit in any one year. Audits are cumbersome, infrequent, and are carried out long after the end of the financial year.

Administrative systems for the VAT in both Morocco and Tunisia are relatively well developed in comparison with those in effect in other countries of the region. Recent IMF staff analyses of VAT administrations in Morocco and Tunisia indicated an efficiency ratio for domestic VAT collection of about 65 percent. This ratio, which is comparable to that of Portugal, can be raised, but only gradually; any improvement will have to follow an enhancement of institutional capacity, modernization of systems and procedures, and skill development of tax personnel. Nevertheless, over the medium term, the ratio can be raised, especially if the above administrative improvements are reinforced by a simplification of the VAT structure itself (consolidation of rates, elimination of exemptions, and broadening of the base). For example, a 10 percentage point improvement in the efficiency of the VAT would generate nearly 1 percent of GDP in revenue in both Morocco and Tunisia.

In short, the key *tax and tariff policy* reforms needed to help the SMR countries address the challenges of the association agreement are:

- The introduction of broad-based, modern VATs in the remaining countries of the region (Lebanon, Libya, and Syria) and the reform of existing VATs through consolidation of rates (Algeria, Morocco, and Tunisia), removal of exemptions, and generally broadening the tax base (Egypt and Jordan).

- The reform of excises through the introduction of ad valorem rates or proper adjustment for inflation, to help ensure revenue buoyancy, and through increases in the taxation of petroleum products in countries where these are sold far below comparable international levels.

- The simplification of the business profits tax through the adoption of a single rate in the neighborhood of 35 percent and the elimination of special tax exemptions.

- Adjusting the top marginal rates for personal income tax to a level comparable to the business profits tax rate (through reductions in Algeria, Libya, Morocco, and the WBGS, and increases in Lebanon from 10 percent and Syria from 17.25 percent) and limiting the number of deductions and exemptions.

- To help smooth the transition to the more liberal trade regime envisaged under the association agreements, tariff reforms should proceed in the direction of further reducing maximum rates and the number of rates to no more than three nonzero rates while simplifying the structure and limiting exemptions. These reforms would preferably need to be generalized to non-EU countries to minimize the risks of trade diversion. Customs administration reforms already underway in Morocco and Tunisia need to be completed and similar reforms implemented in the other states of the region.

The reform of *tax administration* in the region would be most effective if preceded by a simplification and rationalization of the tax systems as indicated above. Specific tax administration reforms that merit particular attention are the following:

- Restructuring existing organizations along modern, functional lines and giving special emphasis to the most productive taxes and to the largest taxpayers

- Simplifying and modernizing systems and procedures and the introduction of efficient management practices

- Expanding computerization, based on simplified and rationalized procedures, to facilitate the rapid processing of declarations, and the more effective use of the taxpayer databases to strengthen audit and enforcement

- Reorienting the audit strategy toward the VAT, focusing on short, well-designed, and targeted interventions

- Ending the separation of assessment and collection in the francophone countries of North Africa, which has led to inefficiencies, evasion, and the buildup of tax arrears

- Attracting and developing quality staff resources by providing intensive in-house and external training, better pay incentives, and greater autonomy for tax officials

Revenue Shares in the SMR Countries

Although the features of a liberal trade regime can be readily distinguished from those of a more restrictive one, it is difficult to devise an unambiguous measure of the degree of trade liberalization in an economy.[14] Given the focus of this chapter, a useful measure may be the *effective tariff rate*, which is relatively easy to compute and may be traced over extended periods. By relating changes in effective tariffs to changes in the share of import tariff receipts in total tax revenue over time, one can explore the possible impact of changes in the trade regime on trade tax shares. Taking a global view of trends in effective tariff rates, most countries appear to have achieved some liberalization of their trade regimes in recent decades.[15] Table 8.3 shows that OECD countries liberalized the fastest, with the average effective tariff declining from 5.84 percent in 1975 to 1.82 percent in 1995. Non-OECD countries on average reduced their effective tariff rate from 15.74 to 13.47 or by 15 percent over the 20-year period.

SMR countries also underwent steady trade liberalization by this measure, with the (unweighted) average effective tariff declining from 21.03 percent in 1975 to

TABLE 8.3. EFFECTIVE TARIFFS BY WORLD REGIONS, 1975–95
(In percent)

	1975	1980	1985	1990	Last available year
All countries	12.70	11.28	12.17	11.18	10.14
OECD countries[a]	5.84	3.95	3.28	2.80	1.82
Non-OECD countries	15.74	14.26	15.85	14.60	13.47
Non-OECD African countries	19.62	17.66	19.11	18.76	16.98
Non-OECD Asian countries	14.05	12.04	15.58	16.48	13.44
Non-OECD Middle Eastern countries	16.47	14.33	14.07	10.70	11.39
Non-OECD Western Hemisphere countries	12.37	12.31	13.66	11.27	10.91

a. Excluding the Czech Republic, Hungary, Luxembourg, and Poland.
Sources: IMF, *Government Finance Statistics* (various years); IMF 1997.

13.23 percent in 1990 (Table 8.4). However, since then there appears to have been a reversal, as the average effective rate rose to 15.31 percent in the latest year for which data are available. This increase is due largely to a reversal of the downward trend in Algeria, Egypt, and Jordan. In Algeria, the increase reflects the impact of the tariffication of quantitative restrictions, a sharp currency devaluation, and improvements in customs administration. Another factor may have been a shift in the composition of imports toward those more heavily taxed products in recent years. Improvements in customs administration may explain some of the increases in the cases of Egypt and Jordan, but in the absence of any major exchange rate movement and no evident shift in the structure of imports, the increase in effective tariffs in these two cases must be due to reclassification of imports and additional levies in the form of surcharges and other fees.

Although over extended periods tariff reform tends to reduce a country's reliance on trade tax receipts, in the short run, the impact of trade liberalization on budgetary revenue may be ambiguous. Indeed, starting from a highly restrictive trade regime, tariff reforms could lead to an *increase* in budget receipts from customs duties. For example, the tariffication of quantitative restrictions, by transferring rents previously collected by traders to the budget, could increase budget revenue. Similarly, reductions in excessively high tariff rates and exemptions could limit the incentive (or the opportunity) for evasion and raise import tax receipts. Simplification of tariff structures could facilitate customs administration and improve collections. When tariff reform is carried out in conjunction with an exchange rate devaluation, as is often the case, the domestic currency value of imports rises and, for a given tariff structure, customs receipts may increase after the devaluation.

TABLE 8.4. EFFECTIVE TARIFFS IN SELECTED COUNTRIES OF THE MIDDLE EAST
AND THE SMR, 1975–95
(Percentage)

	1975	1980	1985	1990	Last available year[a]
Selected non-OECD Middle Eastern countries					
Bahrain	2.26	2.24	3.53	2.61	3.61
Iran	9.49	20.93	11.23	6.49	12.28
Israel	—	4.43	4.96	1.58	0.63
Oman	0.12	1.32	3.68	3.36	3.07
Pakistan	19.54	24.61	25.53	31.65	28.73
Unweighted average	7.85	10.71	9.79	9.14	9.66
SMR countries[b]					
Algeria[c]	9.34	8.08	10.81	12.79	16.98
Egypt	43.24	25.84	28.57	9.58	16.72
Jordan	11.94	16.47	14.05	9.51	12.31
Lebanon	—	—	—	—	16.72
Morocco[c]	25.38	26.32	15.37	19.08	14.92
Syria	16.40	11.56	—	8.43	9.93
Tunisia	19.84	20.91	29.97	19.98	19.62
Unweighted average	21.03	18.20	19.75	13.23	15.31

— Not available.
a. Last available year is 1995 for most countries, but when this information is not available the last available year is used.
b. Libya and the WBGS are excluded for lack of data.
c. Data provided by the country authorities and IMF staff estimates.
Sources: IMF, *Government Finance Statistics* (various years); IMF 1997.

Over the long run, however, and once the highly restrictive features of a trade regime are eliminated, further reductions in tariff rates toward those prevailing in
industrial countries invariably lead to reductions in the shares of trade taxes in total
tax receipts. For those SMR countries that have signed (or will sign) free trade
association agreements with the EU, such an outcome is inevitable.

On a global scale, revenue components as a share of GDP for the major world
regions clearly indicate a steady decline in reliance on trade taxes in the past two
decades, with the world average decreasing from 4.2 percent of GDP in 1975 to 3.2
percent of GDP in the mid-1990s (Appendix Table 8.A.6). As expected, OECD
countries reduced their reliance on trade taxes to negligible proportions as they
completed the liberalization of their trade regimes and built up their domestic tax
capacity through tax reform. For all non-OECD countries combined, the ratio of
trade taxes to GDP declined from 5.3 percent in 1975 to 4.3 percent for the latest
year available. It is worth noting that this drop was due entirely to the virtual elimination of export taxes, as the ratio of import duties to GDP, although it varied over
the period, was nearly unchanged in the mid-1990s from its value in 1975.

For purposes of this chapter, a more relevant measure is the share of *import duties in total tax receipts*, and, in this regard, the data in Appendix Table 8.A.7 provide useful indications. For non-OECD countries, the data show some decline in the share of import duties in total tax receipts in contrast to no change when the share of import duties is related to GDP (implying that nontrade taxes rose faster than GDP over the period). Among the developing regions, two (the African and Asian groups) reduced their relative reliance on import duties between 1975 and the mid-1990s, whereas the other two (the Middle Eastern and Western Hemisphere groups) did not. All regions drastically reduced their reliance on export tax receipts over the 20-year period. When the trends in the shares of trade taxes for each of the regions during this period are gauged against the corresponding trends in effective tariff rates, differences arise, indicating that, even in the long run, tariff reductions do not imply a one-to-one relationship with declines in import tariff receipts. The disparity is due to a number of factors, including the response of import demand (more broadly, the balance of tradables and nontradables) to tariff reductions, changes in the structure of the economy over long periods, the impact of macroeconomic policies that may have accompanied tariff liberalization, and possibly other factors.[16]

The SMR countries, which, as indicated, have undergone steady trade liberalization, have also reduced their reliance on trade taxes in relation to GDP and as a share of total tax receipts, although a rising trend seems to have set in since 1990 (Table 8.5). In those countries for which long-term data are available, the ratio of trade taxes to GDP declined steadily from 6.30 percent in 1975 to 4.53 percent in 1990 before rising to 5.45 percent in the mid-1990s. At this ratio, reliance on trade taxes remains relatively high—much higher than other Middle Eastern countries and only slightly below non-OECD African countries. A similar relationship emerges from a comparison of the shares of trade taxes in total tax revenue (Table 8.6). Thus, although the SMR countries have liberalized their trade regimes in recent years, the progress remains modest and, more strikingly, may have been reversed in a few cases since 1990.

A closer look at the revenue structure of SMR countries in a global context confirms a relatively high reliance on trade taxes, but it also indicates strong revenue performance in the area of consumption taxes. The SMR region's revenue from this source is equivalent to 6.98 percent of GDP in the most recent years for which data are available (1994–96)—higher than any other non-OECD region (Table 8.7). This relatively good performance is due principally to the introduction of a VAT in six of the nine SMR countries, which replaced complex systems of consumption taxes, but also to the relatively high rates of excises. By contrast, the productivity of direct taxation, at 3.75 percent of GDP, is the lowest among the world's regions, reflecting the narrow bases on which direct taxes are assessed and the weakness of the region's collection and enforcement capacity. One feature that stands out in the SMR revenue structure is the relatively high share of nontax revenue to total budgetary receipts, a feature common to other Middle Eastern countries. Whereas in the OECD countries, nontax revenue constitutes less than 10 percent of total receipts, and in the non-OECD regions, about 20 percent, the comparable

TABLE 8.5. TAXES ON INTERNATIONAL TRADE IN SELECTED COUNTRIES OF THE
MIDDLE EAST AND THE SOUTHERN MEDITERRANEAN REGION, 1975–95
(As percentage of GDP)

	1975	1980	1985	1990	Last available year[a]
Selected non-OECD Middle Eastern countries					
Bahrain	2.61	2.18	3.00	2.42	2.79
Iran	2.62	2.52	2.26	2.43	2.39
Israel	—	1.88	2.61	0.64	0.19
Oman	0.23	0.53	1.19	0.80	0.95
Pakistan	5.11	5.60	5.01	5.92	4.88
Unweighted average	2.64	2.54	2.82	2.44	2.24
SMR countries[b]					
Algeria[c]	3.30	1.83	1.73	2.11	3.37
Egypt	10.97	8.12	5.57	3.16	3.76
Jordan	7.52	8.79	7.01	7.01	7.23
Morocco[c]	4.20	4.83	3.74	4.69	5.00
Syria	4.69	3.82	—	1.62	3.05
Tunisia[d]	7.14	7.79	9.49	8.61	8.39
Unweighted average	6.30	5.86	5.51	4.53	5.13

— Not available.
a. Last available year is 1995 for most countries, but when this information is not available, the last available year
is used.
b. Libya and the WBGS are excluded for lack of data.
c. Data provided by the country authorities and IMF staff estimates.
d. Includes VAT on imports.
Source: IMF, *Government Finance Statistics* (various years).

ratios for Middle Eastern countries is 42.2 percent and for the SMR countries, 38.7
percent. As indicated earlier, these high ratios reflect heavy regional dependence on
government income from the exploitation of energy resources or from ownership of
productive enterprises. The relatively high nontax receipts have enabled the SMR
group of countries to attain one of the highest regional revenue-to-GDP ratios in the
world (24.4 percent) despite an unremarkable tax effort. The tax-to-GDP ratio is
15.0 percent, somewhat higher than in non-OECD Asia but lower than in either
Africa or Latin America. As the SMR countries proceed to liberalize their economies over the medium –to long term, nontax revenue is bound to decline. In view of
the relatively high expenditure ratios built into these countries' fiscal systems,[17]
failure to reduce spending and/or improve the tax effort points to a potential revenue
shortfall and an increased risk of fiscal deterioration in the future.

Table 8.8 shows the revenue structure of the individual SMR countries and confirms observations made earlier. Morocco and Tunisia and, to a lesser extent, Egypt
and Jordan, have relatively well-developed tax systems and generate high tax revenue in relation to GDP (in the range of 16–25 percent of GDP); however, in most

TABLE 8.6. TAXES ON INTERNATIONAL TRADE IN SELECTED COUNTRIES OF THE
MIDDLE EAST AND THE SMR, 1975–95
(As percentage of tax revenue)

	1975	1980	1985	1990	Last available year[a]
Selected non-OECD Middle Eastern countries					
Bahrain	18.08	49.70	40.82	30.31	28.27
Iran	29.22	36.70	24.76	33.58	29.11
Israel	14.29	4.75	6.53	2.21	0.62
Oman	1.71	4.86	9.93	7.75	11.49
Pakistan	46.71	41.94	40.66	44.44	31.83
Unweighted average	22.00	27.59	24.54	23.66	20.26
SMR countries[b]					
Algeria[c]	8.06	4.96	4.58	14.34	29.05
Egypt	39.44	26.40	25.10	18.89	16.63
Jordan	52.22	61.38	44.67	37.62	34.45
Morocco[c]	20.01	23.75	18.99	20.59	19.80
Syria	40.82	36.26	—	9.67	15.85
Tunisia[d]	31.37	32.30	38.32	35.87	33.47
Unweighted average	31.99	30.84	26.33	22.83	24.88

— Not available.
a. Last available year is 1995 for most countries, but when this information is not available, the last available year is used.
b. Libya and the WBGS are excluded for lack of data.
c. Data provided by the country authorities and IMF staff estimates.
d. Includes VAT on imports.
Source: IMF, Government Finance Statistics (various years).

other cases, heavy reliance on nontax receipts helps to augment modest collections from weak tax systems. This is the case especially in Libya, Syria, and Lebanon, which have yet to introduce a broad-based consumption tax. As noted earlier, trade taxes constitute an important share of total tax receipts in Lebanon, Jordan, Tunisia, and Morocco, although in the case of the last two, a reasonably well-developed domestic tax system should facilitate the transition toward a more liberal trade regime with reduced reliance on import tariffs. As noted earlier, revenue from direct taxes remains relatively weak, and the ratio of direct tax receipts –to GDP of 3.75 percent for the region as a whole, low by international standards, is buoyed by the case of Egypt, whose high ratio of 6.16 percent is due to the exceptional importance of tax collections from the oil sector, the Suez Canal, and central bank profits.

Concluding Observations

The decision by several SMR countries to proceed to establish a free trade area with the EU, although carrying some risks, provides these countries with the opportunity

TABLE 8.7. REVENUE STRUCTURE IN WORLD REGIONS, 1994–95

	Total revenue	Tax revenue	Other revenue	Taxes on income, profits and capital gains — Total	of which: Individual	of which: Corporate	Domestic taxes on goods and services — Total	of which: General sales, turnover, or VAT	of which: Excises	International trade taxes — Total	of which: Import duties	of which: Export duties	Property taxes
As percent of GDP													
Unweighted average													
OECD	33.62	30.36	3.27	9.01	7.54	2.42	10.32	6.24	3.17	0.56	0.56	0.00	0.71
Africa	20.13	16.40	3.73	4.62	2.19	2.37	5.54	2.85	1.83	4.77	4.19	0.31	0.28
Non-OECD Asia	19.62	14.41	5.21	4.91	1.81	2.74	5.81	2.94	1.96	2.52	2.39	0.12	0.12
Non-OECD Western Hemisphere	20.74	17.42	3.32	3.77	1.02	2.25	6.22	3.63	2.03	3.72	3.66	0.06	0.40
Middle East (including Israel)	27.01	15.61	11.40	5.36	2.58	2.99	5.48	2.60	1.86	2.98	3.02	0.07	0.37
Middle East (excluding Israel)	25.38	12.95	12.43	3.56	0.39	2.93	4.09	0.59	1.95	3.44	3.48	0.08	0.37
Mediterranean[a,b]	24.41	14.96	9.45	3.75	1.39	3.15	6.98	4.90	2.47	4.21	4.09	0.12	0.31
As percent of total revenue													
Unweighted average													
OECD	100.00	90.28	9.72	26.79	22.44	7.19	30.69	18.56	9.43	1.67	1.66	0.00	2.11
Africa	100.00	81.48	18.52	22.95	10.85	11.79	27.50	14.14	9.08	23.69	20.79	1.55	1.41
Non-OECD Asia	100.00	73.44	26.56	25.02	9.25	13.95	29.64	15.00	10.01	12.86	12.20	0.63	0.62
Non-OECD Western Hemisphere	100.00	83.98	16.02	18.18	4.89	10.85	29.99	17.51	9.77	17.95	17.63	0.29	1.92
Middle East (including Israel)	100.00	57.80	42.20	19.86	9.56	11.08	20.30	9.62	6.90	11.03	11.17	0.26	1.39
Middle East (excluding Israel)	100.00	51.02	48.98	14.05	1.54	11.55	16.10	2.32	7.67	13.55	13.73	0.33	1.47
Mediterranean[a,b]	100.00	61.29	38.71	15.35	5.68	12.91	28.61	20.07	10.14	17.25	16.75	0.50	1.27

a. Data provided by the country authorities and IMF staff estimates.
b. Data refer from 1994–96; for Libya, data are for 1994–95; for the WBGS, for 1995–96.
Sources: IMF, Government Finance Statistics (various years); IMF, International Financial Statistics (various years).

TABLE 8.8. SMR COUNTRIES: CENTRAL GOVERNMENT REVENUE STRUCTURE, 1994–96
(As percentage of GDP)

| | Total revenue | Tax revenue | Other revenue[a] | Taxes on income, profits and capital gains | | | Domestic taxes on goods and services | | | International trade taxes | | | Property taxes |
| | | | | | of which: | | | of which: | | | of which: | | |
				Total	Individual	Corporate	Total	General sales, turnover, or VAT	Excises	Total[b]	Import duties	Export duties	
Algeria	31.02[a]	11.52	19.49	2.78	1.51	...	4.91	...	0.97	3.45	3.45	...	...
Egypt	24.88	17.05	7.83	6.16	0.70	5.46	4.57	4.57	...	3.37	3.37	...	0.01
Jordan	30.24	16.65	13.59	3.31	1.21	2.10	7.09	...	...	5.90	5.77[b]	...	...
Lebanon	16.26	11.52	4.74	1.65	1.36	...	...	...	...	7.34	6.83	...	1.26
Libya[c]	24.75[d]	7.32	17.43	...	...	...	...	...	...	...	...	...	...
Morocco[e]	24.52[f]	24.52	—	5.90	2.75	2.03	10.61	5.71	4.87	4.31	4.30	...	0.03
Syria[g]	25.29[d]	11.12	14.17	3.85	0.78	3.03	0.97	0.63	0.34	2.63	2.43	0.19	0.19
Tunisia	25.48[h]	20.06[h]	5.42	4.69	...	...	9.82	5.34	3.54	4.57	4.45	0.05	0.35
WBGS[i]	17.24	14.87	2.37	1.64	...	...	10.89	8.24	2.65	2.11	2.11	...	0.02
Unweighted average[j]	24.41	14.96	9.45	3.75	1.39	3.15	6.98	4.90	2.47	4.21	4.09	0.12	0.31

a. Including hydrocarbon revenue.
b. Including additional tax on imports.
c. Data are for 1994–95.
d. Including oil revenue.
e. Calendar year data through 1995; starting 1996 fiscal year data are for July/June. The 1996 calendar year data are estimated by averaging fiscal year data for the first half of 1996 and 1996–97.
f. Excluding privatization.
g. General government.
h. Excluding social security and payroll taxes.
i. Data are for 1995–96.
j. The components do not add up to the unweighted averages of tax revenue because detailed data are not available for all countries.
Sources: Data provided by the country authorities and IMF staff estimates

to deepen and accelerate fiscal reforms and thus enhance the economic benefits of a more liberal trade regime. Fiscal reforms in general, that is, reforms affecting both revenue and expenditure, contribute to macroeconomic stability, a condition for realizing the benefits of trade liberalization, while enhancing national savings and facilitating productive investment and growth. Tax and tariff reforms, the focus of this chapter, reinforced by institutional modernization and capacity building in customs and tax administration, would ensure more durable improvements in revenue mobilization and allow the SMR countries to reduce their reliance on the taxation of imports. Equally important, these reforms would help reduce economic distortions and improve the efficiency of resource allocation, thereby promoting higher rates of sustainable growth.

On the expenditure side, structural reforms may also need to be undertaken. Given the relatively high levels of government spending and persistent deficits in the SMR, fiscal consolidation could further reduce the pressure on resources and stimulate private sector activity. A larger role for the private sector could, among other things, contribute to greater flexibility in adapting the region's economies to the more competitive environment of freer trade and wider economic integration with the EU. Reform of government spending would not only help eliminate the less productive government activities, but by shifting spending priorities toward investment in essential physical and human capital, it could stimulate higher rates of sustainable growth.

Fiscal reforms in the context of, or as a response to, trade liberalization are not carried out in isolation but are generally accompanied by other reforms in the macroeconomic and structural areas. Although trade liberalization in the SMR countries would, in the context of the association agreements with the EU, proceed gradually, the more vigorous liberalization episodes have required, or at least been accompanied by, exchange rate devaluations. In such cases, to guard against possible erosion of the benefits of an exchange rate action and prevent a possible deterioration of the external current account, monetary and fiscal policies generally need to be somewhat more contractionary than otherwise. To further enhance the benefits of trade liberalization, structural reforms are also required. These commonly include the introduction of greater flexibility in labor markets, an improved regulatory environment, and reform of the banking system and of state institutions, including more vigorous privatization of enterprises. Finally, if the SMR countries are to overcome the adverse consequences of the "hub-and-spoke" problem inherent in current agreements with the EU and benefit more fully from the rules of origin for promoting exports, they should more quickly eliminate the existing barriers to the movements of capital, labor, and products among themselves and establish policies and institutions to achieve closer regional integration.

Several of the SMR countries have already made considerable progress in reforming their fiscal systems and liberalizing their economies. However, these countries remain heavily dependent on international trade taxes. The implementation of the association agreements with the EU will increasingly compel the signatory states in the SMR to find alternative sources of revenue and, simultaneously, to confront a more competitive trade environment. A more vigorous reform of domestic tax systems, as outlined in this chapter, will therefore become increasingly urgent, both for its revenue mobilization potential and for its likely impact on economic efficiency. The benefits to the SMR from closer trade and economic relations with the EU, in terms of inward investment, greater efficiency, and economic growth, could be considerable. However, as the experience of trade liberalization elsewhere clearly indicates, these potential gains can be realized only if the SMR countries accelerate and deepen ongoing fiscal and macroeconomic reforms and reinforce them with needed structural and institutional reforms.

Appendix

TABLE 8.A.1. TUNISIA: REVENUE LOSSES FROM REDUCTIONS IN IMPORT DUTIES ON EU TRADE
(In millions of 1995 Tunisian dinars)

	1996	1997	1998	1999	2000	2001	2002	2003	2004	2005	2006	2007	2008
List 1	35.7[a]	35.4[b]	35.4	35.4	35.4	35.4	35.4	35.4	35.4	35.4	35.4	35.4	35.4
List 2	0	35.3	52.9	70.6	88.2	117.6	117.6	117.6	117.6	117.6	117.6	117.6	117.6
List 3	0	24.3	36.4	48.5	60.7	72.8	84.9	97.1	109.2	121.3	133.5	145.6	151.7
List 4	0	0	0	0	13.3	25.5	37.7	49.9	62.1	74.3	86.5	98.7	110.8
Total	35.7	95.0	124.7	154.5	197.6	251.3	275.6	300.0	324.3	348.6	373.0	397.3	415.5

a. Loss resulting from taxation of capital goods (EU and non-EU origin) at zero rate.
b. Loss resulting from completely phasing out tariffs on all products on the list. Regular taxation resumed as of January 1, 1997 for non-EU countries.
Sources: Tunisian Directorate of Customs and IMF staff estimates.

TABLE 8.A.2. TUNISIA: REVENUE LOSSES FROM REDUCTIONS IN IMPORT DUTIES AND THE ELIMINATION OF COMPENSATORY DUTIES ON EU TRADE
(In millions of 1995 Tunisian dinars)

	1996	1997	1998	1999	2000	2001	2002	2003	2004	2005	2006	2007	2008
Customs duty losses	35.7	95.0	124.7	154.5	197.6	251.3	275.6	300.0	324.3	348.6	373.0	397.3	415.5
DC[a] losses	19.0	28.3	32.2	32.2	32.2	32.2	32.2	32.2	32.2	32.2	32.2	32.2	32.2
Total	54.7	123.3	156.9	186.7	229.8	283.5	307.8	332.2	356.5	380.8	405.2	429.5	447.7
Percent of GDP	0.3	0.7	0.9	1.1	1.3	1.6	1.8	1.9	2.1	2.2	2.4	2.5	2.6

a. Compensatory duty.
Sources: Tunisian Directorate of Customs and IMF staff estimates.

TABLE 8.A.3. MOROCCO: REVENUE LOSSES FROM REDUCTIONS IN IMPORT DUTIES—NO TRADE DIVERSION
(In millions of Moroccan dirhams)

	Year 1	Year 2	Year 3	Year 4	Year 5	Year 6	Year 7	Year 8	Year 9	Year 10	Year 11	Year 12
Import duties	430	566	701	1,019	1,202	1,384	1,568	1,751	1,935	2,119	2,303	2,487
Fiscal levy	399	694	1,110	1,395	1,507	1,619	1,731	1,853	1,976	2,099	2,222	2,345
VAT	122	200	277	408	462	516	569	625	682	738	794	850
Total	951	1,460	2,088	2,822	3,171	3,519	3,868	4,229	4,593	4,956	5,319	5,682
(as percent of GDP)	0.3	0.5	0.6	0.8	1.0	1.1	1.2	1.3	1.5	1.6	1.7	1.8

Sources: Data provided by Moroccan Directorate of Customs and Indirect Taxes and by IMF staff estimates.

TABLE 8.A.4. MOROCCO: REVENUE LOSSES FROM REDUCTIONS IN IMPORT DUTIES —TOTAL TRADE DIVERSION
(In millions of Moroccan dirhams)

	Year 1	Year 2	Year 3	Year 4	Year 5	Year 6	Year 7	Year 8	Year 9	Year 10	Year 11	Year 12
Import duties	582	836	995	1,446	1,690	1,935	2,179	2,425	2,672	2,917	3,163	3,410
Fiscal levy	540	955	1,371	1,937	2,089	2,240	2,391	2,553	2,715	2,877	3,039	3,201
VAT	168	280	392	577	649	965	793	868	943	1,017	1,092	1,167
Total	1,290	2,071	2,758	3,960	4,428	5,140	5,363	5,846	6,330	6,811	7,294	7,778
(as percent of GDP)	0.4	0.6	0.8	1.3	1.4	1.6	1.7	1.8	1.9	2.1	2.3	2.4

Sources: Data provided by Moroccan Directorate of Customs and Indirect Taxes and by IMF staff estimates.

TABLE 8.A.5. LEBANON: CUSTOMS REVENUE LOSSES IMPLIED BY TARIFF DISMANTLEMENT, 1996
(In billions of Lebanese pounds)

Tariff rates	EU imports, 1996	By year												
		1	2	3	4	5	6	7	8	9	10	11	12	13
2	1,199	24.0	24.0	—	—	—	—	—	—	—	—	—	—	0.0
5	502	25.1	25.1	25.1	25.1	25.1	23.1	21.1	19.1	17.1	14.0	10.0	5.0	0.0
10	1,035	104.0	104.0	104.0	104.0	104.0	95.2	87.0	79.0	70.4	56.0	41.4	21.0	0.0
15	335	50.3	50.3	50.3	50.3	50.3	46.2	42.2	38.2	34.2	27.1	20.1	10.1	0.0
20[a]	524.1	113.2	113.2	113.2	113.2	113.2	96.4	88.1	80.0	71.3	57.0	42.0	21.0	0.0
25	134	33.4	33.4	33.4	33.4	33.4	31.0	28.0	25.4	23.0	18.0	13.4	7.0	0.0
30	237.2	71.2	71.2	71.2	71.2	71.2	66.0	60.0	54.1	48.4	38.4	29.0	14.2	0.0
35	57	20.0	20.0	20.0	20.0	20.0	18.2	17.0	15.1	14.0	11.0	8.0	4.0	0.0
40	0.5	0.2	0.2	0.2	0.2	0.2	0.2	0.2	0.1	0.1	0.1	0.1	0.0	0.0
50[b]	204	199.2	199.2	199.2	199.2	199.2	183.3	167.3	151.4	135.4	108.0	80.0	40.0	0.0
80	11	8.4	8.4	8.4	8.4	8.4	8.0	7.0	6.4	6.0	5.0	3.4	2.0	0.0
100	0.3	294.0	0.3	0.3	0.3	0.3	0.3	0.3	0.2	0.2	0.2	0.2	0.1	0.0
Total customs revenue from the EU		648.3	648.3	624.4	624.4	624.4	567.0	518.0	468.2	419.0	333.0	246.4	123.2	0.0
Memorandum items:														
Implied gross revenue loss[c]		—	—	-24.0	-24.0	-24.0	-82.0	-131.0	-180.2	-230.0	-315.3	-402.0	-521.1	-648.3
As a percent of total customs revenue		—	—	-1.9	-1.9	-1.9	-6.4	-10.3	-14.1	-18.0	-24.8	-31.5	-41.2	-50.9
As a percent of total revenues		—	—	-0.8	-0.8	-0.8	-2.7	-4.3	-6.0	-7.6	-10.5	-13.3	-17.4	-21.5
As a percent of GDP		—	—	-0.2	-0.2	-0.2	-0.5	-0.9	-1.2	-1.5	-2.1	-2.6	-3.4	-4.2

— Negligible.

a. Includes imports of cars of which imports from the EU generated customs revenue of LL75 billion in 1996.

b. Includes imports of some petroleum products that are taxed at ad valorem tariff rates of 50 percent but assessed according to the max—min valuation procedure. Data provided by country authorities.

c. The gross revenue loss is the maximum loss to result from the application of the tariff reduction schedule to EU imports under static conditions and in the absence of any offsetting measures.

Source: IMF staff calculations based on data submitted by the Lebanese High Customs Council, and limited to the period of January 1–September 30, 1996.

TABLE 8.A.6. TAXES ON INTERNATIONAL TRADE IN WORLD REGIONS, 1975–95
(As percentage of GDP)

	1975	1980	1985	1995	Last available year[a]
Trade taxes					
All countries	4.21	4.20	4.20	3.38	3.24
OECD countries	1.23	1.02	0.89	0.68	0.61
Non-OECD countries	5.30	5.25	5.36	4.46	4.34
Non-OECD African countries	6.67	6.25	6.56	5.49	5.61
Non-OECD Asian countries	3.80	4.76	5.25	4.35	3.76
Non-OECD Middle Eastern countries	5.01	4.25	4.08	3.48	3.64
Non-OECD Western Hemisphere countries	4.28	4.68	4.48	4.05	3.82
Import duties					
All countries	3.24	3.36	3.44	3.12	3.01
OECD countries	1.18	0.86	0.80	0.65	0.59
Non-OECD countries	4.00	4.20	4.38	4.15	4.04
Non-OECD African countries	4.98	5.02	5.45	5.30	5.21
Non-OECD Asian countries	2.78	3.07	3.76	3.85	3.32
Non-OECD Middle Eastern countries	4.34	4.11	3.88	3.27	3.54
Non-OECD Western Hemisphere countries	3.08	3.80	3.69	3.72	3.61
Export duties					
All countries	0.85	0.73	0.49	0.23	0.16
OECD countries	0.05	0.14	0.04	0.02	0.02
Non-OECD countries	1.14	0.93	0.66	0.31	0.23
Non-OECD African countries	1.61	1.14	1.06	0.34	0.31
Non-OECD Asian countries	0.71	1.26	0.71	0.49	0.43
Non-OECD Middle Eastern countries	0.56	0.09	0.05	0.04	0.05
Non-OECD Western Hemisphere countries	1.00	0.82	0.40	0.31	0.08

a. Last available year is 1995 for most countries, but when this information is not available, the last available year is used.
Sources: IMF, *Government Finance Statistics* (various years); IMF, *International Financial Statistics* (various years).

TABLE 8.A.7. TAXES ON INTERNATIONAL TRADE IN WORLD REGIONS, 1975–95
(As percentage of tax revenue)

	1975	1980	1985	1990	Last available year[a]
Trade taxes					
All countries	26.36	25.92	24.00	21.71	19.42
OECD countries	5.70	4.83	3.42	2.66	2.16
Non-OECD countries	33.63	32.85	31.21	29.10	26.42
Non-OECD African countries	41.23	36.77	35.54	33.77	32.46
Non-OECD Asian countries	29.59	32.99	33.07	27.34	23.98
Non-OECD Middle Eastern countries	29.39	31.26	29.86	28.89	26.91
Non-OECD Western Hemisphere countries	26.89	27.76	24.88	25.63	21.46
Import duties					
All countries	20.21	19.88	19.02	18.68	17.05
OECD countries	5.38	3.78	3.16	2.57	2.10
Non-OECD countries	25.51	25.25	24.65	25.22	23.21
Non-OECD African countries	30.87	28.35	27.85	28.75	27.36
Non-OECD Asian countries	23.06	21.21	23.44	21.83	18.88
Non-OECD Middle Eastern countries	25.35	30.26	28.64	26.98	26.35
Non-OECD Western Hemisphere countries	19.15	21.02	19.84	23.06	20.25
Export duties					
All countries	5.07	5.11	3.44	1.98	1.36
OECD countries	0.28	0.95	0.12	0.06	0.05
Non-OECD countries	6.78	6.50	4.62	2.75	1.91
Non-OECD African countries	9.34	9.03	8.22	5.08	4.03
Non-OECD Asian countries	4.63	6.60	3.70	2.10	2.04
Non-OECD Middle Eastern countries	3.14	0.60	0.29	0.19	0.28
Non-OECD Western Hemisphere countries	6.50	6.00	2.87	2.28	0.41

a. Last available year is 1995 for most countries, but when this information is not available, the last available year is used.
Sources: IMF, *Government Finance Statistics* (various years); IMF, *International Financial Statistics* (various years).

Notes

1. This chapter is based on the author's presentation given at the "Middle East Economic Forum" held in Marrakesh, May 15–17, 1997. I wish to thank A.M. Abdelrahman, Adrienne Cheasty, Liam Ebrill, Julio Escolano, Reint Gropp, Janet Stotsky, and the staff of the Middle Eastern Department for helpful comments and suggestions, and A. Wolde Mariam for valuable research assistance.

2. This refers to the tendency for trade and investment flows from third countries to become even more concentrated in the EU as a way of accessing individual markets in the SMR, partly because of weak economic links among the SMR states themselves but also because the EU has pursued separate agreements with each of the SMR countries. (See Galal and Hoekman 1997.)

3. See Nabli (1996) for a comprehensive survey of trade liberalization experiences.

4. It is worth noting that trade liberalization does not necessarily imply revenue loss. For example, starting from a highly restrictive trade regime, certain trade liberalization measures (for example, the tariffication of quantitative restrictions and reductions in excessively high tariff rates, which may have encouraged evasion) could initially lead to *higher* tariff receipts. However, most SMR countries are liberalizing from moderate protection levels and tariff reductions, therefore implying the loss of revenue for most countries in the region.

5. Excises and VAT on imports, where applicable, are also collected at customs, the latter being normally assessed on a tax base that *includes* tariffs. To the extent that tariffs are eliminated, VAT assessments and collections at customs would also be expected to decline.

6. When measured in relation to GDP, the revenue losses would be highest for Lebanon and Tunisia, the latter mainly because of its relatively high ratios of tax revenue to GDP and EU imports to total imports.

7. See Devarajan and others (1997) for a fuller analysis of the main direct and indirect revenue effects. For a more comprehensive treatment of the revenue impact of trade liberalization, see Ebrill, Stotsky, and Gropp (Forthcoming).

8. Rutherford, Rutström, and Tarr did not measure the revenue loss directly but took it to be equivalent to the additional VAT collections that would be needed to restore revenue neutrality.

9. This assumption may not be as unrealistic as it first appears. Since 1976, trade between Tunisia and the EU countries has been progressively liberalized and the ratio of imports from these countries to total imports has remained in the range of 65–75 percent through 1995, with an average of 70.3 percent. A similar trend has also been observed for Morocco and to a somewhat lesser extent for Algeria.

10. Other features of Lebanon's economy and the terms of its agreement under discussion with the EU also make the gains from a closer trade association with the EU appear relatively less attractive. See Martin (1999).

11. Nontax revenue can still be an important component of a reformed tax system. For example, the user fees that would result from the appropriate commercialization of the supply of government services in areas such as health and education would count as nontax revenue. Moreover, profits realized by parastatals in a perfectly competitive market environment could also be considered a durable source of revenue, although such cases are likely to be rare. Of course, in countries rich in energy resources such as Algeria and Libya, nontax revenue is likely to remain significant for some time.

12. These are to be phased out beginning in June 1998, when Morocco applies the terms of the World Trade Organization.

13. It should be noted that some exemptions are legal and represent common practice (for example, diplomatic franchise, imports by nongovernmental organizations); some are either unnecessary or economically inefficient, even when legal (for example, targeted investment incentives), and in these cases, revenue losses can be reversed by amending existing legislation. However, some revenue losses due to exemptions represent abuse of privilege or outright fraud.

14. In a recent IMF staff study, a 10-point index of trade liberalization was computed for 27 developing countries combining the effects of import tariffs and nontariff barriers (NTBs). Five classifications of import tariffs and three classifications of NTBs were used to construct the index, with the most open import tariff and NTB regimes assigned a "1," the most restrictive a "10" (see IMF [1998]).

15. See Ebrill, Stotsky, and Gropp (Forthcoming) for further analysis of this point.

16. For more discussion of this and related points, see Ebrill, Stotsky, and Gropp (Forthcoming).

17. The average expenditure ratio in the SMR countries (excluding Israel) during 1994–96 was 31.2 percent, compared with 30.5 percent for the OECD countries and 18.9 percent and 28.1 percent for non-OECD Asian and African countries, respectively.

References

Abed, George T., Liam Ebrill, Sanjeev Gupta, Benedict Clements, Ronald McMorran, Anthony Pellechio, Jerald Schiff, and Marijn Verhoeven. 1998. "Fiscal Reforms in Low-Income Countries: Experience Under IMF-Supported Programs." IMF Occasional Paper No. 160. International Monetary Fund, Washington, D.C.

Alonso-Gamo, Patricia, Susan Fennell, and Khaled Sakr. 1997. "Adjusting to New Realities: MENA, the Uruguay Round, and the EU-Mediterranean Initiative." IMF Working Paper 97/5. International Monetary Fund, Washington, D.C.

Alonso-Gamo, Patricia, Annalisa Fedelino, and Sebastian Paris Horvitz. 1997., "Globalization and Growth Prospects in Arab Countries." IMF Working Paper 97/125. International Monetary Fund, Washington, D.C.

Dean, Judith M., Seema Desai, and James Riedel. 1994. "Trade Policy Reform in Developing Countries Since 1985: A Review of the Evidence." World Bank Discussion Paper 267. World Bank, Washington, D.C.

Devarajan, Shantayanan, Delfin S. Go, Sethaput Suthiwart-Narueput, and John Voss. 1997. "Direct and Indirect Fiscal Effects of the Euro-Mediterranean Free Trade Agreements." Unpublished. World Bank, Washington, D.C.

Ebrill, Liam P., Janet G. Stotsky, and Reint Gropp. Forthcoming. "Revenue Implications of Trade Liberalization: Statistical Evaluation and Case Studies." International Monetary Fund, Washington, D.C.

Galal, Ahmed, and Bernard Hoekman, eds. 1997. *Regional Partners in Global Markets*. London: CEPR.

Havrylyshyn, Oleh. 1997, August. *A Global Integration Strategy for the Mediterranean Countries: Open Trade and Market Reforms*. Washington, D.C.: International Monetary Fund.

Hoekman, Bernard, and Simeon Djankov. 1997. "Towards a Free Trade Agreement with the European Union: Issues and Policy Options for Egypt." Working Paper No. 10. Egyptian Center for Economic Studies, Cairo.

International Monetary Fund. 1997. *World Economic Outlook, May 1997: Globalization Opportunities and Challenges*. World Economic and Financial Surveys. Washington, D.C.

———. 1998. *Trade Liberalization in IMF-Supported Programs*. World Economic and Financial Surveys. Washington, D.C.

———. Various years. *Direction of Trade Statistics Yearbook*. Washington, D.C.

————. Various years. *Government Finance Statistics.* Washington, D.C.

————. Various years. *International Finance Statistics.* Washington, D.C.

Martin, Will. 1999. "Assessing the Implications for Lebanon of Free Trade with the European Union." In B. Hoekman and J. Zarrouk, eds., *Catching Up with the Competition: Trade Opportunities and Challenges for Arab Countries.* Ann Arbor: University of Michigan Press, forthcoming.

Moukarbel, Iskandar. 1996. "The Proposed Free-Trade Agreement Between Lebanon and the European Union Countries: Evaluation and Recommendations." Unpublished.Association of Banks of Lebanon, Beirut.

Nabli, K. Mustapha. 1996. "A Comparative Perspective on Trade Liberalization in the Magreb Countries in the Context of the Free Trade Area Agreements with Europe." Unpublished. University of Tunis and North African Bureau of Economic Studies, Tunis.

Nsouli, Saleh M., Amer Bisat, and Oussama Kanaan. 1996. "The European Union's New Mediterranean Strategy." *Finance and Development* 33 (September):14–17.

Page, John, and John Underwood. 1997. "Growth, the Maghreb and the European Union: Assessing the Impact of the Free Trade Agreements on Tunisia and Morocco." In Galal and Hoekman 1997.

Rutherford, F. Thomas, Elisabeth E. Rutström, and David Tarr. 1993. "Morocco's Free Trade Agreement with the European Community." World Bank Working Paper 1173. Washington, D.C.

Saidi, Nasser. 1996. "Lebanon and European Union at the Crossroads: An Interim Assessment of the Partnership Agreement." Unpublished.Association of Banks of Lebanon, Beirut.

Chapter 9

Enforcement of Product Standards as Barriers to Trade: The Case of Egypt[1]

Hanaa Kheir-El-Din
Cairo University

Crossing international borders gives rise to transaction costs that are not faced by domestic producers. Even in the absence of formal trade barriers such as tariffs, quotas, or bans, cumbersome administrative procedures and customs clearing can act as trade impediments. Export checks and import clearance procedures may impose a considerable burden on producers, traders, and investors, in addition to consumers. Imposition of costly procedural requirements to assure that imports satisfy formal specifications and national product standards can be especially burdensome for importers.

The Role of Standards in Egypt

Product standards and technical regulations are meant to facilitate trade and production and to ensure health and safety of consumers. Buyers of final and of intermediate goods want to know the specifications of these goods in terms of their characteristics—reliability, uniformity, safety of use. This information may be conveyed by individual producers and traders but is increasingly ensured through developing common product standards underwritten by recognized expert bodies. Compliance with such standards is usually voluntary, particularly if the standard relates to the quality of the product. Quality is an issue to be settled between the buyer and seller and is usually reflected in the price of the product.

However, the government may enforce mandatory standards or product specifications (technical regulations) to ensure the health and safety of consumers, animal or plant life, or the environment. Numerous international bodies have been created over time with the mandate to develop common and compatible standards in various areas. Major standards developing bodies include the International Organization for Standardization (ISO), the International Telecommunications Union (ITU), the Centre Européen de Normalisation (CEN), the International Electro-Technical Commission (IEC), and the Food and Agricultural Organization of the United Nations (FAO).

While standards are extremely useful for buyers and sellers and have been shown to be an important source of economic growth and consumer welfare, they may be a potential nontariff barrier (NTB) to trade when they are applied in a discriminatory fashion to favor domestic production against foreign competition. This explains why a number of international agreements require members to move toward adopting international standards and accepting foreign testing and certification. Two international agreements are of particular relevance for Egypt: WTO and the European-Mediterranean Partnership Agreement.

The WTO Agreement on Technical Barriers to Trade (TBT) seeks to ensure that technical regulations and standards as well as testing and certification procedures in member countries do not create unnecessary obstacles to trade. It further encourages the use of international standards when they exist and the mutual recognition of national conformity assessment. It also requires that procedures for determining the conformity of products with national standards be fair and equitable between domestically produced goods and equivalent imported goods.

A complementary agreement is that on the Application of Sanitary and Phytosanitary Measures (SPS), which concerns the enforcement of food safety and animal and plant health regulations. This agreement also encourages members to adopt international standards, guidelines, and recommendations where they exist. This agreement, while recognizing the right of governments to protect the health and safety of consumers, stipulates that any measure applied should be limited to protecting human and animal or plant life or health and should not unjustifiably discriminate between members where similar conditions prevail.

Although the Euro-Mediterranean Agreement (EMA) that is being negotiated between the government of Egypt (GOE) and the European Union (EU)—which is to replace the preferential trade and technical assistance programs and the financial protocols that have been developed since the 1970s—is not likely to require the harmonization of standards and the mutual recognition of conformity assessment procedures, it will require substantial reform of the current Egyptian system of standardization and quality control if the EMA is to function effectively.

Egypt's current system of standards and practices reflects a history of inward orientation and a strategy of import substitution implemented by a dominant public sector since the beginning of the 1960s. Many standards and regulations were created not only to protect consumers from unsafe products but also to enforce quality standards that are not relevant to health and safety considerations. Authority to impose quality standards or specifications was given to several ministries.

With the Open Door Policy of the 1970s, Egypt started following a more out-ward-looking orientation; since the mid-1980s, as a result of increasing structural imbalances and the accumulation of external debt, the pace of economic reform has been accelerated. This encouraged increased participation of the private sector and a greater reliance on market forces, foreign trade, and foreign technology. Trade barriers were reduced: tariffs were lowered and rationalized; and NTBs (bans, let-ters of credit suspensions, prior approvals by specified authorities, servicing facili-ties requirements, public import monopolies, and prior import deposits) removed or considerably liberalized (Kheir-El-Din and El-Dersh 1992). These reforms increased the visibility of other regulatory interventions that restricted trade, including the enforcement of product standards. A list of products covering 1,550 tariff lines was made subject to mandatory quality control requirements (World Bank 1997).

Review of the Current System of Standards and Quality Control

The system of standards setting, quality control, and inspection in Egypt has been the subject of consultations with the United States and with the EU and its member states. It has been the subject of exhaustive review by joint teams of the GOE, USAID, and consultants. This section draws on the results of these studies (Nathan Associ-ates 1996, 1997, 1998a, 1998b) to describe the status quo in Egypt in this area.

Creation of Standards

The current system of standards and quality control includes several governmental bodies with direct control over the creation and enforcement of standards. They are the Ministry of Industry and Mineral Wealth (MOI), the Ministry of Supplies and Foreign Trade (MOTS), the Ministry of Health (MOH), and the Ministry of Agri-culture (MOA). In addition, the Atomic Energy Organization (since the Chernobyl accident) also has inspection responsibility for food products, and the Ministry of Scientific Research has recently participated more actively in the standards system.

In Egypt, every product has a standard. The standards are either uniquely Egyp-tian or they follow an international standard (ISO, IEC, and so forth) or a national norm that has been developed in an OECD country. The Egyptian Organization for Standardization and Quality Control (EOS) is the recognized national standards body. It is under the jurisdiction of the MOI and is the sole authority for elaboration of Egyptian national standards for industrial products, testing and measurement equipment, and methods of testing and inspection. The EOS also has responsibility for testing and inspection of materials and products, certification of products (it issues conformity marks and quality marks), technical consultation and training concerning standardization, and liaison with international, regional, and foreign cor-responding organizations. The EOS is authorized to develop, adopt, and publish standards and codes of practice as Egyptian standards. It can amend or revoke such standards or codes. It is charged with operating in accordance with internationally recognized systems and principles.

To develop an EOS standard, at the end of each year by circular letter, the EOS requests from all relevant ministries and other interested parties (including trade and industry associations and importers) proposed new standards or revisions to existing ones that are needed or desired. After examination by EOS technical committees and with reference to international norms, a draft standard is prepared and circulated among the groups involved in requesting or revising standards, and a final draft standard is prepared and submitted to the EOS. If approved, it is signed by the MOI, and then the standard becomes a *voluntary* Egyptian standard.

Officially, Egyptian standards are voluntary, except for those related to public health, safety, and consumer protection. A standard is made *mandatory* by ministerial decree issued by the MOI mandating the relevant standard. An EOS standard may also be made mandatory by ministerial decree by other agencies.

In practice, there are additional channels through which standards are effectively rendered mandatory. Through a series of mandatory technical specifications and regulations embodied in ministerial decrees from not just the MOI, but also the MOTS, MOA, and MOH, product coverage by mandatory standards has been extended to a vast array of goods; some 1,550, or 25 percent, of all tariff lines—of which about half are foodstuffs—are subjected to quality control. The lists of products covered by "quality control" inspection reported by customs and by the EOS in the publication *Mandatory Standards* do not coincide. Moreover, they go beyond conventional norms of consumer protection.[2] When enforced, they give rise to considerable economic costs. Once applicable duties have been paid on goods subjected to inspection requirements, at least 1 percent of each consignment must be sampled and inspected for compliance with the relevant Egyptian standards.

Input into the standards creation process varies by product. A particularly intricate process is that of the creation of standards for food and agricultural commodities. Three ministries and five public organizations are involved in the establishment of regulatory standards and technical specifications in Egypt for food and agricultural products. These are:

- the MOTS through the EOS

- the MOH through the Food Control Department and the Nutrition Institute

- the MOA through three public organizations: the Veterinary Medical Services, Plant Protection and Quarantine, and the Central Laboratory for Food and Feed.

In addition, the General Organization for Import and Export Control (GOIEC) and the Atomic Energy Organization also apply standards for the control of food and agricultural products.

Control of food and agricultural products in Egypt is achieved through a set of product standards and technical specifications that are made mandatory through implementing laws and decrees. While these official product standards and technical specifications cover many if not most situations, they do not cover them all, particularly in the food and agriculture field. In cases where EOS standards or ministerial technical specifications do not exist, ministries indicate that international norms apply. Specifically, product standards and technical specifications (that is, permitted food additives, pesticides, microbiological criteria) of the EU, the United Kingdom, Germany, France, the United States, Japan, and *Codex Alimentarius* and ISO can be used. In practice, the situation is often very different.

Although the MOH has the ultimate responsibility to ensure public health, the large number of product standards, the often vague nature of the quality attributes that have a regulatory status, and the multiplicity of agencies involved in ultimately accepting or rejecting the product make the current system cumbersome and costly. Substantial reforms are required to increase transparency and ensure due process, thereby making the system both efficient and in compliance with the WTO.

As far as manufactured commodities are concerned, mandatory product standards are less complex than for food and agricultural commodities. In the past, a standard was simply made mandatory on request by the EOS. Currently, there is a trend away from such comprehensive standards in favor of performance standards. There are now 138 mandatory product standards being enforced for reasons of quality control. The objective is often one of consumer protection from lower-quality products, especially, but not exclusively, imports. Many of the standards are more specific than the applicable, comparable international standard. Pressure to make a standard mandatory can emanate from anywhere, but it is typically channeled through the EOS to the MOI and through GOIEC to the MOTS.

The Enforcement of Mandatory Standards
In cases where health and safety are legitimate concerns, the current system—when implemented—frequently suffers from mandatory compliance rules that are nontransparent and redundant. Substantial disincentives are created for investment, production, and trade.

For food and agricultural products, control in Egypt is shared by the five previously mentioned agencies and their dependent organizations. The focus is primarily on imported food products, although exports often also have to meet mandatory EOS standards (and which may as a result inhibit export production). Domestic markets are also checked, particularly by the MOH to ensure that products not meeting EOS standards are not sold. However, there is evidence that standards applied to imports may differ from those applied domestically. As an example, the frozen meat standard appears to apply only to imports; similar meat products produced domestically are ignored.

Each food control authority operates in a similar manner characterized by a head office in Cairo with field offices located throughout Egypt. The importation process for most food products is cumbersome and restrictive. It involves at least 30 different steps (SRI International 1997). The entire import process comprises five broad stages, each one consisting of multiple steps. These stages are preshipment requirements, initial import procedures, product inspection and testing, appeal procedures, and final clearance.

The inspection and testing stage involves the notification of all required food inspection agencies. Up to four agencies may be involved. All food consignments will be inspected by the Atomic Energy Organization (for irradiation), the GOIEC (for quality), and the MOH (for safety and quality). MOA and the Veterinary Medical Services will be involved for all meat, poultry, seafood, and dairy products (for safety and quality). Appropriate forms must be completed separately with each agency. With the exception of frozen meat and poultry, each agency samples and tests the consignment independently. For frozen meat and poultry, a combined sampling is done but testing is still done independently by each agency. *All* agencies must approve the shipment before release is granted. Failure by any one of the agencies to clear a sample results in the rejection of the whole shipment. The MOH grants the final release of the consignment.

A problem directly related to multiple agency inspection and mandatory inspection of each consignment is the excessive loss of product that occurs. In addition, a substantial portion of the resources devoted to inspection and testing involves factors that have no bearing on the safety of the product but are rather devoted to quality testing—particularly testing by the GOIEC.

Rejection of consignments may be appealed by the importer. This requires the submission of a notice to appeal, the resampling and reanalysis of the product, and an often lengthy review by the MOH Technical Review Committee for Import Appeal. This review process is time consuming, generally doubling or tripling the clearance time.

A particular problem for importers concerns mandatory shelf life requirements. The EOS sets shelf life standards for a multitude of products, including many food items. These are periods after which a product may not be sold. The periods set do not necessarily reflect actual shelf life of the product, even under the climatic conditions prevailing in Egypt. They restrain trade because the limitations placed on the allowable shelf life are sometimes alleged to be excessively short, especially as products may not be imported if more than 50 percent of the allowed shelf life has already expired. Delays caused by inspection, testing, and other import clearing procedures can result in shortening the remaining shelf life for a product to such an extent that the importer has little time to move the product to the market. Without an absolutely guaranteed market for the product, the standards can effectively prohibit imports. While shelf life dates are important, especially for food products subject to spoilage and deterioration, they are better left as an issue to be determined by the producer with government oversight to ensure implementation.

Monitoring and enforcement of mandatory standards for manufactured goods is vested in three agencies: the Department of Industrial Control (MOI), which monitors domestic compliance to EOS-recognized mandatory standards at the factory level; the Department of Control (MOTS), which inspects for fraudulent products domestically; and the GOEIC (MOTS), which is responsible for monitoring the EOS mandatory standards for imported and exported goods.

Domestically produced products and their production processes must be in compliance with mandatory standards issued by the EOS. Factories are checked at least once a year by the Department of Industrial Control. Failure to comply can result in administrative shutdown. Imports and exports of manufactured products are less regulated than are food products. However, since 1990, mandatory inspection by the GOEIC has increased to more than 100 product groups from the 17 products previously inspected. This was partially due to lifting import bans on certain products and easing import licensing procedures: in effect, quality control replaced the import bans and became an NTB (Kheir-El-Din and El-Dersh 1992).

When controlled products move through the ports, the GOEIC samples each lot. It is allowed by law to take up to 1 percent of a consignment for sampling, and can take another 2 percent if the product is initially rejected. Importers and exporters complain of long delays, unclear procedures, and excessive sampling. Testing of industrial products sometimes takes a long time, especially if the required equipment is not available. Importers who regularly buy the same product from the same foreign suppliers are subjected to inspection of every shipment received. For some products, the fees involved are significant. Fees charged for inspection are based on either the weight of or the units in a consignment. They range from 0.5 piaster per kilogram to a maximum of E£10,000 per consignment. Fees for goods intended for retail sale are at least twice as large as those applied if the goods are not prepared for retail sale.

Problems and Economic Costs of the System

The current system is disruptive to producers and traders. In part this is due to ill-conceived goals and the design and history of the system, and in part it is due to problems of implementation. The system imposes large welfare losses in the aggregate and has made it costly and difficult for producers to obtain inputs required for export production. Major problems with the system are that quality is confused with safety, there are multiple centers of authority, there is a lack of transparency and consistency, compliance costs are higher than necessary, and there is significant negative overall impact on the economy.

Quality Confused with Safety

The standards set by the EOS and made mandatory by various agencies for a large number of products combine safety and health-related elements with quality-related elements. While the former provide a legitimate rationale for governments to intervene (determine whether products should be allowed to circulate), the latter do not. The mandatory use of quality standards, particularly by the GOEIC in its evaluation of imported and exported products, unnecessarily restricts product variety on the Egyptian market and goes beyond the legitimate role of governments in setting product standards.

This is most obvious in the food sector, where physical characteristics of products such as size, shape, color, and texture are frequently subject to mandatory requirements, as are excessive composition elements such as fat or sugar content. The problem extends to the manufactured goods sectors, where the amount of ink in a ballpoint pen or the length of matches is a mandated requirement. EOS standards often also contain quality norms that are vague, subject to interpretation, and restrict the ability to produce and/or import and export a variety of products. As much as two-thirds to three-quarters of Egypt's regulatory analytical capacity has been said to be devoted to quality testing. Because emphasis is set on products' quality, attention and resources available for helping to ensure product safety are reduced; this may actually lead to a greater level of unsafe products existing within Egypt than would otherwise be the case. Because the focus of testing is on product quality, laboratory instrumentation and technical expertise are inadequate for safety testing.

Many countries impose mandatory product standards to ensure safety or avoid economic fraud. However, the EOS standards combine a mixture of quality and compositional standards and of safety standards that is both inappropriate and unnecessary. Standards seem to be used for multiple purposes: for product identification, for the purpose of tariff classification, for identification of counterfeit products to prevent fraud, to protect the consumer against spoiled products, and for "quality" more generally. A careful review of all applied standards and the acceptance of existing international norms (the *Codex*, ISO, IEC, and so forth) are necessary to improve the Egyptian system of standards control.

Multiple Centers of Authority

Egypt maintains a regulatory system involving multiple governmental agencies. Its impact is felt most in the importing of food products. Multiple problems exist within the current importing system that lead to extended clearance times, loss of product, uncertainty as to the standards to apply, excessive costs of container unloading charges, port and warehouse rental charges, labor costs in clearing product, and dispute resolution.

As mentioned, up to five agencies can be involved in inspection, sampling, and testing of food products. Importers must not only file regular customs documents but must additionally file import documents with—and pay fees to—each agency. Product inspections are almost always carried out independently, with the exception of frozen meat and poultry. Each agency obtains its own samples and independently tests the product. Delays of two to four days to inspect the product are not uncommon. Duplicative testing is the rule. All consignments are sampled, regardless of compliance history, although the international norm samples consignments based on compliance history of the product, the country of origin, and the compliance performance of the importer, exporter, and shipper. Inspection is carried out by a technical committee of three individuals and leads to an excessive use of manpower.

The system of multiple inspection, sampling, and testing must be discontinued. A single agency should have the responsibility for testing food imports. Similarly, a single agency should have the responsibility to examine manufactured (nonfood) products. Sampling based on compliance history of a product should be implemented. Quality testing should be eliminated. This in turn requires a comprehensive review of existing standards to ensure that these are centered on health- and safety-type rationales, are justified, and are worded in performance terms rather than specifying design characteristics. Single inspectors—rather than committees—should be responsible for conformity assessment.

Lack of Transparency and Due Process

One of the most important difficulties with the existing quality control system for imported products, as well as for domestic and exported products, is the lack of transparency and due process in setting and enforcing the regulations. Transparency requires that all affected parties know clearly what regulations apply to a product and are informed and consulted in advance of proposed changes that will be made and the rationale for such changes. There should also be no uncertainty, at the time of importation, how a product will be classified and what technical requirements will be applied.

Due process refers to the process by which laws, decrees, standards, and technical specifications are made and implemented so that all affected parties can have advance knowledge of proposed laws, decrees, technical specifications, and proposed changes to them; can provide input into the decisionmaking process, and can have a legitimate mechanism of appeal. Without due process, transparency cannot be achieved. The absence of transparency and predictability in Egypt is not only a source of economic loss, but also implies that Egypt does not meet the requirements of the WTO in this area.

High Compliance Costs

The prevailing system of Egyptian standards and product safety entails costs of compliance that are high by international standards and imposes many unnecessary costs on consumers and producers. These costs result from laboratory deficiencies, limited testing capabilities, port delays as a result of excessive and unnecessary sampling and testing, unnecessarily rejected consignments, product wastage due to excessive sampling, multiple fees paid for duplicative procedures, and the need (incentive) to provide informal payments to officials to speed clearance.

A sample survey of 33 producers and traders (3 public and 30 private) was conducted by Nathan Associates in 1996 and the results systematically compiled. It showed that:

- More than half the firms surveyed encountered problems or delays in securing raw materials due to GOE product standards or technical regulations.

- Fewer than one-quarter of the firms said that they could comply and did with Egyptian standards and technical regulations.

- About three-quarters of the firms encountered business difficulties in attempting to comply with the existing system of standards and technical regulations.

It is worth noting that most of the firms surveyed were well aware of the importance of quality and used Total Quality Management (TQM) practices within the firm.

Economic Impact of the Current System

Some preliminary estimates of the economy-wide impact of the current quality control system based on the cost estimates reported in the survey and field interviews have been attempted (Nathan Associates 1996). The results suggest that the cost impacts are largest for food-related and consumer goods' producers and traders and smallest for industrial products and pharmaceuticals. Using World Bank estimates that about 25 percent of Egyptian tariff lines are subjected to some form of mandatory technical regulations, it has been estimated that:

- Direct and indirect additional costs to affected producers and traders vary between 5 percent and 90 percent according to industry, with the highest costs for food products and imported final consumer goods.

- Exports are lowered by 9 percent to 12 percent, as the system of quality control raises import costs of raw materials, intermediate inputs, and capital goods; market access to the regionally important Euro-Med market is reduced; and the incentive for foreign and domestic investment is lowered.[3]

All in all, Nathan Associates estimate that the aggregate welfare loss of the current system exceeds 1 percent of GDP, reflecting higher import costs, lower exports, reduced product variety and availability, reduced access to best available technology, and the waste of government resources expended on duplicative and unnecessary activities.

Harmonization and Cost of the Current System in an Integrating World

Using a system of standards that is not compatible with international norms gives rise to a variety of costs for the economy. These costs could be avoided through harmonization with widely used codes and practices. Standards are dynamic in that they are continually being developed and modified as technology and markets evolve. Thus, international standards (*Codex*, ISO, and so forth), while aiming at reducing uncertainty, evolve in response to technical change and expectations of producers and traders. They are increasingly used to coordinate production and distribution. This points to the importance for Egypt of coordinating its rules and regulations with its major trading partners.

Gains from Coordination of Standards within the EMA

One of the potential gains for Egypt from joining the EMA emanates from a reduction in administrative costs in dealing with other members. Membership in the EMA may facilitate recognition of administrative requirements for product standards, testing and certification procedures, and customs documentation, including that currently required by the GOIEC, MOH, and MOA. In a simulation analysis of the potential gains to Egypt, Konan and Maskus (1997) calculate the amount of overall gain associated with a reduction in administrative barriers. Hoekman and Djankov (1997) argue along the same lines, although they do not quantify the impact of an Egypt-EU Free Trade Agreement (FTA).

The more integrated the economy into the regional market, the larger is the investment inflow into the economy. A potentially negative outcome would result if the Egyptian economy is not reasonably harmonized with the EU, as the FTA that eliminates tariffs on EU exports to Egypt could result in reduced investment and product sourcing from EU countries instead. The facts that FDI in export manufacturing in Egypt is still very small and the European market accounts for over half of Egypt's nonoil exports emphasize the importance of harmonization of standards for Egyptian industry and reduction of compliance costs.

Furthermore, with increased competition facing Egypt within the European market and domestically from direct imports, Egyptian producers will be threatened by internal and external competition. As Egypt's competitors are increasingly using harmonized European standards to enhance their competitive advantage, it becomes compelling for Egyptian firms to join in the process of market integration. This is all the more urgent given that the process of integration of the wider European market (including Central and Eastern European countries as well as Turkey) is evolving rapidly at the political, economic, and business level. This process is also spreading to southern Mediterranean countries such as Morocco and Tunisia. Of course, as the market grows, the use of voluntary product and service standards to guide business relations within the private sector will certainly also continue to rise.

The current Egyptian system for standardization acts as a barrier against integrating into the regional markets and, even more, into the global market. This points to the necessity of reconsidering the system and aligning it with international norms as represented by ISO guidelines and CEN processes. Reviewing the basic characteristics of standardization in Europe as compared with Egypt is necessary. Standards and technical regulations in Egypt are not conducive to increasing trade and investment between European and Egyptian firms. Maintaining tight administrative control of the economy—as reflected by the current system of standards in Egypt— is incompatible with attempting to achieve export-led economic growth.

Consistency of the Current GOE Practices with Commitments to the WTO

As mentioned earlier, the Uruguay Round agreements include two subsidiary agreements, the TBT and the SPS. All 134 members of the WTO (among which is Egypt) are required to abide by the provisions of both the TBT and SPS agreements. These agreements require countries to use international standards except where the standard is an ineffective or inappropriate means for the fulfillment of the legitimate objectives pursued (TBT) or a more stringent standard can be scientifically justified (SPS).

The most relevant requirements of the TBT agreement for the Egyptian system of quality control are the following:

- Treating imports no less favorably than domestic products (national treatment).

- Ensuring that technical regulations are not prepared or adopted with a view to or with the effect of creating unnecessary obstacles to international trade.

- Where relevant standards or their completion is imminent, members must use them, or their relevant parts, as a basis for their technical regulations.

- All members must play a full part in the preparation by appropriate international standardizing bodies of standards for products for which they have adopted, or plan to adopt, technical regulations.

- Members must give "positive consideration" to accepting the regulations of other members if they are equivalent, even if different.

- Technical regulations should be based on product performance rather than design or descriptive characteristics.

- All proposals to create new standards must be published, notified to the WTO Secretariat, and allowed a reasonable interval before entering into force, except in cases of urgency for safety, health, environmental protection, or national security.

As noted above, in a number of respects, Egypt is not in conformity with the various requirements of the WTO. Reforming the system to be consistent with these requirements would help to reduce the costs of the present system.

Conclusion and Recommendations

Although it is legitimate that governments interfere to ensure safety and integrity of products produced domestically, or those imported or exported, the system applied by the GOE is complex, superfluous, and costly. Substantial changes must be introduced within the current system to provide for a more dynamic and efficient economy, to offer Egyptian consumers greater product variety and quality, and to allow Egypt to meet its obligations, especially under the GATT/WTO. These changes point to the following main directions of reform required by the current system in Egypt (see also Nathan Associates 1998a, 1998b):

- Streamline the system to conform to the WTO TBT agreement. The most important obligations under this agreement are the requirements that each member adopt international standards as a basis for its own standards and abide by the national treatment principle.

- Make product quality attributes a voluntary matter to be dealt with by the market, and limit mandatory technical product regulations to instances where this is justified to achieve safety, health, and environmental objectives.

- Reform the operation of the MOTS and GOIEC by elimination of inspecting and testing for quality, ensuring that products that have already been inspected by another agency of the GOE are not reinspected, and creating a register of repeatedly imported or exported products and exempting these products from testing.

- Establish interministerial cooperation to avoid duplicative sampling and testing and to avoid inconsistent application of regulations. Harmonization of standards and regulations with international norms would greatly help in this direction.

- Require acceptance by the MOTS and GOIEC of precertification and preinspection. The GOE should consider immediate and unilateral recognition of International Safety Marks (precertification) for all nonfood products that guarantee the safety of the products by a thorough international system of inspection and minimize safety risks. Preinspection at ports of export, while not as efficient as precertification, is preferable to inspection in Egypt upon arrival. An internationally accredited entity can ensure that goods are inspected before being exported to Egypt, using the Egyptian standards where required. This would ensure speedier inspection and testing in addition to ensuring accuracy and reducing consumer risks.

Streamlining the system of product standards, technical regulations, and inspection and testing for conformity along the lines prescribed above will have the benefit of reducing barriers to trade and lowering import and export transactions costs. This would stimulate both imports and exports and should result in lower consumer prices in addition to reducing consumer risk. Furthermore, harmonized standards lead to international recognition of both quality and safety standards, which would enable Egyptian manufacturers to export their products much more freely.

Practical steps toward implementing these reforms in the short term could include:

- Reducing the number of imported products requiring inspection at the port of entry by releasing without further testing or inspection products bearing an internationally recognized product certification safety mark and products that have been preinspected or tested in the country of origin by an accredited laboratory, when accompanied by certificates of compliance (see below). Products tested by an Egyptian-accredited inspection company recognized by the GOIEC should also be released without further inspection. In all cases, inspection by the GOIEC (or the substitute body proposed below) should be limited to spot checks. For noncertified and non-prespecified products, the GOIEC would continue to inspect and test products at the port of entry in its own laboratories or through a recognized third party.

- Creating of a register of repeatedly imported products that meet Egypt's requirements and that have a good record of compliance. Inspection of items on this list should be limited to spot checks.

- Requiring that inspection and checking be undertaken by a committee from customs and security bodies. The committee will confine its checking of each consignment for security reasons and illegal products. The importer presents customs with the necessary documentation to clear the shipment. After review, customs will either clear the shipment for release or will direct the consignment to other bodies for inspection and testing.

- Establishing a system for identification and recognition of competent inspection and testing companies. These companies should be made known to all importers and manufacturers, and certificates of compliance based on the results of their inspection and testing should be accepted by Egyptian authorities.

- Speeding up the process of harmonization of Egyptian standards with existing internationally recognized standards (ISO, IEC, *Codex,* and so forth). New standards developed by these bodies should be directly adopted in those instances where it is deemed necessary to make the norms mandatory. A national body should be created to determine what products are to be regulated and whether technical regulations are required. The recently formed Egyptian Accreditation Council might be able to fulfill this function.

- Establishing a national product conformity and consumer protection body, combining GOIEC and EOS functions into a single national inspection and testing organization. This body would provide certificates of conformity to international safety marks and to Egypt's technical regulations for both externally and domestically manufactured products. It would avoid costly contradictions in test results arising from separate government inspection bodies and eliminate costly duplication of effort in the prevailing inspection process. This body would also provide spot-check services in response to requirements of consumer protection and authorities responsible for the quality and safety of products supplied in the Egyptian market.

These recommendations would streamline the inspection and testing processes for imported goods—which suffer the most from the current enforcement system—without compromising consumer safety, public health, or environmental protection. The resulting cost savings to industry and to the government would enhance trade and promote economic activity.

Notes

1. This chapter relies extensively on the findings of four studies by Nathan Associates: "Research Study on the Quality Control System in Egypt," July 1996; "Egypt: Review of Selected Egyptian Organization for Standardization (EOS) Food and Manufactured Durable Goods Standards with Respect to International Norms," October 1997; "Egypt: Review of Selected Egyptian Organization for Standardization (EOS) Food Standards with Respect to International Norms," March 1998; and "Pilot Study for Pre-Certification of Imported Products," March 1998.

2. Nathan Associates (1998a) report that the official list of inspected and tested items provided by the GOIEC contains 130 line items, 26 of which are foods and agricultural products. The list contains categories or groups of products that do not appear to have any safety, public health, or environmental implications. A study to compare this list to the 320 to 340 mandatory standards issued by the EOS would be useful.

3. The costs in terms of reduced employment from the current system are twofold. Reduced investment and trade translate into employment reduction of corresponding magnitudes. Furthermore, since imports tend to be more capital intensive relative to exports in Egypt, the current system of quality control, by effectively protecting import-competing activities at the expense of export-oriented firms, encourages investment in relatively capital-intensive industries.

References

Hoekman, B., and S. Djankov. 1997. "Towards a Free Trade Agreement with the European Union: Issues and Policy Options for Egypt." In A.Galal and B. Hoekman, eds., *Regional Partners in Global Markets: Limits and Possibilities of the Euro-Med Agreements.* London: CEPR and ECES.

Kheir-El-Din, H., and A. El-Dersh. 1992. "Foreign Trade Policy in Egypt, 1986—1991." In S. El-Naggar, ed. , *Foreign and Intratrade Policies of the Arab Countries.* Washington, D.C.: International Monetary Fund.

Konan, D. E, and K. E. Maskus. 1997. "A Computable General Equilibrium Analysis of Egyptian Trade Liberalization Scenarios." In A. Galal and B. Hoekman, eds., *Regional Partners in Global Markets: Limits and Possibilities of the Euro-Med Agreements.* London: CEPR and ECES.

Nathan Associates for the USAID/DEPRA Project. 1996, July. "Research Study on the Quality Control System in Egypt." Cairo.

Nathan Associates for the USAID/DEPRA Project. 1997, October. "Egypt: Review of Selected Egyptian Organization for Standardization (EOS) Food and Manufactured Durable Goods Standards with Respect to International Norms." Cairo.

Nathan Associates for the USAID/DEPRA Project. 1998a, March. "Egypt: Review of Selected Egyptian Organization for Standardization (EOS) Food Standards with Respect to International Norms." Cairo.

Nathan Associates for the USAID/DEPRA Project. 1998b, March. "Pilot Study for Pre-Certification of Imported Products." Cairo.

SRI International. 1996. *Industry Diagnostics and Roadmaps to Increase Egypt's Export Performance.* Cairo.

World Bank. 1997. *Country Economic Memorandum, Egypt: Issues in Sustaining Economic Growth, Main Report.* Vol. II. Report No. 16207 EGT. Washington, D.C.

Chapter 10

Electronic Data Interchange, Trade Facilitation, and Customs Reform[1]

Benita Cox and Sherine Ghoneim
The Management School
Imperial College for Science, Technology and Medicine, London

The increasing competitive pressures from both global and domestic markets are forcing nations to adopt new trade practices and standards. Nations need to adjust to new methods of trade information exchange, open up their telecommunications systems, and learn to take full advantage of harmonized procedures, standards, and practices for trade documentation. The role of electronic commerce and electronic data interchange (EDI), in particular, is rapidly evolving in the face of increasing pressure from global markets to provide standardized methods and practices for international trade. A general term to describe these changes in international trade administration is "trade facilitation."

With the gradual removal of international trade barriers and the increasing interdependence between international markets, EDI is expected to play a significant role in facilitating international trade (Farhoomand and Pace 1995). EDI is the most prevalent form of electronic commerce supporting trade transactions across various industry sectors on a national and international level. EDI, as a system of exchanging standardized trade-related information, is not only a fundamental information technology (IT) business process reengineering tool (Swatman 1994; Swatman, Swatman, and Fowler 1994; Venkatramann 1991), but also a key electronic commerce technique for a reengineered trade facilitation process (Schware and Kimberley 1995), especially with respect to customs and excise applications. Experts forecast a million users of EDI by the end of the year 2000. Recent statistics suggest that EDI users (excluding financial EDI users) are estimated to be in the region of 170,000 users, 70 percent of whom are in the United States and Europe.[2]

At the national level, the simplification and speeding up of trade information flows offers significant national benefits. Singapore claims that properly applied trade facilitation is already saving it in excess of 1 percent of its gross domestic product ($700 million in 1994) each year. As a result, reengineered trade processes based upon trade facilitation principles and EDI have become a global phenomenon (Schware and Kimberley 1995). An increasing number of nations are in the process of developing their EDI industry, and there is a rapidly growing need for the development of national frameworks and implementation guidelines.

Developing nations, therefore, find themselves in the position of having to rapidly adapt their traditional trading practices if they are to be able to participate fully in international trade. Although Western countries have expended much energy in recent years defining international trade standards and founding the EDI and electronic commerce infrastructure, for developing nations, barriers to developing their national EDI industries and electronic trading communities are both different and more complex than in more developed nations.

While there are a number of lessons to learned from mature Western EDI markets, these models are not necessarily appropriate for developing countries. For example, the literature suggests that EDI successes in the United Kingdom were primarily driven by the retail and manufacturing industries, which could benefit from an advanced state of EDI service provision and telecommunications deregulation. In the case of Egypt, there is not only an absence of the required EDI industry service provision and electronic commerce infrastructure, but also much less in the way of interorganizational cooperation and communication of the type existing between retail and manufacturing in the United Kingdom.

The main objectives of this chapter are twofold: First, to identify the factors that influence success in IT-facilitated trade processes, particularly within the framework of introducing EDI to nations in the early stages of formulating their EDI and electronic trading policies; second, to identify nation-specific requirements within a multidisciplinary implementation framework and determine the respective policy implications. For concreteness, the focus of attention will be on the necessary conditions for using EDI to improve the operation of customs in Egypt.

Schware and Kimberley (1995) note that, "The purpose of best practice within the context of trade facilitation is to replace paper documents with electronic equivalent, but not in an exact substitution." Properly designed, an EDI system will streamline documentation procedures and retool practices among the parties involved in the trade and transport procedures. The concept of replacing paper documents with EDI, representing much of the detail with codes and harmonized processes (trade facilitation), and the simplification of procedures (reengineering) represents the complete IT-facilitated trade process.

Developing a national EDI adoption framework should not be confined to addressing technical requirements. To maximize potential benefits, a national strategy will have to take into account the context in which the development of the EDI industry is undertaken. It must consider the nation's particular political and economic goals and constraints, the business culture, and sectoral structure as well as the organizational domestic and international requirements that may influence or be affected by the adoption of EDI. Factors that influence and are influenced by EDI adoption on a national, industrial, and organizational level include the *context* (political, economic, and social environments), *infrastructure* (technical requirements and know-how), and the *capacity to change* in developing a national EDI strategy. These elements give rise to what we call the CIC framework, a multidimensional research approach that recognizes the complexity and interrelatedness of the business and technical determinants of successful EDI implementation.

The proposed framework identifies the major criteria to be considered when adopting EDI. Rather then call for a universal EDI strategy, a successful EDI strategy must grow out of a sophisticated understanding of the surrounding business and technical requirements and structure and how they are changing. Only strategies that are tailored to the particular business requirements and existing inter- and intrafirm systems and processes, and that have the flexibility to accommodate change are likely to succeed.[3]

The CIC Framework

Successful development of a national EDI strategy requires that an analysis be undertaken of the *context, infrastructure,* and *capacity to change*.

Contextual Environment for EDI
Successful EDI implementations have been made in response to demand pull conditions: nations adopting EDI were either driven by increased globalization and regional integration pressures translated into trade facilitation initiatives, or by national business requirements. Business requirements on a national, industry, and corporate level have been particularly important in successful EDI adoption. The 'contextual" influences will not only vary from one nation to another, but also according to specific industry requirements, differences in corporate objectives, and the role of government in the economy.

Infrastructure and Know-How
Technical infrastructure involves not only information technology resources, but also telecommunications platforms and legislative aspects to govern interorganizational relations. At the national level, the legislative framework as well as the national information technology and telecommunications infrastructure, in general, and the role of value-added networks and coordinating bodies, in particular, have to be investigated.

Capacity to Change
Exploiting EDI's technical capacity to accommodate changing business and technical requirements has been identified as a critical success determinant in developing

an EDI strategy. In this chapter, "capacity to change" refers to EDI's technical ability to accommodate changing business and technical requirements.

The Case of Egypt

Contextual Environment for EDI

A number of factors influence the decision to adopt EDI on a national level. These factors stem from the political, economic, social, and technical environment (Figure 10.1).

POLITICAL ENVIRONMENT

It is crucial that due attention be given to the political environment into which EDI is to be introduced. Of primary importance is the role of government in establishing successful national EDI strategies. Singapore is a clear example of a successful government-sponsored EDI initiative, whereas Latin America has achieved limited success with trade facilitation initiatives primarily because of the lack of serious government intervention (Schware and Kimberley 1995). In Europe, there have been a number of initiatives, both national and international, aimed at establishing European-wide EDI policies and standards. The European Commission has, for example, allocated ECU 30 billion to spend over the next 10 years to establish a pan-

FIGURE 10.1. EDI CONTEXTUAL PRESSURES

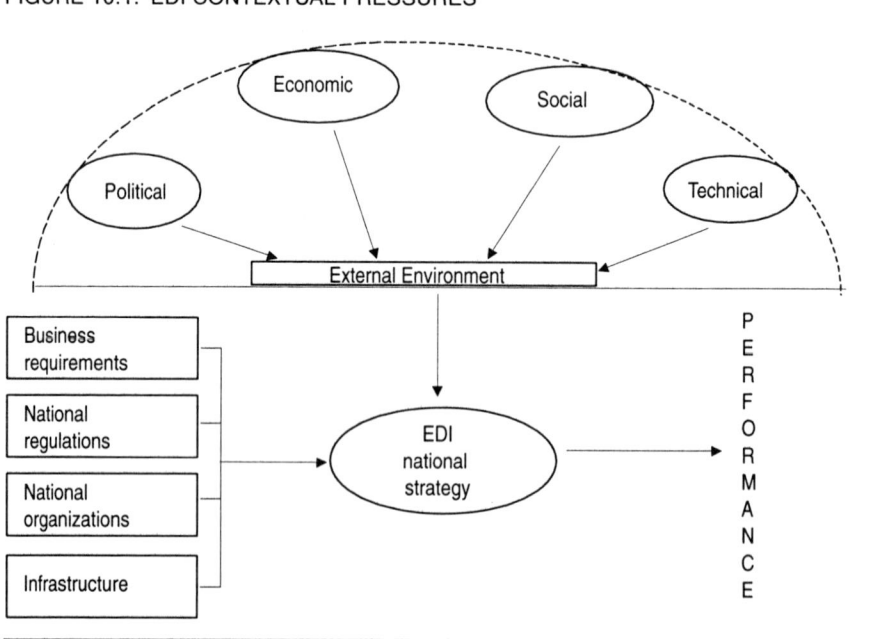

European EDI infrastructure. Likewise, Egypt is under pressure to extend IT policy in general and EDI specifically.

A World Bank study conducted in 1995 endorsed the use of EDI and electronic commerce as critical components in trade facilitation. Based on this study, recommendations were put forward to the Egyptian Cabinet of Ministers in May 1997 that identified a number of immediate priorities to boost Egypt's trade performance as part of a continued pursuit of trade and the promotion of foreign direct investment (FDI). These recommendations were primarily concerned with introducing customs, inspection, and regulatory and procedural reforms to strengthen Egyptian competitiveness in the world markets; accelerate the pace of moving goods into and out of the country; improve the reliability of importing and exporting processes; and generally reduce the transaction costs of exporting. Although considerable effort has been made by the Egyptian government to enhance the transparency of trade procedures, this remains problematic. The Egyptian government has now lent its support for the implementation of EDI but sees its role as a regulatory one, securing funding and providing the required infrastructure, rather than implementational.

ECONOMIC ENVIRONMENT

Trade liberalization and economic transformations around the world in recent years have increased the pressure to review existing systems used for processing trade documentation. There is an urgent need to achieve faster economic growth, which depends in part on the ability of firms to participate in the world commodity. The government of Egypt is committed to liberalizing imports, promoting exports, and encouraging foreign direct investment. Such development strategies entail removing barriers to trade that require reforming traditional standards, procedures, and agreements, which facilitate international trade.

SOCIAL ENVIRONMENT

Studies have highlighted the power of the business community to drive forward the adoption of electronic trading standards (Banerjee and Golhar 1991; Reekers and Smithson 1994). For instance, in the United Kingdom, the success of the introduction of EDI may largely be attributed to the pressures exerted by the business community to establish standards. The United Kingdom initiated EDI for trade facilitation purposes early in the 1980s. The British Simpler Trade Producers Board (SITPRO) and the U.K. Article Numbering Association worked toward developing TRADACOMS, which is a national standard and caters to domestic business requirements.

Egypt is coming under increasing pressure from the business community to adopt information technologies, which will allow it react more flexibly and promptly to changing market demand. As a result of recent increased awareness of the business benefits associated with electronic commerce in general and EDI in particular, members of the business community in the Federation of the Egyptian Industries

(FEI) and members of various chambers of commerce are pursuing different av-
enues to acquire new trading technologies.

As a member of the United Nations Conference on Trade and Development
(UNCTAD), Egypt is a participant in the trade efficiency program designed to enhance trade systems and services through the creation of a network of Trade Points
in each of the participating nations. Besides creating trading networks, Trade Points
also provide trading facilities and linkages, and promote the introduction of EDI.

Egypt as an emerging market is also a recipient of aid, particularly allocated to
electronic systems upgrading and IT-specific technology transfer. Technical pressures to adopt information technologies (such as electronic commerce and EDI) and
new logistics (such as just-in-time inventory control) were primarily supply driven
in the early 1990s by international organizations in an attempt to exploit the funds
allocated.

Lack of awareness of the potential business impact of such technologies, on the
one hand, and lack of domestically rooted demand-driven initiatives, on the other,
substantially delayed serious developments to establish national value-added service networks in Egypt.

Infrastructure

The extent to which a nation is able to adopt a new technology is heavily dependent
on the state of its existing infrastructure. "In 1985, Egypt had the vision to develop
solid strategy to build the information infrastructure" (El Sherif 1996). Part of this
strategy was achieved through establishing information and decision support centers at both central and local government levels. In addition, nationwide databases
were developed and major improvements in both telecommunications and informatics
were achieved. Strategic alliances were formed with international, high–profile,
world-leading organizations in information technology and close bilateral cooperation with European Union countries was established to share experience and know-
how (El Sherif 1996). In addition, Egypt has participated in UNCTAD's Trade
Efficiency Program, aimed at establishing a worldwide network of trade facilitation
centers called Trade Points. These Trade Points are laboratories where the latest
information and telecommunications technologies, such as EDI, are applied to trade
(UNCTAD 1992). However, Trade Points' plans to introduce EDI to the Egyptian
market did not materialize. Trade and information technologies have been confined
to data provision; Trade Point services, located within the Ministry of Industry, are
limited to the provision of datasets and reports on national and international trade
trends.

EDI services in Egypt are limited to access to international service providers.
Neither the philosophy nor the facility is available on a national basis. Use is confined to a limited number of multinationals committed to communicating with par-

ent companies or trading partners. Dependence is primarily on one service provider. Experience in those countries where EDI has been successfully implemented highlights the importance of the role of EDI coordination authorities and value-added network service providers. Organizations such as EDIform in the Netherlands and the EDIA (EDI Association) in the United Kingdom play a crucial role in coordinating activities. Egypt, likewise, requires the appointment of a national EDI service provider as well as a single, well-funded, one-stop trade promotion agency with strong affiliations and networking capacity with various trade bodies.

Capacity to Change

Another major determinant of the success of a national EDI strategy is the initiator's awareness of EDI's capacity to accommodate nation-specific, changing business and technical requirements. International trade processes are typically characterized by complexity and redundancy. Some document-handling procedures are surrounded by 500-year-old practices. A typical international trade transaction can take as many as 150 different documents to process (Schware and Kimberley 1995). Meyers and Canis (1991) indicate that there are estimates of paperwork in international trade costing some 7 percent of the value of the goods traded. This complexity is not only a result of the multiplicity of organizations involved in the supply chain, but also a product of multiple data entries.

Although EDI can play an effective role in reengineering such processes, environmental constraints are likely to inhibit such changes. For example, India, where resistance to change is strong, committed itself in 1993 to domestic EDI usage, but in 1995 there were no more than 200 users in the region (Schware and Kimberley 1995).

The ability to satisfy changing market requirements, and the flexibility required to meet changing demands for products and services, are important determinants of a firm's competitiveness. The infrastructure and procedures that enable both importers and exporters to access and exchange products and information efficiently and effectively are critical to a nation's competitive position and capacity. Achieving the necessary process change in the area of international trade procedures represents a major challenge in trade facilitation initiatives.

Initiators awareness should not be confined to the technical ability of EDI to streamline procedures as a part of a major reengineering strategy, but also encompass the potential for EDI to accommodate change. A phased approach to account for the existing environmental constraints should be adopted. This is the approach underlying the proposed EDI solution for the Customs and Excise Authority in Egypt discussed below.

The Egyptian Customs and Excise Authority

Egypt's Customs and Excise Authority (CEA) was established in the early 19th century (1819) as the formal gateway for imports and exports. The CEA has focused, since its inception, on generating revenues for the national treasury through duties applied to imports and exports. Customs duties alone have accounted for approximately 30 percent of tax revenues over the past five years and 12 percent of all government revenues (World Bank 1997). Consequently, the efficiency of customs revenue collection is a crucial dimension of the CEA's operation.

As Egypt pursues economic reform and seeks to integrate into the world economy, the role, mission, and objectives of Egypt's CEA is changing. Trade facilitation is becoming much more important. Progress in achieving the desired changes is hindered by numerous inspection agencies and layers of regulations, which slow the movement of goods to and from international markets, hinder trade promotion and administrative efficiency, and encourage theft and fraud.

The introduction of EDI within a trade facilitation framework would not only reap efficiency gains, in terms of use of accelerated, simplified systems and EDI-based pre-clearance of imports and exports, but would also provide the information necessary for decisionmaking with respect to problem solving, facilities scheduling, and planning for maximum use of infrastructure. Such implementation would not only contribute toward Egypt's integration in the global economy, but would also cater to increasing the revenue generated by Egypt's CEA as a result of increased efficiency and enhanced transparency of the procedures involved in international trade.

Egypt is an emerging market that is heavily investing in development and growth strategies based on trade and FDI promotion and streamlining associated processes. EDI provides the capacity to cater to Egypt's trade facilitation requirements and offers the potential for some dramatic national performance, as witnessed by the evidence of success in Singapore.

EDI's role in endorsing national strategies and safeguarding national interests should provide the basis of developing a long-term strategy in spite of the presence of major implementation barriers. As proposed, a simple EDI implementation scenario may be adopted in the short term to overcome immediate problems, cater to information availability, and provide management and control to serve the immediate trading process efficiency requirements.

The Status Quo

The CEA has four geographical directorates: Cairo, Alexandria, Suez, and Aswan. Each directorate has several customs posts—for example, the Alexandria directorate handles both the Alexandria and Damietta seaports in addition to Egypt's western borders with Libya. Each directorate is organized around two functional layers: operational and financial. The operational layer is mainly responsible for the validation of regulatory permits and documentation as well as the valuation of goods and the application of various duties and taxes. The financial layer is primarily concerned with duty collection and management of warehouse transactions. Each directorate has distinct functions and features, reflecting the type and value of goods processed. In terms of transaction volume, the Cairo directorate handles around

300,000 consignments each year, compared with 70,000 for Alexandria. However, in terms of value, Alexandria handles 82 percent of Egypt's total imports and exports.

Since the inception of the process of automation at the CEA, initiated in the mid-1980s through a French government initiative, the focus has centered around Alexandria, which is the largest revenue generator.[4] Since then, only 12 other customs posts have been automated. The majority of outlets are still based on manual processes.

Problems of information flow within the CEA are typical of those encountered by institutions involved in international trade, namely, lack of detailed data and a series of complex processes in need of streamlining. Analysis of the existing flow of information through the CEA suggests that improvements can be made with respect to logistics and data handling, which would result in substantial financial savings.[5] Areas of reform have focused on the requirement for detailed data, streamlining processes, and organizational challenges.

REQUIREMENT FOR DETAILED DATA

There is a fundamental requirement for detailed product information. The existing systems cater only partially to such a requirement. As a result, there is often inconsistency and discrepancy in the information reported, particularly with respect to the estimated versus the actual revenue collected.

STREAMLINING PROCESSES

A long and tedious paper-based system, by definition, lends itself to error. The presence of multiple agencies and multiple layers within each agency in the processing of information results in inconsistency in the data reported. Lack of systems transparency and consistency in procedures in applying and interpreting regulations contributes to systems complexity and ambiguity.

Customs officials indicate that clearance procedures could be streamlined and that substantial savings in the attendant time and costs could be achieved. The government is seeking to introduce new procedures that use modern information technology that will effectively facilitate trade.

ORGANIZATIONAL CHALLENGES

Major strategic and organizational barriers exist that impede the adoption of EDI. First, the existing organizational and cultural setup of the CEA is complex and rigid. There is considerable resistance to altering inter- and intraorganizational power relations. Second, many customs posts are still manually operated and have a grace period of one to three months to complete any one operation and report data to the central computing system. Managers of such posts fear that change is likely to inhibit any fundamental structural reengineering programs. Third, the strategic alliance in place with the French organization in charge of operating and maintaining the central computing department in Alexandria is funded by the French government, which has recently renewed its funding and maintenance contract of the system through 1999. This alliance does not allow for any tampering with the existing system, nor is it flexible.[6]

A Possible Approach

Given the existing organizational and cultural constraints at the CEA, a staged approach to introducing EDI within the Customs and Excise Authority in Egypt is clearly required. Although a fully fledged EDI implementation strategy, together with a fundamental business process reengineering initiative, may contribute significant benefits to the CEA, the given constraints do not allow for such privilege. However, an initial phased approach leading eventually to business process redesign may be introduced through the simple application of an EDI system, external but parallel to the CEA flow of information processes, which shadows the data processed. This would be transparent to the public, but avoid the major threats associated with a new implementation. A three-phase approach to meet CEA-specific barriers and challenges is proposed below.

PHASE I—EDI INTRODUCTION

This initial stage of EDI implementation should aim at capturing detailed consignment details without tampering with the existing systems. In this introductory stage, EDI is used to shadow existing processes. A warehouse audit control system would ensure the capture of detailed consignment data, which can be electronically processed and await the goods' release authorization. This can subsequently be deducted from the debit manifest according to the consignment details. This minor alteration does not interfere with any of the operational layer processes but provides a number of benefits:

- Detailed line items will be received from the shipper before docking, which will provide immediate access to information; cut down on time delays; include a complete record of information, including customs code and product description; and provide control of warehousing inventory.

- The automatic tracking of products in process versus products released will be much better controlled and thus reduce opportunities for inconsistent data or discrepancy. Similarly, dumping processes will be better controlled.

- Audit for valuation of import goods could take place in advance, since details of a shipment would be available before the actual docking of the goods. This will enhance the systems' transparency.

This proposed system would also provide a more centralized audit of the functions of the CEA and help set the stage for expanding this pilot phase to a full and comprehensive EDI implementation. The pilot could be further extended to provide an enhancement to the existing paper process by enabling a preset form to be printed for importers upon submission of consignment.

Although the proposed initial phase of EDI is confined to producing accurate data and providing initial information control, it provides the potential to streamline business processes and improve control over identified system loopholes.

PHASE II—EDI DEVELOPMENT AND DIFFUSION

The second stage of the proposed solution aims at establishing the foundation for developing the national EDI community. This phase would be set up at the operational level and would entail the use of a PC terminal at the initial stage of the clearance process. A unique reference could automatically be generated on the Import Clearance Application Form, which would result in the elimination of the final CEA central registration process in Alexandria. This would also facilitate communication with the importer or his or her broker, increase efficiency (avoid data inconsistency and procedural delays), and enhance the CEA's services. Networking of PCs may be considered at a later stage. Such application would, however, require development and upgrading of the skills, knowledge, and expertise of existing staff.

PHASE III—ESTABLISH AN EDI GATEWAY

Ultimately, the CEA would benefit from the implementation of a full-fledged EDI implementation. Such implementation would involve simplifying processes, removing excessive and obsolete controls, shortening and easing lines of communication, and using both bar coding and EDI for rapid, accurate transfer of data between computers. It would also require alignment with trading partners' systems and the adoption of international electronic commerce standards. Given the existing constraints, this may only be considered as a long-term strategy.

Business Requirements

In line with the CIC framework, the proposed development of an EDI strategy is demand driven to cater to national requirements. The phased nature of the implementation solution is driven by business requirements to fulfill the trade facilitation initiatives, integrating the core business application identified as the information contained within shippers' documents. A phased approach is also needed in recognition of CEA-specific barriers and challenges. The first phase's "parallel shadowing" will improve system accountability, enhance CEA access to detailed data, and indirectly help control theft and fraud. In the second stage—community development—the use of EDI is extended to importers to enhance efficiency and promote an electronic trading culture. The third stage—development of a CEA EDI gateway—will result in a full-fledged EDI operation based on a business process redesign and quality management strategy. This will bring Egypt in line with international efficiency standards. Unlike the initial implementation phases, implementing a corporate EDI gateway would involve fundamental changes in procedures and processes.

Role of Government

The regulatory role of government, and its endorsement of developing EDI through securing funding and required infrastructure, is critical in project ramp up. The government of Egypt has played a leading referee role rather than an implementational one in the initial stage of introducing EDI. Following on from the Singapore experience, government endorsement of electronic trade in general and EDI in particular will be instrumental in promoting and institutionalizing EDI adoption nationwide.

Trading Partners' Requirements

To ensure successful implementation, incorporating trading partners' requirements is also crucial. The success of Her Majesty's Customs and Excise Authority in the United Kingdom in endorsing electronic trading has been partly due to addressing and integrating trading community requirements in all activities related to the collection and dissemination of information (Sawhney and Williams 1994). Such a partnership can be seen as a fundamental requirement to facilitate later phases of EDI implementation and community development. Accommodating trading partners' requirements, particularly in terms of standards compatibility, is crucial in developing the EDI community.

Technical Strategy

Technology transfer with a view to developing a national EDI industry in general or adopting EDI on an organizational or institutional level is not problematic. In fact, some technical alternatives, such as using EDI on the Internet, can be adopted immediately. However, in order to successfully and systematically develop a national EDI community, it is important to have a national vision and a clear strategy. This strategy should not be confined to technical aspects, but also include the know-how critical to successful development. Examples are the role of value-added network services (VANS), EDI associations, and coordinating bodies in founding a national EDI industry.

Widespread use of the Internet is potentially providing small and medium-sized enterprises with a cost-effective means of adopting EDI. There are some serious legal and security implications related to the use of electronic trading on the Internet, which lie beyond the scope of this chapter, but technically the Internet may provide an interim stepping-stone toward the full, appropriate adoption of electronic trading.

Conclusion

Introducing EDI within trade facilitation initiatives, in customs and excise applications specifically, will not only reap efficiency gains but also embrace national goals to integrate into the global economy and increase revenues generated as a result of increased efficiency. Critical to successful EDI implementation is accommodating the contextual environment and not confining the strategy to technology transfer in building the EDI industry. The foundation must be demand driven to cater to specific national requirements—defined within a clear national strategy, as in the case of Singapore. It is estimated that successful implementation of EDI within the CEA in Egypt may result in increasing the revenue generated by the authority by $350 million annually.[7]

The success of a national EDI strategy will primarily depend on integrating business requirements, government intervention, infrastructure efficiency, and capacity to change to cater to changing market and technical requirements. The main policy implications of our analysis are summarized below.

A demand-driven national EDI strategy must be based on well-defined national business and economic needs and requirements. It should incorporate international requirements to streamline trade processes, which will reduce the trade information processing cycles to a minimum critical path, thereby achieving economies of scale and scope and maximizing competitive advantages (Schware and Kimberley 1995). It should also cater to the requirements of national industry sectors, based on their perceived competitive and efficiency benefits. Unless there is recognition of business drivers as the main motivational factors to adopt EDI, limited benefits will emerge.

Increase awareness and enhance EDI-specific education. Expert knowledge of business requirements and EDI capacity is a prerequisite to successful implementation. An awareness and education program is an important key to success. Lack of such a program is likely to cause failure and delay EDI implementations (Schware and Kimberley 1995). Promoting EDI education will contribute toward human capacity building. It will not only help develop the skills and expertise required for maximizing the use and potential of EDI implementations, but also cater to tailoring EDI use to national requirements and constraints.

Government must be instrumental in developing the EDI industry infrastructure, particularly in the early stages of development. The government's capacity to alter regulations to accommodate electronic trading requirements, secure funds, or act as a catalyst in developing the EDI community by endorsing an intergovernmental and/or public sector electronic trading strategy is invaluable. Development of the infrastructure does not necessarily need to be centrally funded by the government, but could be in the form of an endorsement or partnership with the private sector. The most important aspect is to institutionalize electronic trading and ensure an environment conducive to community development.

National infrastructure development is needed. A primary requirement for developing a national EDI industry is the availability of a sufficiently sophisticated, competitive, and reliable data communications network and VANS, as previously discussed. Although the EDI technology itself is transferable, local expertise is still required to apply domestic requirements, definitions, and restrictions. This is applicable in terms of defining EDI applications and standards as well as in developing the marketing and community development strategies. Developing the infrastructure should also take into account the know-how transfer to include factors critical to successful EDI adoption on a national level, including the role of VANS and EDI associations.

Capacity to change. The national strategy should include an institutional mechanism for monitoring and tracking changing business and technical requirements in order to cater to the required changes—in legislation, for example— effectively and efficiently.

Notes

1. The authors would like to thank Mr. Hatem Zorkani for his invaluable input to the study of the Customs and Excise Authority in Egypt.

2. Kimberley, P. 1998. Paul Kimberley and Associates, Sydbey, Australia. Unpublished internal report.

3. This study builds on Cox and Ghoneim (1996, 1997, and 1998).

4. Zorkani, Hatem. 1996. Adviser, Cabinet Information and Decision Support Center and Consultant to CEA Efficiency Development Program. Personal communication.

5. Zorkani, Hatem. 1997. Adviser, Cabinet Information and Decision Support Center and Consultant to CEA Efficiency Development Program. Personal communication.

6. Zorkani 1997.

7. Zorkani 1997.

References

Banerjee, S., and D. Y. Golhar. 1991. *Electronic Data Interchange in U.S. firms: A Survey*. Report. Drexel University.

Cox, B. and S. Ghoneim. 1996. "Drivers & Barriers to Adopting EDI: A Sector Analysis of UK Industry." *European Journal of Information Systems* 5:24–33.

———. 1997. "Developing a National EDI Strategy." In P. Banerjee, R. Hackney, G. Dhillon, and R. Jain, eds., *Business Information Technology Management: Closing the International Divide*. Har-Aanad Publications PVT Ltd.

———. 1998. "Strategic Use of EDI in the Public Sector: The HMSO Case Study" *Journal of Strategic Information Systems*.

El Sherif, Hisham. 1996. "Electronics and IT—The Road to Development." *German Arab Trade*. German Arab Chamber of Commerce Report. Cairo.

Farhoomand, A. F., and E. Pace. 1995. "An Exploratory Investigation of Electronic Commerce Use in International Trade". In G. Doukidis, B. Galliers, T. Jelassi, H. Kremar, and F. Land, eds., *Proceedings of the 3rd European Conference on Information Systems.* Athens, Greece.

Fowler, D. C., P. M. C. Swatman, and P. A. Swatman. 1994. "A Corporate EDI Gateway: A Centralised Approach to Integrating EDI." In *Proceedings of the "ACIS'94"—5th Australian Conference on Information Systems.* Melbourne, Victoria.

Meyers, R. B., and R. J. Canis. 1991. "Preparing for the 21st Century with EDI and Bar Coding." *EDI World* 1(12):35–40.

Reekers, N., and S. Smithson. 1994. "EDI in Germany and the UK: Strategic and Operational Use." *European Journal of Information Systems* 3(3):169–78.

Sawhney, V., and A. Williams. 1994. "Electronic Data Interchange in Government: The Business Opportunities." *Report, CCTA.* The Government Centre for Information Systems, London.

Schware, R., and P. Kimberley. 1995a. "Information Technology and National Trade Facilitation: Making the Most of Global Trade." World Bank Technical Paper 316. Washington, D.C.

Schware, R., and P. Kimberley. 1995. "Information Technology and National Trade Facilitation: Guide to Best Practice." World Bank Technical Paper 317. Washington, D.C.

Swatman, P. M. C. 1994. "Business Process Redesign Using EDI: The BHP Steel Experience." *Australian Journal of Information Systems* 2(1):55–73.

Swatman, P. M. C., P. A. Swatman, and C. Fowler. 1994. "A Model of EDI Integration and Strategic Business Re-engineering." *Journal of Strategic Information Systems* 3(1):41–61.

UNCTAD. 1992. *Report on the Creation of a Trade Point in Egypt, Preparatory Mission,* pp. 20-22 Unpublished. Geneva

Venkatramann, N. 1991. "IT-Induced Business Change." In M. S. Scott Morton, ed., *The Corporation of the 1990s: Information Technology and Organisational Transformation.* Oxford University Press.

World Bank. 1997. *Promoting Outward Orientation through Exports, Arab Republic of Egypt, Country Economic Memorandum—Egypt: Issues in Sustaining Economic Growth—Main Report.*

Chapter 11

Free Zones in the Middle East:
Development Patterns and Future Potential

Kishore Rao
The Services Group, Inc.

Free trade zones have been used internationally to promote exports, attract foreign direct investment, and spur economic growth. Modern free zones are recent variants of the traditional freeport or free zone concept, which has been in existence for several centuries. Free zones were established to encourage *entrepôt* trade, mostly within harbors among international trade routes. Early examples of free zones include Gibraltar (1704), Singapore (1819), Hong Kong (1848), Hamburg (1888), and Copenhagen (1891).

Since the first modern zone was established in the United States in 1945,[1] the number of zones worldwide has multiplied rapidly (Table 11.1). In the space of just three decades, more than 850 free zones are operating in some 100 countries, directly employing almost 30 million workers, and accounting for over $250 billion in global trade.[2] Zones are found in virtually every major trading country, including the United States.[3]

The generic free zone concept has evolved over time. There are several types of zones found internationally, including export processing zones (EPZ) (industrial free zones for export manufacturing industries), and commercial free zones (for trading, warehousing, and other *entrepôt* activities). Free zones and their variants continue to be an internationally recognized customs concept under the international Kyoto Convention.[4]

Several countries in the Middle East were early adopters of free zones. Egypt, Syria, Israel, and Jordan, for example, established free zones in the 1960s and 1970s, at about the same time that zones were set up in the Philippines, the Dominican Republic, and elsewhere. Yet, with a handful of exceptions, the economic contribution

TABLE 11.1. GROWTH IN FREE ZONE ACTIVITY WORLDWIDE

	1970s	1998
Number of countries	30+	100+
Number of zones	80	850
Number of private zones	None	600+
Total global trade	$10 billion	$250 billion +
Total direct employment	1.5 million	27.0 million

Sources: World Export Processing Zone Association (WEPZA) and The Services Group (TSG) estimates.

of free zones in the Middle East has been negligible compared with zone programs in the Far East and Latin America. This chapter examines the reasons behind the limited contributions of Middle Eastern zones, particularly in terms of manufactured exports.

Profile of Free Zones in the Middle East

History and Current Status

Despite being among the first countries to host modern free zones, the Middle East and North Africa (MENA) region has historically accounted for a small share of global free zone activity. Of the 850 industrial estate–style free zones worldwide, fewer than 5 percent are in the MENA area.[5] Most zones are found in North America, East Asia, and Latin America. Currently, there are 47 zones operating in the region (Table 11.2). Although statistics are unreliable, these zones represent an even smaller share of global free zone export and employment.

Leading free zone locations in the region are Egypt, Turkey and the United Arab Emirates (UAE). Zones in these countries account for the vast majority of total free zone exports and employment. Countries of the Arabian Gulf, in particular, have emphasized free zone development over the past decade.

MENA free zones generally share a number of characteristics that are unlike most zones internationally. These include:

- *Commercial rather than industrial orientation.* Most zones are oriented to trading and warehousing. Industrial and manufacturing activity is quite limited. There are few industrial free zones or export processing zones, per se.

- *Strong government role.* Government has taken the lead in developing and operating zones, generally on a heavily subsidized basis.

- *Limited role in trade and investment strategies.* Countries have not generally focused on free zones as a mechanism for export generation and foreign investment promotion. Most zones have a marginal economic impact.

TABLE 11.2. PROFILE OF OPERATIONAL MENA ZONES

	Start date	No. of zones	Exports	Employment
Cyprus	1980	1 public	$47 million	300
Egypt	1976	7 public	$400 million	70,000
		1 private		
Iran	1989	4 public	—	—
Israel	1969	3 public	—	—
Jordan	1973	4 public	—	3,000
Kuwait	1995	1 private	—	700
Lebanon	n.a.	1 public	—	n.a.
Libya	n.a.	1 public	—	—
Morocco	1994	1 public	$40 million	7,000
Syria	1971	6 public		
Turkey	1985	4 public	$600 million	8,000
		2 private		
UAE				
Ajman	1988	1 public	—	5,000
Dubai	1985	2 public	$2.4 billion	35,000
Fujairah	1987	1 public	—	2,000
Sharjah	1995	2 public	$80 million	3,000
UAQ	1988	1 public	—	700
West Bank/Gaza	1997	1 private	—	1,000
Total		40 public		
		7 private	—	—

n.a. Not applicable.
— Not available.
Note: Figures are latest available for industrial estate free zones. They exclude individual factories with free zone status operating outside of enclaves.
Source: TSG estimates based on official data.

- *Poor reputations.* Many MENA countries have viewed zones with suspicion and skepticism. Many zones are associated with marginal trading activities, small-scale businesses, and smuggling, rather than a strong focus on export manufacturing.

However, after years of relative dormancy, the last decade has seen expanding free zone activity. An increasing number of countries, in the Gulf and beyond, are establishing free zones (see Box 1). Even Saudi Arabia, which has traditionally viewed the whole country as a free zone, is in the process of establishing export zones in Yanbu and Jeddah.

In large part, the major factor behind the resurgence of zones has been the notable experience of the Jebel Ali Free Zone in Dubai. Established in 1985, Jebel Ali has been able to attract almost 2,000 international companies, create 35,000 jobs, and generate over $4 billion in exports. It has been a major factor behind the diversification of the UAE economy from an almost total reliance on exports of petroleum and related products.

BOX 11.1. FREE ZONES IN MENA ARE MULTIPLYING

Abu Dhabi: Free zone being established on Saadiyat island.

Bahrain: Two free zones planned.

Egypt: Four private zones planned in the North Suez area.

Iraq: Free zone being planned in Basra.

Jordan: Two QIZs designated; Aqaba freeport in planning.

Kuwait: Private zone planned at airport.

Lebanon: Planning for seven new private zones is underway.

Oman: Free zone development at Salalah port is underway.

Qatar: Free zone planned at Doha.

Ras Al Khaimah: Free zone being developed.

Saudi Arabia: Zones possible in Yanbu and Jeddah.

Tunisia: Plans for two free zones are underway.

Turkey: New zone approved at Black Sea port of Hopa.

West Bank and Gaza: Private zone operating in Gaza; plans for three new zones are underway.

Yemen: Private free zone being developed in Aden.

The perceived success of Dubai has led to "copy-cat" projects in each of the Emirates, as well as other members of the Gulf Cooperation Council (GCC). Some of these are "greenfield" projects requiring very large investments. Others are conversions of existing industrial estates or related facilities. Saudi Arabia, for example, is evaluating the feasibility of establishing a free zone in the Yanbu Industrial City, which already houses the giant Saudi Arabian Basic Industries Corporation (SABIC).

The other center of current zone activity is Jordan and the West Bank and Gaza. Jordan is promoting the Qualified Industrial Zone (QIZ) program of the United States.[6] The existing Al Hasan industrial estate received QIZ designation from the U.S. government last year; new QIZs are being established in Karak, Aqaba, and elsewhere. Cross-border zones are being established with Israel in the West Bank and Gaza. The Gaza Industrial Estate is already operational, and planning for a high-tech zone is advanced in Tulakarem in the West Bank. The Palestinian Industrial Estates and Free Zone Authority has plans for private zones in at least 20 locations in the West Bank and Gaza.

Economic Impact

INTERNATIONAL

The economic impact of zones internationally has been widely debated.[7] The basic rationale for zones has been to stimulate exports, foreign investment, and job creation. In developing countries, free zones have been used to offset the antiexport bias of economic policies and experiment with policy reforms.[8] Many developed countries continue to rely on the mechanism to enhance competitiveness and promote foreign investment.[9]

Table 11.3 profiles leading examples of successful and unsuccessful free zone programs. Several aspects are notable. First is the fact that the United States is the world's leading promoter of free zones. The 240 foreign trade zones in the United States employ almost 400,000 workers and generate some $16 billion in exports. Second is that free zones are especially prominent in relatively small countries. A leading example is the Dominican Republic, which has 47 operational zones, with a population of only 11 million. Costa Rica, with a population of 4 million, is another example. The employment importance of free zones has been especially pronounced in smaller countries (Table 11.4). The impact on gross exports is more significant than on employment. However, the net foreign earnings of zone operations are much lower. Net exports range from a low of 10–25 percent in most countries, to a high of 63 percent in Taiwanese zones. The net foreign exchange impact of zones depends on the extent to which strong supply and sourcing relationships with companies located outside of zones exist.

MIDDLE EAST

The impact of zones in the Middle East has not been examined in detail. Unfortunately, reliable data on zone performance do not exist. However, available data suggest that the economic importance of free zones to most MENA countries is very

TABLE 11.3. FREE ZONE SUCCESSES AND FAILURES

	Start date	No. of zones	Exports (billion $)	Employment
Successful Programs				
United States	1945	240	$16 billion	370,000
China	1979	150	$15 billion	300,000
Indonesia	1973	110	$3.5 billion	150,000
Philippines	1969	83	$7.2 billion	180,000
Thailand	1981	26	$4.7 billion	120,000
Dominican Republic	1968	47	$1.2 billion	190,000
Costa Rica	1981	9	$0.8 billion	40,000
Unsuccessful Programs				
India	1965	6	$1.0 billion	90,000
Bangladesh	1980	5	$0.5 billion	80,000
Pakistan	1980	2	$0.3 billion	40,000
Jamaica	1973	3	$0.3 billion	11,000
Jordan	1973	4	—	3,000
Guatemala	1973	7	$0.04 billion	3,000

— Not available.
Note: Figures exclude single-factory free zones located outside industrial estate-free zones.
Sources: The Services Group; World Bank; WEPZA; National Association of Free Trade Zones.

TABLE 11.4. EMPLOYMENT AND EXPORT IMPACT OF ZONES

	National exports (%)	*National employment (%)*
Bangladesh	10.5	< 1
Costa Rica	9.9	1.5
Dominican Republic	56.0	4.7
Malaysia	11.6	1.4
Mauritius	60.0	17.1
Philippines	35.0	< 1
South Korea	3.0	< 1
Sri Lanka	70.0	2.4
Taiwan	4.0	1

Note: Figures exclude private or single-factory free zones located outside industrial estate free zones. Net exports are zone exports minus imports.
Sources: Madani 1998, May, and author's estimates.

limited (Table 11.5). Middle Eastern zones are a very small source of employment. Like most zone programs internationally, zone jobs account for less than 1 percent of total national employment in most MENA countries. This is less the case among zones in Gulf countries, where free zones are an important source of employment, particularly in nontraditional industries. The contribution to national exports is generally more significant, particularly in smaller countries, such as Cyprus, the UAE, and so forth. But even here, zone exports represent less than 10 percent of total national exports.

At the same time, it is clear that the economic impact of free zones is far more significant in the smaller Gulf countries, compared with larger countries of the re-

TABLE 11.5. ECONOMIC IMPACT OF MENA ZONES—SELECTED COUNTRIES

	Total zone exports	*National exports (%)*	*Total zone employment*	*National employment (%)*
Cyprus	$47 million	3.70	300	0.10
Egypt	$400 million	4.50	70,000	0.50
Jordan	n.a.	—	3,000	0.27
Morocco	$40 million	0.04	7,000	0.11
Turkey	$600 million	2.30	8,000	0.04
UAE				
Dubai	$2.4 billion	7.20	35,000	10.10
Sharjah	$80 million	2.40	3,000	1.80

n.a. Not applicable.
— Not available.
Note: Figures are latest available for industrial estate free zones. National exports for the UAE refer to UAE total exports rather than for each Emirate.
Source: Estimates by The Services Group.

gion such as Egypt, Turkey, or Morocco. The free zones in the UAE, for example, have become the primary source of employment, inward investment, and exports in nonoil industries. The Jebel Ali free zone, for example, accounts for well over half of nontraditional exports from Dubai, and the vast majority of foreign investment in non-oil- and defense-related activities.[10] The growth of the zone has been above international norms. Inward investment in the zone doubled between 1988 and 1990, and has grown at a rate of about 150 companies per year since then, reaching more than 1,800 companies in 1998.[11] Purchases of zone-based enterprises from the domestic market exceeded $700 million in 1997.[12]

The Sharjah free zones have been particularly important in stimulating the manufacturing industry in the Emirates. According to a recent report, Sharjah accounted for 41 percent of all manufacturing units registered in the Emirates; most of these are located in the Emirates' free zones.[13] Ajman has become the center for textile and apparel manufacturing, most of which is centered in its free zone.

Despite these obviously positive attributes, the UAE free zones have been criticized on three grounds. First, the majority of free zone enterprises are engaged in trading and commercial activities, rather than manufacturing and more value-added activity. More than 70 percent of Jebel Ali's companies, for example, are registered as traders. Second, the free zones employ primarily expatriate labor, particularly from the Indian subcontinent. These workers are paid wages that are below levels paid to UAE citizens. As a result, low-wage-dependent activities—such as apparel assembly—are "artificially" sustained. Third, it is unclear that the free zones have a net positive economic benefit to the country, given the large public sector expenditures required for their establishment. Development of the Jebel Ali free zone, for example, required government capital investment of about $2 billion. It is not clear that this has yielded a positive return, given the strong package of incentives provided to enterprises—including zero taxes and subsidized facilities and services.

Major Factors Influencing the Performance of MENA Zones

The generally poor performance and limited economic impact of MENA zones are the result of a large number of factors. Some of these are common to free zones in other parts of the world, but a number are unique to the region. This section briefly analyzes these factors, before outlining some major recommendations for implementation by policymakers.

Basic Concept

At the most basic level, MENA zones have failed to keep up with the evolution of the free zone concept. Free zones were traditionally developed as isolated enclaves, both in terms of the underlying policy framework and in terms of geographic location. Access to a generous set of incentives and privileges was tightly controlled. Qualifying firms typically had to be 80–100 percent export oriented (for EPZs), engaged in recognized manufacturing activities, and at times only foreign owned.

Zones were physically located in relatively remote areas or near transport hubs, viewed primarily as "growth poles" for regional development.

This rather rigid concept has changed quite fundamentally over the past decade, reflecting the new emphasis on integrating free zones with the domestic economy, and viewing zones as a catalyst for the liberalization and modernization of the host economy. One aspect of this has been the liberalization of the traditional free zone concept to encompass a broader range of activities, directed at both export and local markets. Commercial and manufacturing zones have evolved into large-scale special economic zones and freeports. EPZs have changed from the traditional "pure EPZ" concept of industrial estates solely for export-oriented manufacturers, to various "hybrid" EPZs (Table 11.6).

The other major development is the establishment of specialized zones catering to specific sectors or industries. Most Latin American countries have commercial free zones for transshipment and other trade services; Malaysia has a separate law governing these zones. Science and technology parks have been established in Taiwan (China), Singapore, China, and elsewhere. Zones catering to specific industries like petrochemicals, forestry products, and gems and jewelry, are found in Thailand and Malaysia. Financial service zones have been established in Israel and Malaysia.

MENA zones have continued to be developed and viewed as enclaves, not integrated with their host countries. The location of many zones has been for political rather than economic reasons. Most Jordanian, Syrian, and Egyptian zones, for example, were located at quite remote sites. Access to incentives is tightly restricted, usually through the application of cumbersome and lengthy investment approval processes. Government domination of zone development and operation has restricted the number and vitality of zones. Zones have not specialized to cater to the needs of specific groups of industries.[14]

The net effect of these factors has been to greatly restrict zone activity and circumscribe their economic impact. A critical number of zones—or the establishment of a single, large-scale project such as a Freeport—has failed to materialize. The lack of critical scale is a major competitive weakness of the region's free zone programs.

Development Approach

Another major factor in the Middle East is the fact that most zones have been located, developed, and operated by the government. This has resulted in:

- *Poor locations.* The choice of location of many public zones was based on political rather than economic considerations. Many zones were located in very remote areas, entailing huge public sector outlays.

- *Inadequate development and operation of zones.* In many cases, zone physical development was not phased, facilities were heavily subsidized or poorly designed, and facilities were poorly maintained or not promoted. While

TABLE 11.6. CHANGING FREE ZONE CONCEPTS—SELECTED COUNTRIES

	Pure EPZ	Hybrid EPZ	Pure FTZ	Commercial free zone	Special economic zone	Freeport	Science-technology park
Northeast Asia	Taiwan, China Korea, Rep. of	China		China Japan	China		China Japan Taiwan
Southeast Asia	Indonesia Vietnam Philippines	Indonesia Philippines Thailand Vietnam	Malaysia	Malaysia	Philippines	Indonesia Malaysia Philippines	Malaysia Singapore
South Asia	Bangladesh India Pakistan Sri Lanka						India
MENA	Cyprus Morocco Gaza		Egypt Iran Jordan Turkey UAE	Iran Israel Jordan Kuwait Lebanon Syria			

Note: A country listed in more than one category means that several free zone concepts are available in that location. Pure EPZs are those that permit entry of EPZ-registered firms only, and exclude those registered under other schemes. Hybrid EPZs are divided into a fenced-in EPZ area open only to EPZ-registered firms, and a general industrial estate is open to all firms. Pure FTZs are for industrial or commercial users, without an export requirement.
Source: The Services Group.

affluent countries like the UAE can maintain world standards without operating on a cost-recovery basis, zones in countries like Jordan, Egypt, and Syria have languished.

- *Unfair competition for private zones.* Where private zones have been attempted, most face unfair competition from government-run free zones operating on a subsidized basis. This is a major factor facing private zone development efforts in Turkey, Egypt, Jordan, and elsewhere.

In contrast, the most notable trend over the past 15 years has been the growing number of privately owned and operated zones and industrial estates worldwide. While Latin America still accounts for the largest number of private zones, an increasing number are found in East Asia, especially the Philippines, with 80 operating economic zones and another 30 under development.

The increasing role of the private sector in zone development is changing the way in which the public and private sectors interact in zone development. In traditional projects, the government provides on- and off-site infrastructure, facilities, and basic services. To facilitate private zone development, innovative public-private partnership approaches have been established.[15] This is almost completely absent in the Middle East.[16]

Uncompetitive Policy Frameworks

A major reason behind the poor performance of some MENA zones has been uncompetitive and restrictive policy frameworks. While the investment incentives provided are generous, restrictive provisions and bureaucratic procedures erode their effectiveness. As a result, many manufacturers have not chosen to locate in the region's free zones, in favor of general industrial estates. There are several main policy issues:

- restrictive controls on free zone activity and cumbersome regulations

- exclusion on merchandise processed in Arab zones from preferential treatment under bilateral and regional trade agreements

- flaws in fiscal incentives provided free zone firms.

RESTRICTIVE PROVISIONS AND CONTROLS

The regulatory framework governing free zone activity, and the efficiency with which it is implemented and administered, have proven to be one of the key determinants of free zone success or failure worldwide. The cornerstone of a successful free zone program is the transparency and comprehensiveness of the incentives offered and the automaticity of their application, without the need for elaborate qualifying criteria.

The core policies and procedures of the MENA zones are not competitive from this perspective, with the notable exception of the free zones in the UAE and Kuwait. These latter zones have built their success on the removal of obstacles to foreign investment, and deregulation and simplification of procedures.

In sharp contrast, the free zone programs of most other countries are highly restrictive in terms of limits on foreign ownership, ownership and control of buildings and real assets, customs procedures, and the like. In Jordan and Egypt, it has proven easier to operate outside of free zones than within. The Jordanian free zone program is a particularly negative example. To date, the free zone program has been unable to contribute in a meaningful way toward exports, job creation, or economic growth. Reasons for this poor performance are largely attributable to a number of fundamental flaws in the existing free zone law and regulations:[17]

- *Lack of private sector development of zones.* The law provides a total government monopoly for zone development, financing, operation, and regulation.

- *Restrictive treatment of real assets.* Firms are unable to own land within free zones, hold title to leasehold improvements, or dispose of real assets after lease expiration. As a result, firms cannot use real assets for collateral financing and must hand over such property to the Free Zones Corporation after lease expiration.

- *Inappropriate application of extraterritoriality principles.* The law provides for an extreme concept of extraterritoriality. As a result, free zone products are not granted national certificates of origin except under a fixed, 40 percent value-added test. No mechanism exists for granting certificates of origin under the importing country's rules of origin provisions. Free zone merchandise is completely excluded from regional trade agreements. Free zone firms have also been denied access to foreign exchange financing of import and transit operations or the Central Bank's rediscounting scheme, except on an exceptional basis.

- *Burdensome local sales and sourcing provisions.* Sales into the domestic market are impeded by transaction-specific authorization requirements by the Ministry of Industry and Trade and by cumbersome customs procedures. Furthermore, purchases by free zone companies from the domestic market are not considered indirect exports and thus can be admitted only on a duty-paid basis.

Other weaknesses are found in terms of elaborate procedures and heavy documentation. In Jordan, three government agencies are involved in the inspection and clearance of free zone merchandise, including the customs department. Until recently, the investment application for free zone status in Egypt was 40 pages long, and investment approvals took anywhere from 12 to 24 months.

FLAWS IN PACKAGE OF FISCAL INCENTIVES

While restricting free zone activity, MENA zone programs also offer a package of fiscal incentives that is typically far more generous than available elsewhere. Some of these have only limited effectiveness and impose significant costs on government budgets.

As shown in Table 11.7, most MENA zones offer a zero tax environment. Corporate income taxes are exempted for a period of 5–15 years, or exempted in perpetuity in the case of Turkish free zones. Personal income taxes on expatriate workers are exempted or reduced significantly. Free zone companies in the UAE zones are able to import expatriate labor and pay them wages and other benefits below that mandated by law for UAE citizens.[18] Turkish zones continue to prohibit strikes and lockouts within free zones, although such practices are against international labor standards.

A competitive weakness of these programs is their continued reliance on tax holidays. While this is less of an issue among the oil-rich Gulf countries that do not impose corporate or personal income taxes in general, this policy leads to significant distortions, as shown by international experience (see Box 2).

BOX 11.2. SOME DRAWBACKS OF TAX HOLIDAYS

A tax exemption is of little benefit if the company is not making profits, which is usually the case in the initial years of operation. Firms that are profitable from the outset might not have needed incentives in the first place.

Tax holidays can facilitate income shifting from non-tax-exempt enterprises to tax-exempt companies through transfer pricing of intercompany transactions.

Tax holidays reduce the appeal of debt financing of capital investment by removing the benefits of interest deductibility. This equity funding bias is accentuated if dividends of tax-exempt firms are also exempt from personal income tax.

Tax exemptions tend to benefit investments with a short-term time horizon. Longer-term projects that generate profits beyond the tax holiday period do not benefit, unless firms are permitted to accrue and defer asset depreciation deductions beyond the tax holiday period.

Tax exemptions do not benefit investors from many OECD countries that tax income on a global basis, unless a "tax sparing" agreement is in place.

Source: Mintz 1990 and UNCTAD 1995.

TABLE 11.7. FREE ZONE INCENTIVES—SELECTED COUNTRIES

	Jordan	Egypt	Turkey	Dubai
Corporate profit tax exemption	100% for 12 years	100% for 5–15 years	100% in perpetuity	100% for 15 years, renewable for 15 years
Foreign ownership restrictions	Controlled	Some controls	None	None
Capital and profits repatriation	Restricted for Jordanian companies	Unrestricted	Unrestricted	Unrestricted
Property, local, and social taxes	100% exemption	100% exemption	100% exemption	100% exemption
Tax on dividends	None	100% exemption up to 5% of dividend value	100% exemption	100% exemption
Management of foreign currency earnings	Unrestricted for non-Jordanian companies	Unrestricted	Unrestricted	Unrestricted
Duties and other import and export charges	100% exemption	100% exemption	100% exemption	100% exemption
Personal income taxes	100% exemption	No exemption	No exemption	100% exemption
Sales to local market	Allowed subject to prior approval and duty payment	Unrestricted, subject to full duty payment	Unrestricted, subject to full duty payment	Unrestricted, subject to full duty payment
No. of days to receive free zone license	60 days	90–120 days	n.a.	One week
Other			Prohibition of strikes and lockouts for 10 years	Liberal work visa and expatriate salary policies

TRADE EXCLUSIONS ON FREE ZONE MERCHANDISE

A major drawback faced by all Arab countries is that free zone merchandise is subject to a blanket exclusion under current regional agreements. In other words, products processed in an Arab free zone cannot qualify for entry into any existing bilateral or regional trade agreements. Legally, the exclusion of free zones has its roots in a 1982 Arab League decision[19] that initially spelled out those exclusions for Arab trade agreements–at that time, a series of bilateral trade protocols.

Conceptually, free zone products are excluded from Arab trade agreements because free zone firms benefit from an unprecedented duty-free import advantage. It is argued that by also granting these firms preferential trading access, free zone firms could threaten both competing exporters not located in free zones and domestic producers in the importing country. But this argument ignores the fact that domestic firms can benefit from a number of duty-free import schemes (temporary admission, duty drawback, bonded warehouses) that allow domestic exporters to import duty-free inputs *and* gain preferential export market access, thus providing the double benefit to domestic manufacturers that is denied to free zone firms. This inconsistency is one of the reasons why manufacturing investment in many of the area's free zones has been limited.

Even worse, this blanket exclusion against free zone merchandise has been included in the recent Greater Arab Free Trade agreement, contrary to the practice of most other regional trade agreements that generally permit free zone access (Table 11.8). While treatment varies, in general, free zones are eligible for preferential access, therefore treated on the same basis as other duty-deferral schemes. In three of the four agreements, free zone goods may become eligible for preferential access in member states to which they are exported by paying duties before exportation, in the country in which they are located, on the nonoriginating parts or components of zone products.[20]

The net effect of the Arab League regulation has been extremely restrictive. Free zone–based manufacturers cannot access regional markets on a preferential basis.

TABLE 11.8. FREE ZONE ACCESS UNDER REGIONAL TRADE AGREEMENTS

Regional trade agreement	Is treatment or processing in zone eligible for preferential access?	Are zones treated the same as other duty-deferral regimes?	May duty be paid in exporting country for zone goods to become eligible for preferential access?
NAFTA	Yes	Yes	Yes
Mercosur	No	No	No
EFTA	Implied yes	Yes	Implied yes
CARICOM	Implied yes	Yes	Implied yes

Note: NAFTA: North American Free Trade Agreement; EFTA: European Free Trade Agreement; CARICOM: Caribbean Economic Community.
Source: Data compiled by The Services Group.

Weak Zone Administrative Bodies

The weak performance of some programs can also be traced to weak government bodies established to develop and operate zones and regulate free zone activity. This is the case especially of older programs such as those in Jordan, Egypt, and Syria, where zone regulatory authorities lack the basic power, autonomy, and funding to function effectively. The Jordanian Free Zones Corporation, for example, suffers from limited autonomy—even establishment or alteration of a lease rate requires approval of the Cabinet. This organization and many others lack control over their budgets and have restrictive civil service limitations on remuneration and employment conditions. These factors have led to chronic overstaffing—in Egypt, the free zone authority at one point had 4,000 employees.

In other parts of the world, free zone administrative regulatory bodies are being restructured. A variety of institutional frameworks has been used for free zone regulation, development and management (Table 11.9). But the focus of these regulatory bodies has changed significantly in many countries. With the entry of the private sector into zone development, most countries have either set up specialized public sector free zone development and management agencies, or increasingly have divested the physical project development function to the private sector and transformed their free zone authorities into purely regulatory and promotional bodies.

International experience has shown that countries embarking on private free zone development find it difficult to reconcile the divergent functions of zone management, regulation, and investment promotion. In many free zone–sponsoring countries, conflicts of interest have arisen when regulatory bodies are also engaged in zone development activity, especially when existing public zones would directly compete against new private zones. Opportunities for perceived and actual conflict of interest are multiplied when the entity charged with guiding and monitoring free zone performance is simultaneously one of the free zone operators being monitored.

TABLE 11.9. FREE ZONE REGULATORY BODIES

Country	Type of body	Private sector representation on board	Zone development/ management	Zone regulation	Zone promotion
Costa Rica	Public corporation	Yes, majority private	No	Yes	Yes
Dominican Republic	Government agency	Yes, majority private	No	Yes	Yes
Indonesia	Government agency	Yes, 2 representatives	Yes	Yes	No
Philippines	Public corporation	Yes, 1 representative	Yes	Yes	Yes
Taiwan	Government department	No	Yes	Yes	Yes
Thailand	Public corporation	No	Yes	Yes	Yes

Source: Official data compiled by The Services Group.

Many free zone authorities are becoming more user responsive by reorganizing themselves as corporate entities (to get out of civil service limitations) and have substantial private sector participation at the board of directors level. An example in Asia is Thailand's Industrial Estate Authority, but this approach is more commonly found among the industrial free zone programs in Latin America (notably, Costa Rica and the Dominican Republic).

Conclusions and Recommendations

This chapter has shown that the relatively weak economic performance of free zones in the MENA region is the result of numerous factors in the policy and incentive framework, development approach, and institutional structure regulating zone activity. With the exception of the Gulf countries, MENA governments have not emphasized free zone development. They have instead adopted an extreme view of extraterritoriality that has transformed free zones into centers of marginal trading and commercial activities, rather than a focus for investment promotion and export manufacturing.

At the same time, the potential for free zone development in the region is enormous. Free zones remain a highly effective means of attracting foreign direct investment and generating nontraditional exports. The increasing trend toward private sector development and operation of zones offers governments a unique opportunity to facilitate rapid investment and export growth, while reducing public sector outlays.

The rationale for free zones is not diminishing in the context of regional economic integration and WTO accession and implementation. The case for dynamic free zones in the MENA region is actually stronger in the context of trade liberalization.

First, even with the full implementation of the Uruguay Round, tariff and nontariff barriers will remain in most countries. MENA exporters will need to compete with exporters in other countries who are operating in a duty- and tax-free environment. Second, even with lowered tariffs, antiexport biases will not be removed. Various policy distortions, procedural inefficiencies, and infrastructural inadequacies will deter exporters. Many of these problems can be directly addressed only over the long term. This places importance on the continued development of focused investment and export promotion mechanisms such as the Freeport.

The prevalence of free zones in industrialized countries with open economies also underscores the importance of the concept to competitiveness. The 240 U.S. foreign trade zones are a particularly prominent example. Many companies choose an FTZ location because of important advantages of operating in a flexible, duty-free environment (see Box 3). Operating costs are lower as a result of reduced insurance, security, and overhead costs. Cash flow is enhanced by the ability to postpone duty payments until entry into the domestic customs territory. FTZs in the United States have been critical in enabling manufacturers to operate "just-in-time" systems. In fact, most vehicles manufactured in the United States are located in FTZs or have factories with FTZ status. Mechanisms such as free zones that provide efficiency advantages are even more important, even with the advent of modern production concepts and approaches and the reduction of tariff and nontariff barriers. This is one reason why these programs have been introduced and expanded in a number of industrialized countries, including Japan, Canada, France, and the Republic of Korea—in addition to the United States.

Realizing the economic potential of free zones in the MENA region, however, is not a simple task. It will require implementation of number of actions in a range of areas. These include

- working with the Arab League to remove exclusions on free zone merchandise and developing WTO-consistent origin certification policies

- assisting governments in rationalizing free zone incentive policies and developing competitive legal frameworks with streamlined and simplified procedures

- preparing a competitive concession agreement between the host country government and the zone developer that enshrines a "partnership" approach to zone development and operation

- streamlining free zone government administrative bodies to enhance operating flexibility, increase private sector representation, and outsource functions and services to the private sector

---

BOX 11.3. ADVANTAGES OF USING A U.S. FOREIGN TRADE ZONE

- Improved cash flow through payment of duties upon shipment out of the warehouse or factory instead of receipt into the facility.
- No customs duties on scrap, waste, or obsolete materials.
- Option of paying customs duties on the imported materials or the final product shipped from the zones, whichever is less.
- No customs duties owed on the value to labor, overhead, or profit incurred in zone processing in the United States.
- No customs duties owed on exported merchandise.
- Ability to hold all goods in a duty-free environment until needed.
- FTZ may be used for quality-control inspections to ensure that only merchandise that meets only U.S. specifications is imported and that duty is paid.

Source: National Association of Foreign Trade Zones.

- assisting area governments in developing and implementing more innovative free zone concepts, including Freeports, technology parks, and industrial clusters

- ensuring that new private zones do not face unfair (subsidized) competition from existing public zones, and privatizing existing government-owned free zones.

In short, these initiatives will work only when there is sufficient political will backing the projects and an effective technical support is provided.

Notes

1. The first modern industrial free zone in a developing country was established in Shannon, Ireland, in 1959. This was followed by the Kaoshiung export processing zone in Taiwan in 1962.

2. WEPZA 1997, updated by TSG estimates.

3. There are more than 240 foreign trade zones in the United States. In 1998, these zones employed more than 370,000 persons and generated some $16 billion in exports (National Association of Foreign-Trade Zones 1998).

4. The International Convention on the Simplification and Harmonization of Customs Procedures of 1979 (Kyoto Convention) defines free zones as being "part of the territory of a State where any goods introduced are generally regarded, insofar as import duties and taxes are concerned, as being outside the Customs territory and are not subject to the usual Customs control. In commercial free zones, goods are admitted pending subsequent disposal; goods admitted to industrial free zones may be subjected to authorized processing operations."

5. International Labor Organisation 1998, drawing upon WEPZA (1997).

6. The QIZ offers duty- and quota-free access to the U.S. market for products manufactured by qualifying enterprises located in a designated enclave. Products must meet certain criteria to qualify under the program. This includes a 35 percent minimum content rule, 11.7 percent of which must be of Jordanian origin and 7–8 percent from Israel; the remainder to reach the 35 percent value-added requirement can be from U.S., Jordanian, Israeli, or West Bank and Gaza sources.

7. See Madani (1998, May) for a review of the most recent literature.

8. World Bank 1992.

9. In addition to the United States, Canada has at least 10 free trade zones, and at least 9 so-called "foreign access zones" have recently been established in Japan.

10. The establishment of the zone has also been an important factor in making the Dubai port the 10th largest in the world. Between 1992 and 1997, total container traffic through the Dubai ports more than doubled (Jordan 1999a).

11. Data provided by Jebel Ali Free Zone Authority (JAFZA).

12. JAFZA Chairman Sultan Bin Sulayem, quoted in *Gulf Business*, August 1999.

13. "Sharjah Exports Leap 24 Percent," *Gulf News*, September 5, 1999.

14. Turkey has taken the lead in establishing specialized zones—one caters exclusively to the leather industry, the other is a financial services zone in Istanbul. Information technology parks are being planned in Lebanon and Jordan. A large scale Freeport and special economic zone is set to be established in Aqaba, Jordan.

15. Cash-strapped governments have turned to private developers for not only on-site infrastructure and facilities (that is, internal roads, utilities, common facilities, factory buildings, and so forth) but even off-site infrastructure connections. Unlike the usual practice in other countries, many Southeast Asian private zone developers have had to finance external access roads, power line connections, water and sewage treatment plants, and other facilities, to meet the requirements of their zone-based tenants.

16. Development of the private free zone in Shuwaikh entailed prolonged negotiation with the Kuwaiti government. Many factors, including the institutional resistance of the ports and customs authorities, had to be overcome by the private development group.

17. Rao and Li 1995.

18. Expatriate workers are housed in dormitories on site in most of the UAE zones.

19. The Agreement for Facilitating and Developing Trade Exchange between Arab States as published in the Official Gazette, No. (3217), page 344, dated March 1,1984, was approved by the Economic and Social Council Decision No. 848-d dated February 27, 1982.

20. Exporters from U.S. free zones under NAFTA pay duties (usually at their option) at the duty rate applicable to the materials in the condition as received in the zone, or at the duty rate applicable to the manufactured product in the condition at the time of removal. However, that duty rate is applied only to the imported materials contained in the manufactured product.

References

Jordan, Barry. 1999a. "Free But Not Always Easy." Gulf Business 3(9).

———. 1999b. "Zone Clones." Gulf Business 4(4).

Madani, Dorsati. 1998, May. "A Review of the Role and Impact of Export Processing Zones." Unpublished paper. World Bank, Washington, D.C.

Mintz, Jack M. 1990. "Corporate Tax Holidays and Investment." *World Bank Economic Review* 4(1).

Rao, Kishore, and Lim Pao Li. 1995, May. "Facilitating Private EPZ Development in Jordan." Unpublished report. World Bank, Washington, D.C.

United Nations Conference on Trade and Development. 1995. "Incentives and Foreign Direct Investments." Background report. Geneva.

World Bank. 1992."Export Processing Zone." Industry and Development Division, World Bank, Washington, D.C.

Index

U

unemployment, 7, 24, 184
United Arab Emirates, 169
   free zones, 251, 256
United States
   Egypt, 128–129, 131
   free zones, 249, 260–261
Uruguay Round (UR) Agreement, Egypt,
   119, 125–126, 127

V

valuation, 238
   Jordan, 143
value-added network services (VANS),
   240, 241
value-added tax (VAT), 191–192
   Morocco, 174
   Tunisia, 171

W

wine, 108
withholding tax, Morocco, 174
World Trade Organization (WTO), 261
   Egypt, 223–224, 225
   Jordan, 142
   Saudi Arabia, 153, 154, 162